Economic Report on

Africa

2012

Unleashing Africa's Potential as a Pole of Global Growth

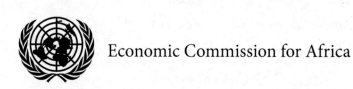 Economic Commission for Africa

 African Union

Ordering information

To order copies of *Unleashing Africa's Potential as a Pole of Global Growth* by the Economic Commission for Africa, please contact:

Publications:
Economic Commission for Africa
P.O. Box 3001
Addis Ababa, Ethiopia

Tel: +251 11 544-9900
Fax: +251 11 551-4416
E-mail: ecainfo@uneca.org
Web: www.uneca.org

Cover photos: From top left Stock.xchng/Patrick Hajzler, Herman Brinkman, UN Photo/ Eskinder Debebe, Stock.xchng/Petr Kovar, Ilker, Damian Searles.

Table of Contents

4. Unleashing Africa's Development Capacity   103

5. Mobilizing Resources for Structural Transformation   143

Boxes

Figures

Tables

Acronyms

AERC	African Economic Research Consortium
AfDB	African Development Bank
AIDS	Acquired Immune Deficiency Syndrome
APRM	African Peer Review Mechanism
ATM	Automated Teller Machine
AU	African Union
AUC	African Union Commission
BRIC	Brazil, Russia, India and China
CAADP	Comprehensive Africa Agriculture Development Programme
CEPR	Centre for Economic Policy Research
CFA	African Financial Community
CODESRIA	Council for the Development of Social Science Research in Africa
COMESA	Common Market for Eastern and Southern Africa
DAC	Development Assistance Committee
EAC	East African Community
ECCAS	Economic Community of Central African States
ECOWAS	Economic Community of West African States
EIU	Economist Intelligence Unit
ETF	Exchange-Traded Fund
FAO	Food and Agriculture Organization of the United Nations
FDI	Foreign Direct Investment
FIFA	International Federation of Association Football
FTA	Free Trade Area
FOCAC	Forum on China-Africa Cooperation
G-20	Group of Twenty Finance Ministers and Central Bank Governors
GDP	Gross Domestic Product
GRIPS	National Graduate Institute for Policy Studies
HIV	Human Immunodeficiency Virus
HSRC	Human Sciences Research Council
ICCO	International Cocoa Organization
ICO	International Coffee Organization
ICT	Information and Communication Technology
IDS	Institute of Development Studies
IEA	International Energy Agency

IFPRI	International Food Policy Research Institute
ILO	International Labour Organization
IMF	International Monetary Fund
IPRCC	International Poverty Reduction Center in China
MDGs	Millennium Development Goals
MENA	Middle East and North Africa
MFN	Most Favoured Nation
NEPAD	New Partnership for Africa's Development
ODA	Official Development Assistance
OECD	Organisation for Economic Co-operation and Development
OPEC	Organization of the Petroleum Exporting Countries
OSAA	United Nations Office of the Special Adviser on Africa
OUP	Oxford University Press
PCRD	Post-Conflict Reconstruction and Development
PPIAF	Public-Private Infrastructure Advisory Facility
PPP	Purchasing Power Parity
PRSP	Poverty Reduction Strategy Paper
REC	Regional Economic Community
SADC	Southern African Development Community
SAP	Structural Adjustment Programme
SAR	Special Administrative Region
UN-DESA	United Nations Department of Economic and Social Affairs
UNCTAD	United Nations Conference on Trade and Development
UNDP	United Nations Development Programme
UNECA	United Nations Economic Commission for Africa
UNIDO	United Nations Industrial Development Organization
UNRISD	United Nations Research Institute for Social Development
UNU-WIDER	United Nations University World Institute for Development Economics Research
US	United States
USA	United States of America
WDI	World Development Indicators
WEF	World Economic Forum
WHO	World Health Organization
WTO	World Trade Organization

Acknowledgements

THE ECONOMIC REPORT on Africa 2012, a joint publication of the United Nations Economic Commission for Africa (ECA) and the African Union Commission (AUC), was prepared under the leadership of Abdoulie Janneh, Executive Secretary of ECA, and Jean Ping, Chairperson of AUC, with the active involvement of Maxwell Mkwezalamba, Commissioner for Economic Affairs. The report team benefited from the guidance and supervision of Emmanuel Nnadozie, Director of Economic Development and NEPAD Division (EDND), ECA, and René Kouassi N'Guettia, Director of the Economic Affairs Department, AUC. Jennifer Kargbo, former Deputy Executive Secretary of ECA, and Abdalla Hamdok, Deputy Executive Secretary, facilitated discussion of the theme and drafts of the report.

The ECA team comprised Adam B. Elhiraika (Coordinator), Ndubisi Nwokoma, Bartholomew Armah, Elvis Mtonga, Adrian Gauci, Li Qiang, Jymdey Yeffimo, Malcolm Spence, Simon Mevel, Chrystelle Tsafack Temah, Deniz Kellecioglu, Julianne Deitch, John Sloan, Zheng Jian, Aissatou Gueye, Souleymane Abdallah and Samson Kwalingana. The AUC team comprised Charles Awitor (Coordinator) and Victoria Egbetayo. The AUC team benefited from reflections and input from the following AUC staff: Janet Byaruhanga, Nena Thundu Yihenew Zewdie, Atef Marzouk and Festus Fajana.

The thematic part of the report is based on original chapters contributed by Professor David Olusanya Ajakaiye, Director of Programmes, Foundation for Economics Education, Ibadan, Nigeria (chapter 3); Professor Fantu Cheru, Research Director, the Nordic Africa Institute, Sweden (chapter 4); and Professor Machiko Nissanke of the School of Oriental and African Studies (SOAS), University of London, United Kingdom (chapter 5). ECA and AUC also gratefully acknowledge the assistance of Professors Fantu Cheru and Olusanya Ajakaiye in the substantive editing of the report.

Internal and external reviewers and written reviews by Subregional Offices (SROs) of ECA provided comments and suggestions that have greatly improved the quality of ERA 2012. In particular, the following external reviewers provided insightful written comments on the manuscript: Professor Benjamin Turok, Parliament of the Republic of South Africa; Professor Oliver Saasa, Premier Consult Limited, Lusaka, Zambia; Dr. Winford Masanjala, Ministry of Finance, Lilongwe, Malawi; Dr. Rusuhuzwa Kigabo Thomas, National Bank of Rwanda; Dr. Diop Ibrahima Thione, CREA, Dakar, Senegal; Dr. Yves Ekouves Ekoué Amaizo, Afrology Think Tank, Vienna, Austria and Dr. Degnet Ababaw, Ethiopian Economic Policy Research Institute, Addis Ababa, Ethiopia.

Documents and background material made available by AUC and the Governance and Public Administration Division (GPAD), the Regional Integration, Infrastructure and Trade Division (RITD) and the Food Security and Sustainable Development Division (FSSD) of ECA provided invaluable assistance to the authors of the report.

The report team also benefited from data provided by the African Centre for Statistics (ACS) of ECA.

The report team gratefully appreciates the guidance and support of Doreen Bongoy-Mawalla, ECA Director of Administration and the Publications and Conference Management Section (PCMS) led by Etienne Kabou. The ECA English editorial team comprised Lorna Davidson, Colin Allen, Adjoa De Bordes and Gillian Wolfe while the French translation team comprised Pierre Noel, Amadou Fall, Abou Lawan, Isabel Chaves de Oliveira, Marcellin Zounmenou, Yamadou Keita and Lazhar Slimane. The Documents Control team was led by Marcel Ngoma-Mouaya. Charles Ndungu, Teshome Yohannes and Ferdos Issa handled the design and printing of the report.

The final report was ably edited by Communications Development Incorporated's Bruce Ross-Larson and Jack Harlow. We acknowledge with gratitude their professionalism and thoroughness.

The ECA Information and Communication Service (ICS), led by Adeyinka Adeyemi, and supported by Andrew Allimadi, Mercy Wambui, Aloysius Fomenky and Sophia Denekew, provided invaluable assistance in media outreach, dissemination and policy advocacy around the report.

The following ECA staff, fellows and interns also provided useful assistance to the report team: Agare Kassahun, Rahel Desta, Gerawork Getachew, Shewaye Woldeyes, Siham Abdulmelik, Solomon Wedere, Bekele Demissie, Kamaludeen Muhammad, Malaika Toyo, Adwoa Attakrah, Christian Lambert Nguena and Ruth Hoekstra.

Foreword

THE FIRST DECADE of the twenty-first century has been characterized as the "decade of Africa's economic and political renewal". The continent achieved remarkable progress in economic growth while at the same time expanding the scope for democratic governance in a large number of countries. Growth in Africa averaged more than 5 per cent a year, and the pattern of growth has been generally consistent. A handful of African countries have registered annual growth rates of 7–11 per cent. More important, the continent demonstrated its resilience through its quick and robust recovery from the shocks of the global economic and financial crisis. The year 2011 was no exception, as growth accelerated in most countries despite the political turmoil in North Africa and continued global economic fragility.

The dynamism of African economies has captured the imagination of the world. Having been written off as "the hopeless continent" for decades, Africa is now being courted by powerful economic actors with a keen interest in its natural resources and untapped market. While the new narrative of "a rising Africa" is warmly welcomed, it must be made clear at the outset that the continent's new fortunes are not the outcome of good luck; they are the result of years of hard work and better macroeconomic management. Indeed, the economic revival of the continent is attributed to improved economic and political governance, reduction in armed conflicts, increasing foreign capital inflows (especially direct investment) and improvements in the business climate—as well as rising commodity prices.

A positive portrayal of Africa in international circles is encouraging, but the *Economic Report on Africa 2012* presents a more cautious and nuanced analysis of the continent's growth trajectory. The report situates the story of a rising Africa in a broader context, by pointing out the challenges and opportunities that lie ahead as governments push forward a series of policies to achieve structural transformation in an environment of global uncertainty. The report identifies the key binding constraints for unleashing Africa's productive capacity and proposes a series of bold measures that governments must implement to position the continent as the next pole of global growth and rebalancing.

Finally, the *Economic Report on Africa 2012* argues that sustaining the growth momentum and taking Africa's development potential much further depends on strong political leadership with the capacity to mobilize the population around a common national development vision. This must be complemented by an effective institutional framework that delineates the roles and responsibilities of the three drivers of transformational change—the State, the private sector and civil society—for realizing the common vision and for ensuring mutual accountability.

In a refreshing reassessment of the continent's growth prospects, and echoing the central message of the *Economic Report on Africa 2011* on the developmental State, the report calls for pragmatism, as well as steady and hands-on State guidance. These will lay the conditions for transformative change through improved governance, long-term development planning and industrial policy, as well as enhanced investment in education, infrastructure, technology, agriculture and climate change mitigation and adaptation, all of which aim to foster access of the poor to productive assets and employment opportunities.

It is our hope that this year's report will stimulate lively discussion and debate among policymakers, the private sector, civil society and other stakeholders at the national, regional and continental levels—as well as international development partners and the business community—on how to accelerate Africa's impressive growth performance of the last decade and sustain it over the long term.

Abdoulie Janneh
United Nations
Under-Secretary-General and
Executive Secretary of UNECA

Jean Ping
Chairperson
African Union Commission

Overview

THE EXPERIENCE OF the last decade suggests strongly that Africa is likely to make the twenty-first century its own—an experience woven into this document countless times. Essentially, since the beginning of this century, African countries have shown strong economic growth owing to improved economic management, a generally hospitable international environment and rising prices for their commodity and other strategic minerals.

Growth was interrupted when the 2008 global financial crisis—and steep food and fuel prices—hit the continent. Yet Africa quickly recovered and saw its growth resume at pre-crisis rates, a clear indication of the deep restructuring under way for more than a decade. Several prominent international financial organizations and private think tanks, observing this trend, have stressed Africa's potential to be a "global growth pole"—one that, reflecting its own size and rate of growth, boosts growth in other countries, worldwide. The headline "Africa rising", which appeared on the cover page of *The Economist* news magazine on 3 December 2011, captures the growing optimism about Africa's role in the world.

Still, the continent should not rest on its laurels, as UN-ECA Executive Secretary, Mr. Abdoulie Janneh, warned in his June 2011 address to the African Union Executive Council in Malabo, Equatorial Guinea. The last decade's impressive growth must be examined in a proper context if Africa is to become a global growth pole, for the fact remains that the sources of Africa's growth have changed very little over the years: agriculture and natural resources remain the main drivers, and Africa has diversified its economies in little meaningful way. Moreover, job creation has not matched growth and employment needs. It is therefore important to carefully review Africa's development experience in the recent past, analyse the attributes of a global growth pole, consider the steps—or "imperatives"—that Africa must take to become a global growth pole and identify what it has to do to set free its growth potential.

Thus the theme—and title—of the *Economic Report on Africa 2012* is *Unleashing Africa's Potential as a Pole of Global Growth*, examined in five chapters. Chapter 1 presents a review of the developments in the world economy and implications for Africa. Chapter 2 offers an overview of economic, social and human conditions in Africa in 2011 and prospects for 2012. The remaining three chapters focus on how to harness the continent's productive capacity by taking bold measures to ease the binding constraints that still stifle Africa's potential.

Chapter 3—the focus of the growth pole analysis—looks at Africa's growth in the last half century, particularly the drivers of growth in different development strategies. Through the optic of the global growth pole, it proposes several imperatives that Africa must fulfil, including sustained high growth, as well as economic transformation (mainly of infrastructure, human resources and local entrepreneurship). It also discusses options for capitalizing on the opportunities, and for managing the risks, of the emerging multipolar world and the gradual shift

> *Africa's marginal position in the global economy can be reversed with the right type of political leadership.*

in the resource balance from the developed world to Asia and other developing regions.

In more detail, chapter 4 presents how to unleash Africa's productive potential. Emphasizing that Africa's marginal position in the global economy can be reversed with the right type of political leadership committed to mobilizing all sectors of society around a common national development vision and strategy, the chapter suggests the need for two other elements: a capable and pragmatic bureaucracy and a social compact in which the State, the private sector and civil society are mutually accountable for implementing that vision. The chapter then proposes options for improving political and economic governance, for relaxing constraints from deficits in human capital, infrastructure and local entrepreneurship, for unlocking Africa's agricultural potential, for stepping up regional integration initiatives and for harnessing new partnerships, particularly with the emerging economies of the global South.

Chapter 5 reviews the various resource-mobilizing channels open to Africa given the pressing need to transform itself structurally. It outlines innovative proposals on mechanisms for mobilizing, using and distributing resources for setting a foundation of shared growth and inclusive development. It begins by reviewing past experience as well as new opportunities and challenges facing policymakers in mobilizing and using external resource flows—official and private—for socio-economic structural transformation. The chapter then looks at new financial instruments for mobilizing private savings from international and domestic investors, as well as issues in mobilizing domestic public resources.

Chapter 1: Developments in the world economy and implications for Africa

AFTER A STRONG rebound in 2010, the world economy slowed in 2011 owing to increased risks and uncertainties that are expected to remain in 2012 and beyond. Although the negative effects of the triple crisis of 2007–2009—food, energy and finance—still linger, the euro area sovereign debt crisis has further aggravated structural imbalances in the world economy and cast a doubt on the prospects for sustained growth and a quick recovery.

The depth and complexity of the global crisis have so far defied policy responses from developed-country governments. They kept interest rates low and pursued tight fiscal austerity measures to restore fiscal credibility. Yet long-run structural problems, such as increased income inequality, dysfunctional labour markets and global imbalances in particular, have intensified.

African economies quickly rebounded from the 2008 financial crisis as commodity prices rose and export revenues returned to pre-crisis levels, enabling them to finance the necessary investments. Turmoil in North Africa and the euro area crisis combined to slow growth in 2011, but despite uncertainties some African countries have grown at double digits, reflecting higher commodity prices and strong domestic demand.

The world economy is entering a critical period full of uncertainties and challenges. In the short term, the euro area crisis might push the global economy into another recession with devastating consequences. High unemployment and rising food and energy prices have already

> *The world economy is entering a period full of uncertainties and challenges.*

widened income inequality and stirred up discontent and social instability around the globe.

Africa is not immune to the global crisis, though it is in a much better position to deal with global exigencies than before. The expected slowdown of the world economy may reduce demand for its commodity exports, lower prices and thus reduce its export earnings. However, export diversification in recent years can help the continent to better weather these effects through intra-African trade. Shortfalls in official development assistance could threaten many aid-dependent African countries' social development programmes, but this could also encourage the continent to mobilize local resources and reduce over-dependence on foreign financial assistance.

With the above risks and challenges as their backdrop, Africa's governments need to push through growth-promoting macroeconomic policies in the short run, while adopting long-term development strategies. Specifically, they should increase investments in high-quality education, health and infrastructure that can enhance long-term growth potential—within their fiscal space. Monetary policy has to be accommodative to support growth. All these measures should be combined with policies that provide social protection for vulnerable groups in society, thus consolidating the poverty-reduction achievements of the past decade.

> *African countries must pursue structural transformation to sustain growth, create jobs and reduce vulnerability to external shocks.*

In the long term, African countries must vigorously pursue economic diversification and structural transformation to moderate negative external shocks from the euro debt crisis or volatility in commodity prices (or both) and provide decent jobs for African men and women. In addition, they should intensify efforts to diversify their export destinations, expand economic partnerships (including those with emerging economies) and deepen intra-Africa trade and investment. Crucially, though, Africa can grow faster and become a global growth pole by unleashing its productive potential through aggressively investing in infrastructure and human capital. Such a broad-based, transformative agenda will require each country to have strong political leadership and an effective institutional framework.

Chapter 2: Economic and social developments in Africa and prospects for 2012

THE PACE OF economic growth in Africa weakened in 2011, reflecting the impact of political and social strife in some countries in the north of the continent. Growth in the rest of Africa sustained strong momentum, however, as several countries benefited from increased export earnings, owing to higher global commodity prices and strong export demand, as well as buoyant domestic demand, fuelled by strong public investment, higher agricultural harvests and a recovery of inward capital flows that responded to a more stable economic environment and better economic management. Oil exporters lagged behind non-oil exporters for the first time in five years, and countries in North Africa faltered.

Continental growth is still creating too few jobs, however—unemployment remains high and youth unemployment especially is growing. These failures of growth are because much of the output growth is driven by capital-intensive sectors—and they lack economy-wide links—while the labour-intensive sectors lag behind. Economic growth has not therefore generated the jobs and incomes needed to reduce the high unemployment and poverty on the continent. African countries will have to diversify their sources of growth towards labour-intensive sectors to make inroads in these areas.

Inflation generally rose on the continent, sparked by rising global food and fuel prices. This was most felt in the Horn of Africa, where severe drought and lower food production led to steep increases in food prices. Policy remained generally accommodative though, and few countries (apart from those in East Africa, to limited effect) tightened their monetary stance. Fiscal policy was reasonably expansionary, with many countries sustaining their spending plans in support of public investment spending, but this further widened the aggregate fiscal deficit in 2011.

Growth prospects in the medium term are optimistic, with output for the continent as a whole set to recover strongly in 2012 and thereafter, premised on a return to political stability in North Africa. However, as the global economic slowdown threatens these prospects, they depend on the global economy regaining its growth momentum. Without this improvement, African countries are likely to suffer a setback through reduced exports and inward capital inflows.

But what of the longer term? What should Africa do, so it need not worry about what the rest of the world does?

Chapter 3: Africa as a pole of Global Growth

SINCE INDEPENDENCE, AFRICAN growth has been driven mainly by primary production and export alongside little economic transformation and too much unemployment and poverty. The continent still faces development deficits in infrastructure, entrepreneurship, human resources and science and technology. The last decade, however, has benefited from improvements in macroeconomic management, good governance and control of corruption such that manufacturing, modern financial and telecommunications services as well as tourism are beginning to make significant contributions to growth. During this period, Africa has witnessed a substantial improvement in its economic performance: its gross domestic product (GDP) grew by an average of 5.6 per cent in 2002–2008, making it the second-fastest growing continent in the world at times, behind Asia. Of the world's 15 fastest-growing economies in 2010, 10 were African. More reassuring, it is not only the resource-rich countries that are experiencing this growth—some

Future growth will depend on harnessing Africa's untapped natural resources, youthful population and growing middle class.

African countries that do not boast of oil or mineral wealth are growing as well.

This resurgence is giving rise to Africa's growing recognition as an emerging market and a potential global growth pole. It has prompted African leaders, institutions, development partners and other stakeholders to suggest that future world growth will depend on harnessing Africa's unique features, especially its untapped huge natural resources, youthful population and growing middle class.

African governments need to continue promoting good political governance as evidenced by the downward trend of government hardening and oppression of peaceful demonstrations. The focus was on shared values at the 16th African Union Summit in January 2011, which looked at reforming electoral systems, improving democratic processes and human rights, showing zero tolerance for unconstitutional changes of government, building on the New Partnership for Africa's Development (NEPAD) and its African Peer Review Mechanism (APRM) commitment to establish a more coherent Pan-African Governance Architecture and adopting the African Charter of Values and Principles of Public Service and Administration. There is also international support for initiatives to strengthen rule of law and parliamentary oversight as well as civil society engagement.

Africa has about 12 per cent of the world's oil reserves and 40 per cent of its gold as well as vast arable land and forest resources. These resources, along with rising demand for raw materials from emerging economies especially, make Africa an attractive destination for direct and portfolio investors. Foreign direct investment (FDI) inflows to Africa reached $62 billion in 2009, an almost seven-fold increase in a decade. The uptrend is expected to continue. Meanwhile, rigorous implementation of the African mining vision will strongly improve the development effectiveness of the continent's natural resources.

To make the most of Africa's demographic potential, the youthful population and fast-growing labour force has to be offered comprehensive, innovative skills and knowledge development. This will ensure that they are a blessing and not a source of conflict and insecurity, which would harm the investment climate. This way, Africa will take maximum advantage of ageing populations in advanced economies and rising wages in Asia, thus becoming the next global manufacturing and high-tech services platform.

The high rate of urbanization and the rise of the middle class in Africa will play a major role in growth. The number of middle-class households will increase by half from 2010 to 2020, and by 2030 the top 18 African cities will have a combined spending power of $1.3 trillion. This large, untapped domestic market should attract high domestic and foreign investment.

In order to be a global growth pole, Africa needs to meet certain imperatives: the crucial imperative is to sustain its recent growth rate for at least another two decades. It can do this if it vigorously addresses the development deficits in the structural transformation of output (including industrialization) and trade, infrastructure, human resources and entrepreneurialism, and capitalizes on the opportunities—and manages the risks—of the emerging multipolar world.

If it meets these deficits, Africa may well be able to sustain its recent 5 per cent growth to 2034, by which time, if other countries maintain their recent growth rates, it should account for at least 5 per cent of world GDP (China's position in 2005)—and be regarded as a global growth pole. If the continent were to grow at an average annual rate of more than 5 per cent, it would account for 5 per cent or more of global GDP in a shorter period.

Industrialization is critical. African countries should pursue economic transformation programmes to lift the share of manufacturing to at least 25 per cent of GDP and to restructure services from distributive trades (dominated by informality) towards the more modern services needed to support sophisticated economies (as Africa transits to knowledge-intensive operations). These moves should be complemented by extensive economic diversification where the share of manufacturing exports climbs steeply and the composition of manufactured imports changes towards capital goods, industrial intermediates and components.

Investment in infrastructure is also vital. Better roads, dams and hydropower should translate into increased electricity consumption and tighter transport connections, reducing transaction costs, raising economic productivity and competitiveness and improving living standards. Success in this area would be seen in per capita electricity consumption of 1,129 kilowatt-hours and GDP per unit of energy use of 4, at least; a share of paved roads of at least 44 per cent; and telephone lines and Internet users per 100 people not less than 16 and 6, respectively, in any African country.

Human capital, too, has to be upgraded and secondary and tertiary enrolment should climb to at least 64 per cent and 16 per cent, respectively, matched by quality assurance mechanisms. Adult and youth literacy rates should be at least 77 per cent and 90 per cent, respectively, in any African country. Life expectancy should be 68 years at least and infant mortality 37 per 1,000 live births at most in any African country. Governments should strengthen health systems by allocating greater domestic resources; ensuring the removal of barriers to access to services; overseeing the development, deployment and retention of critical human resources for health; and abolishing

Enhancing good governance is a precondition for Africa's economic and social development.

inequity in access to health care. Current initiatives to re-duce the prevalence and burden of HIV/AIDS and malaria should be sustained in line with achieving the Millennium Development Goals (MDGs).

Finally, all African countries should nurture indigenous entrepreneurs capable of working with foreign counterparts to promote the effective transfer of knowledge and to ensure technological spillovers to African economies.

Beyond these measures, they should capitalize on and manage the opportunities and risks in the emerging multipolar world. The two opposite aspects stem from rising global commodity prices and demand, strategic trade relations with new development partners, FDI from emerging economies, support for infrastructure devel-opment by new partners and development potential of diasporas (beyond remittances). All these interventions require collaboration among stakeholders under the lead-ership and guidance of a developmental State.

Chapter 4: Unleashing Africa's development capacity

SUSTAINING THE CURRENT growth momentum in Africa and unleashing the continent's productive capacity requires innovative and bold actions on many fronts.

Promoting good political and economic governance

Entrenching good governance is a precondition for Africa's development and social progress. Although political and economic governance are improving, much more needs to be done, and key elements include strengthening the insti-tutions of the State to foster predictability, accountability and transparency in managing public affairs; promot-ing free and fair electoral processes; fighting corruption and inefficiency; enhancing public service delivery; and

expanding social protection programmes. Greater effort is needed to expand political space for citizens to take part in decisions and to hold public officials accountable for their actions. It is particularly important that governments create a policy environment supportive of entrepreneur-ship and private sector development, and reduce the cost of doing business by stamping out rent-seeking practices by public officials.

Repurposing education for development

Human capital formation is lagging in Africa, and a fresh approach is needed to bridge the education–employment mismatch (between graduates' academic training and the skills needed in the labour market). Africa's development potential can only be unbridled if governments greatly improve human resources, through a battery of actions to make the educational system relevant to the economy, in-cluding thorough and systematic reform of the educational system, with greater emphasis on quality than quantity. Governments will need to assign greater emphasis to

science and technology, as well as entrepreneurship train-ing that will catalyse the effective unlocking of Africa's productive potential, placing African universities at centre stage. Steps would entail reviewing knowledge produc-tion, the nature and content of knowledge, the place of research and knowledge production (and how to pay for it) as well as the types of partnership that African universi-ties should seek in order to be equal players in the global arena—while remaining locally and nationally relevant.

Promoting technology transfer and innovation for value addition and structural transformation

Technology transfer and innovation are key drivers of eco-nomic and social development in a knowledge economy. They hugely enhance productivity and efficiency, while

lowering the costs of production and information—the keys to unlocking sustained growth, competitiveness and economic transformation. Africa's fast growth in the last two decades has partly been supported by acquisition of mature technology, as seen in the steep increase in the royalties and licensing fees it pays, and imports of capital goods and business services.

To take one example: technology transfer has been at the centre of the rapid diffusion of mobile telephony and wireless technologies in Africa, and has had a profound impact on individuals, firms and governments. It would have had a greater impact if Africa had helped to design, manufacture and build the components and the network infrastructure. Yet Africa is failing to attract foreign private research and development projects or manufacturing investment because of its limited base of technology and intellectual capital. Worse, according to one source, it is going backwards in technology production and ownership.[1]

Five radical steps are therefore needed to ensure that Africa benefits from the world's technological knowledge to meet its challenges of unemployment, poverty and climate change.

First, African countries need to put in place policies and strategies to integrate the three subcomponents of science, technology and innovation in all economic sectors

Technology transfer and innovation are key drivers of productivity growth and development in a knowledge economy.

and government agencies. Second, they should install mechanisms to mobilize, invest and manage funds for these three elements. Third, countries should increase investment in education, particularly in these subcomponents, to develop the necessary skills and talent needed to sustain innovation and entrepreneurship in a knowledge economy. Fourth, they need to upgrade soft and hard infrastructure to serve as a platform for technology transfer and innovation. Finally, they need to strengthen the business environment in order to meet innovative firms' needs through supportive financial, intellectual-property, competition and procurement policies. Such measures would virtually guarantee Africa's future growth, competitiveness and economic transformation.

Reversing underinvestment in infrastructure

Investment in infrastructure is necessary for releasing productive capacity and for improving living standards, yet poor infrastructure remains a major obstacle in Africa. The key constraint is lack of financing, and closing the gap will require action on many fronts. African governments should, for example, harness the domestic financial sector, such as commercial banks, insurance funds, the stock market and pension funds. African central banks should play a catalytic role by introducing incentive-based

risk sharing and by issuing bonds, launching guarantee schemes and adopting new financial instruments to lever their balance sheets. These domestic efforts should be complemented by efforts to attract FDI from emerging economies, such as China and India, with relatively large financial resources as well as the appropriate skills and technology. Governments should also take steps to get more out of existing infrastructure through efficiency gains.

Boosting productivity in agriculture

An African green revolution is a prerequisite for Africa's green industrialization and for its response to climate change. In general, countries have moved up the technological ladder first by developing agriculture and promoting value addition through agro-industries before moving

to heavy industry.[2] In Africa, raising the productivity (and hence profits) of small farmers should be given priority because the majority of rural Africans are engaged in subsistence agriculture. This approach demands high and sustained levels of investment in key public goods,

> *Green-economy develop-*
> *ment strategies are essential*
> *for promoting high and*
> *sustainable growth for*
> *Africa to become a global*
> *growth pole.*

Moreover, national governments need to take resolute steps to empower women farmers through better access to productive assets, land-ownership rights, credit and farming education.

Strategies for agricultural development should run parallel to those which allow countries to industrialize along green lines and to diversify economically, so as to render them less vulnerable to climate change. Green-economy development strategies are essential for promoting high and sustainable growth and for Africa to become a global growth pole. Harmful impacts of climate change fall unduly on the poor and exacerbate inequalities in health, education, labour force participation, and access to food and water. As Africa is far from meeting its own development investment needs from domestic resources, external financial support for mitigation and adaptation is vital.

such as rural roads and irrigation, agricultural research and new technology, support for input-related industries, such as fertilizers and seeds, and new economic links that will create economic opportunities for enterprises in rural areas.

Other interventions likely to increase the productivity of small farmers, in turn adding value and moving economies along the industrialization curve, are securing smallholders' rights in land policies, ensuring incentives for off-farm enterprise job creation, promoting African systems for supporting innovative farming technologies and expanding learning systems for farmers and agro-industries.

It is also imperative to examine the supply- and demand-side factors that may constitute barriers to mobilizing resources in a green economy. Governments can also increase spending on clean technologies and practices and gradually eliminate subsidies for polluting industries. National development plans should have policies that promote output and use of clean products; developing, diffusing and transferring technology are critical for this.[3]

Accelerating regional integration and intra-African trade

Progress in regional integration is mixed, but political commitment on what needs to be done is high. Such integration is an important first step towards global integration, and requires better links among Africa's countries by heavy investments in roads, telecommunications and intra-African financial institutions that will facilitate payments through, for example, regional guaranteed payment systems. African governments should therefore develop trade-related regional infrastructure by encouraging private sector participation (domestic and foreign) into infrastructure. Finally, governments must redouble their efforts to simplify procedures and harmonize policies in a wide range of areas, such as customs, immigration, border control and cargo inspection.

Harnessing new development partnerships through strategic engagement

The rise of powerful southern economic powers such as China and India presents opportunities and challenges. African governments should take an incisive approach towards them and develop a coherent strategy to ensure that trade, investment and finance from these countries serve to accelerate the continent's development potential, promote technological progress, enable capital accumulation and consolidate structural transformation. They should encourage, in particular, investments in infrastructure and agri-business. Moreover, the governments of resource-rich African countries should develop a strong governance framework for the extractive sector (such as gold and oil) to stamp out corruption and avoid the "resource curse". Strengthening governmental negotiation capacity is critical.

> *African governments need to develop comprehensive national and regional strategic frameworks for engagement with external partners and investors.*

Chapter 5: Mobilizing resources for structural transformation

THE LAST DECADE has seen a notable recovery in African countries' capacity to mobilize resources and raise investments, although the continent's growth prospects and its capacity for mobilizing resources remain vulnerable to external shocks.

Given the new opportunities from strong demand for Africa's resources and fundamental changes in the geopolitical landscape, it is vital for Africa to optimize the various channels of mobilizing resources and to improve the mechanisms for using and distributing resources. In this way it can create a foundation for shared growth and inclusive development.

Africa can draw on its experience with traditional aid donors for the challenges in dealing with new players, including investors from emerging economies as well as multinational corporations and international portfolio investors who have recently renewed their interest in resource-rich Africa. To avoid non-productive capital flows (financial and human), African countries should explore mechanisms of repatriation of illicit capital flows and developing new financial instruments for securing private savings from international and domestic investors—encouraging only those likely to contribute to its development. African countries should also seek to improve public resource management and increase the participation of domestic stakeholders in development.

African countries should capitalize on the new opportunities for resources rarely available since independence, but the challenges of turning optimism into reality are equally daunting. In particular, the policy challenge shared by all African countries—resource-poor and resource-rich alike—is how to deploy new resources in socio-economic development and how to make resources for development less volatile and less subject to commodity booms. Their leaders could consider the following lines of action.

Windfalls from commodity booms and newly available resources should be deployed purposely to help diversify and transform economic structures, while resource rents should be distributed to aim for inclusive growth.

African governments should take strategic positions with all the categories of external actors and investors—traditional aid donors, new development partners, multinational corporations and private portfolio investors. They should seize on their newly acquired stronger position by presenting their home-grown development visions and strategies as a basis for negotiations.

For mobilizing private domestic and foreign savings through the financial system, governments should concentrate on deepening financial markets and strengthening the capacity of financial institutions so that mobilized funds are effectively intermediated and used for productive investments and socio-economic development.

It is important to explore and deepen mechanisms of regional cooperation for countercyclical macroeconomic management. This may lead eventually to stabilization or development funds among several countries or Africa-wide.

Finally, it is crucial to forge a productive partnership between the State and domestic stakeholders by eliminating basic considerations of influence in the political economy of public resource management. This will allow governments to tackle the structural weaknesses in generating

domestic public resources that stem from the shallow tax base and heavy reliance on resource-based and trade taxes. Authorities can broaden the tax base by improving the distribution mechanisms through fiscal channels, for example by ensuring better public goods provision and by mainstreaming the informal sector within the formal economy.

Notes

1   http://www.uneca.org/istd/tech_resurgence.pdf.

2   See UNECA and AUC (2009) "Economic Report on Africa 2009: Developing African Agriculture Through Regional Value Chains". UNECA. Addis Ababa. Ethiopia.

3   See UNECA and AUC (2011) "Economic Report on Africa 2011: Governing Development in Africa – the Role of the State in Economic Transformation". UNECA. Addis Ababa. Ethiopia.

Developments in the World Economy and Implications for Africa

AFTER A STRONG rebound in 2010, the world economy slowed in 2011 owing to increased risks and uncertainties that are expected to remain in 2012 and beyond. The negative effects of the triple crisis of 2007–2009—food, energy and finance—still linger, and the euro area sovereign debt crisis has aggravated the structural imbalances in the world economy and cast doubt on the prospects for sustained growth and a quick recovery. The shift of "toxic assets" from private sector to government balance sheets in major developed economies did not relieve the global financial system as expected, but instead worsened government fiscal positions, paced by new global financial turmoil with the onset of the euro area crisis.

The depth and complexity of the global crisis has so far defied the many policy responses applied by the major developed countries, which kept interest rates low and pursued fiscal austerity measures to restore fiscal credibility. Despite these measures, however, long-run structural problems, such as increased income inequality, dysfunctional labour markets and global imbalances, have intensified.

African economies rebounded quickly from the 2008 financial crisis as commodity prices rose and export revenues returned to pre-crisis levels, enabling them to finance the necessary investments. But with the political turmoil in North Africa, coupled with the euro area crisis, growth slowed in 2011. Still, some African countries continued to post double-digit growth, reflecting increased commodity prices and strong domestic demand.

1.1 World growth slowed and unemployment stayed high

THE WORLD ECONOMY grew at 2.8 per cent in 2011, down from 4 per cent in 2010, largely because of decreased demand and greater uncertainty (figure 1.1). Gross domestic product (GDP) growth in developed economies declined from 2.7 per cent in 2010 to just 1.3 per cent in 2011, on both demand and supply factors. Domestic demand, particularly in the developed world, stagnated owing to obstinately high unemployment and depressed consumer and business confidence, as fear of a second recession became widespread. Low growth in the developed world is expected to persist at least until the end of this year (figure 1.1).

The outlook for the world economy remains gloomy, with growth expected at 2.6 per cent in 2012.

In contrast, emerging and developing countries, as well as economies in transition, performed relatively well, but they were not immune to the fallout in the world economy: they faced rising inflationary pressures, increased income inequality and escalating social tensions.

The outlook for the world economy remains gloomy, with growth expected at 2.6 per cent in 2012. The euro area crisis is the most severe downside risk (section 1.7).

Figure 1.1

GDP growth rates of major global regions, 2005–2012 (%)

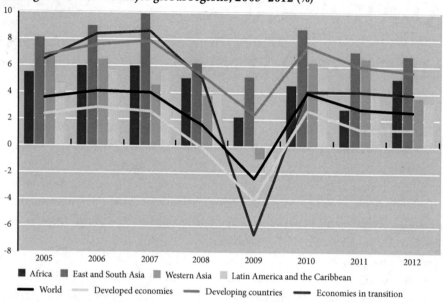

■ Africa   ■ East and South Asia   ■ Western Asia   ▨ Latin America and the Caribbean
— World   — Developed economies   — Developing countries   — Economies in transition

Source: UN-DESA (2011, 2012).

Notes: a. Estimated; b. Forecast.

Growth in the *European Union* (EU) levelled off from 2 per cent in 2010 to 1.6 per cent as the euro area registered only 1.5 per cent growth in 2011 (UN-DESA, 2012). The euro area crisis struck at consumer and business confidence, and lowered private consumption and investment against a backdrop of re-emerging financial turbulence and a bank credit crunch. The EU is expected to register minimal growth of 0.7 per cent in 2012, and the euro area a mere 0.4 per cent.

> *The EU is expected to grow at 0.7 per cent in 2012, and the euro area at a mere 0.4 per cent.*

Growth in the *United States* (US) declined to 1.7 per cent in 2011 from 3.0 per cent in 2010, reflecting continued sluggish private consumption and reduced government expenditure (UN-DESA, 2012). An elevated oil price, high unemployment and persistent deleveraging held down disposable household income. US growth is forecast to slip to 1.5 per cent in 2012. Downside risks lie in fiscal policy choices and the spillover effects of the euro area crisis on still fragile financial institutions. However, some positive signs have emerged in job markets, which might influence the 2012 presidential election and the subsequent economic policy orientation and the pace of the recovery.

Japan's economy switched from 4.0 per cent growth in 2010 to a contraction of 0.5 per cent in 2011, mainly owing to the shock of March's devastating earthquake and tsunami on private consumption and investment (UN-DESA, 2012). Export growth slowed, reflecting the disaster's disruption to supply chains as well as the yen's climb. Post-disaster reconstruction expenditure and rising manufacturing confidence are, however, projected to enable the economy to rebound with 2.0 per cent growth in 2012. In the medium and long term, though, an ageing population, mounting public debt and deflationary pressures will weigh heavily on growth.

The *economies in transition* grew 4.1 per cent in 2011, as in 2010, but still below pre-crisis rates (see figure 1.1). Domestic demand remained weak, as high unemployment and increased household indebtedness constrained private consumption and investment. However, export revenue rose on high commodity prices. The economies in transition are expected to grow 3.9 per cent in 2012, yet they remain vulnerable to spillovers from the euro area crisis owing to their close economic links to that bloc.

In 2011, developed economies' overall fragility weighed heavily on developing countries' growth, which stood at 6.0 per cent, down from 7.5 per cent in 2010; growth is projected to decline further to 5.6 per cent in 2012 (see figure 1.1). Overheating worries have receded, but high unemployment and political turmoil in some countries are still threatening growth prospects. Developing countries have tried to make up for the decline of external demand by stimulating domestic demand and pursuing expansionary policies.

East and South Asia—the world's growth engine—also felt the global economic chill through slackening exports. Growth slowed to 7.1 per cent in 2011 against 8.8 per cent in 2010 (see figure 1.1), despite robust private consumption and investment. Natural disasters affected regional industrial production and supply chains. Growth is projected to further decelerate to 6.8 per cent in 2012 as external demand from developed countries stays depressed.

China and India—the two largest emerging economies—were slowed by headwinds from the world economy in the fourth quarter, though they maintained excellent growth of 9.3 per cent and 7.6 per cent, respectively, in 2011. High inflation eroded Chinese household incomes and government attempts to limit bank credit—stemming from anxieties of an overheating economy—put pressure on private investment. The major risk for China's economy comes from a possible external demand slump, which

would depress export growth. China is forecast to grow 8.7 per cent in 2012.

India's buoyant private consumption was its main growth driver. Rising prices of basic foods, water and electricity have, though, become a source of public protest against government policies. India is expected to keep its growth momentum, at 7.7 per cent in 2012. Low productivity of rain-fed agriculture and a possible reversal of capital inflows are the main risks (EIU, 2011a).

Western Asia's economic growth edged up from 6.3 per cent in 2010 to 6.6 per cent in 2011 (see figure 1.1), mainly on a high oil price and greater social security spending. Increased energy export income and supportive macroeconomic policies propped up growth in oil-exporting countries, while some oil-importers saw recovery led by fiscal stimulus and domestic demand. Others contracted or stagnated because of social and political instability. Growth for the region is expected to decline sharply to 3.7 per cent in 2012 as a result of regional political uncertainties and a possible downward trend in the oil price.

Economic growth in the *Latin America and the Caribbean* (LAC) region decelerated to 4.3 per cent in 2011 from 6.0 per cent in 2010, despite the vigorous domestic demand attributable to favourable labour markets, high commodity prices, global low interest rates and currency appreciation (see figure 1.1).[1] Growth rates were divergent across the region: South American countries continued to benefit from emerging economies' commodity demand, sound economic fundamentals and increased domestic demand. Mexico and the countries in Central America and the Caribbean, in contrast, experienced slow growth, influenced by the weak US economy (EIU, 2011a). The

Even with the lacklustre global backdrop, Africa's economic outlook is quite positive, with growth of 5.1 per cent expected in 2012.

> *High unemployment, especially among youth, characterizes Africa's labour markets.*

LAC region is expected to slow to 3.3 per cent growth in 2012, reflecting a generally unfavourable global economy.

Africa's growth fell from 4.6 per cent in 2010 to 2.7 per cent in 2011 (see figure 1.1), mainly owing to the political turbulence in North Africa. Private investment declined with increased investor risk aversion there, though domestic demand remained robust and exports rose despite a severe drought in other parts of the continent.

Yet even with the lacklustre global backdrop, Africa's economic outlook is quite positive, with growth of 5.1 per cent expected in 2012. The key downside risk lies in export revenues shrinking because of sharply lower world commodity prices and adverse weather.

Persistent high unemployment is the most pronounced outcome of the weak global economy, and the global jobs situation improved little in 2011, despite worldwide government efforts to stimulate growth (table 1.1). After a steep rise in 2009, the developed economies' and EU unemployment rate approached 9 per cent in 2010, and it kept on climbing through most of 2011 (ILO, 2011b). The world unemployment rate for youth—the most vulnerable group in a labour force—declined only marginally to 12.6 per cent in 2011, with potentially destabilizing impacts on societies (ILO, 2011c).

Table 1.1

Unemployment, 2007–2011 (%)

Region	2007	2008	2009	2010			2011		
				CI lower bound	Preliminary estimate	CI upper bound	CI lower bound	Preliminary estimate	CI upper bound
					Rate				
World	5.6	5.7	6.3	5.9	6.2	6.5	5.6	6.1	6.6
Developed economies and European Union	5.8	6.1	8.4	8.5	8.8	9.1	7.9	8.6	9.4
Central and South-Eastern Europe (non-EU) and Commonwealth of Independent States	8.6	8.6	10.4	9.1	9.6	10.1	8.9	9.7	10.6
East Asia	3.8	4.3	4.4	3.9	4.1	4.3	3.8	4	4.2
South-East Asia and the Pacific	5.4	5.3	5.2	4.8	5.1	5.4	4.5	4.9	5.3
South Asia	4.5	4.3	4.4	3.9	4.3	4.6	3.7	4.1	4.4
Latin America and the Caribbean	7	6.6	7.7	7.2	7.7	8.1	6.8	7.4	8.1
Middle East	10.5	10.2	10.3	9.6	10.3	10.9	9.3	10	10.8
North Africa	10.2	9.6	9.9	9.1	9.8	10.5	8.6	9.8	10.9
Sub-Saharan Africa	7.9	7.9	7.9	7.6	8	8.4	7.4	7.9	8.4

Source: ILO (2011a).

Note: *Preliminary estimates for 2010; projections for 2011; CI = confidence interval.*

High unemployment, especially among youth, characterizes Africa's labour market. Although the informal economy provides a cushion for the young unemployed, the youth unemployment crisis can only be addressed through strong, broad-based growth and comprehensive social and economic measures (UNECA and AUC, 2010). Africa boasts the youngest population among the global regions, and youth are the most precious resource for the continent's economic and social transformation. To release their potential, African governments must fulfil their commitments on youth employment and invest resources to address the key factors affecting youth employment, such as a skills mismatch and inadequate access to credit and productive resources (ILO, 2011c).[2]

The world economic slowdown and the global employment crisis are likely to have serious implications for Africa, in both the short and medium term. They could increase pressures on African countries' long-run objectives, such as poverty reduction, by constraining government budgets, which have to be channelled to priority areas such as infrastructure, science and technology and human resource development, as well as industrialization and employment creation (chapter 4). African economies' choice of key development areas will therefore largely determine their medium-term growth trajectory.

1.2 Inflationary pressures mounted

WORLD INFLATION EDGED up from 2.5 per cent in 2010 to 3.7 per cent in 2011, but is expected to ease to 2.6 per cent in 2012, with similar trends for developed and developing economies (figure 1.2). Given such expectations and gloomy global prospects, monetary policy in major economies is likely to remain accommodative in 2012, allowing continued balance-sheet repair in the private and government sectors and supporting world economic recovery.

Figure 1.2

Inflation in major regions and economies, 2005–2012 (%)

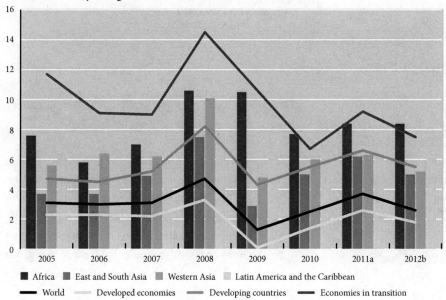

Source: UN-DESA (2011, 2012).

Note: a. Estimated; b. Forecast.

In the developed world, inflationary pressures came mainly from high food and fuel prices (section 1.4). Inflation reached 2.6 per cent in 2011, up from 1.4 per cent in 2010, and is forecast to moderate to 1.8 per cent in 2012 (see figure 1.2).

As in 2011, developed economies are expected to maintain an accommodative monetary stance in 2012 in order to induce domestic demand and stimulate their economies. The US Federal Reserve, for instance, has decided to keep the federal funds policy rate near zero until mid-2014, while the European Central Bank cut its key interest rate twice towards the end of 2011, reflecting its concern over the euro area's growth and employment prospects. Similarly, the central bank of Japan kept its benchmark interest rate near zero and enhanced monetary easing to fight deflation and accommodate the effects of the earthquake on productivity and growth.

For the economies in transition, weakened growth prospects and receding commodity prices alleviated inflationary pressures in the second half of 2011, though inflation was still near double digits (see figure 1.2). Most countries tightened their monetary policies in the light of economic recovery and elevated food and fuel prices.

Inflation in developing countries, which have been under overheating pressures since 2010, went up to 6.6 per cent in 2011, but is forecast to recede to 5.5 per cent in 2012 (see figure 1.2). The injection of excess liquidity into the global economic system by major developed economies drove up nominal world food and energy prices, lifting imported inflation in developing countries. In response, most of the latter postponed monetary tightening or even returned to accommodative monetary policies in 2011. The Reserve Bank of India, for example, kept its benchmark interest rate on hold in December after raising it seven times to fight inflation in 2011; China's central bank lowered its reserve requirement in December, and Brazil cut its interest rate three times in the second half of 2011.

As in other developing regions, inflation in Africa is expected to decline in 2012, though low global interest rates and high food and fuel prices are still likely to subject African countries to inflationary pressures (see figure 1.2). African economies have historically had higher inflation than most other developing regions. Recent downbeat global economic trends support an accommodative monetary policy in most countries on the continent, except for those facing non-food inflationary pressures. In a longer term, however, reforms to economic structures and institutions are essential for controlling inflationary pressures on the continent.

1.3 Fiscal balances improved

THE FISCAL BALANCE improved in almost every major economy or region in 2011 (figure 1.3). Developed economies as a whole cut their fiscal deficit from 7.5 per cent of GDP in 2010 to 6.5 per cent, though the US and Japan still ran fiscal deficits close to 10 per cent.

High food and fuel prices are still likely to subject African countries to inflationary pressures.

Developing economies partly rebuilt their fiscal buffers, using increased commodity export revenues.

The prospects for strengthening the position much further in 2012 do not appear promising on current forecasts, and fiscal consolidation runs the danger of stunting major developed economies' long-term growth prospects. Still, these economies are expected to continue moving that way: the euro area, for example, is forecast to register a fiscal deficit of only 3.1 per cent of GDP as members pursue austerity to regain fiscal credibility.

Figure 1.3

Central government fiscal balances for selected regions and economies, 2005–2012 (% of GDP)

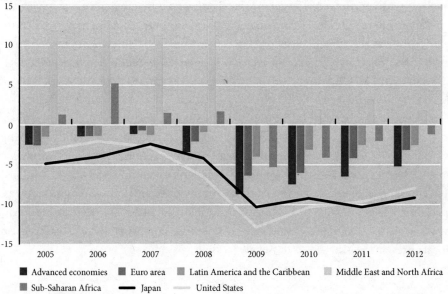

Source: IMF (2011a).

Developing countries may see slightly worsening fiscal positions in 2012 because of reduced demand from developed countries and a possible decline in commodity prices, exacerbated by higher spending on food subsidies and social protection programmes.

Fewer fiscal policy options were available to economies globally in 2011 than the year before. Developed economies, especially the euro area, are facing greater pressure to push through with fiscal austerity, given alarmingly high debt levels. [3] Developing countries' fiscal positions are generally well managed. [4] However, owing to weakened global growth prospects, they are more likely to adopt a neutral fiscal policy stance as prolonged fiscal expansion could exhaust fiscal space, fuel inflation, crowd out private investment and threaten their long-term growth potential.

Fiscal retrenchment by the world's major economies is likely to have short- and medium-term negative impacts on African economies, mainly through two channels. First, fiscally vulnerable African countries have to face much higher demand for sovereign debt yield in global markets as investors reassess sovereign debt risks in light of the euro area crisis. Second, on the aid front, developed economies might greatly reduce and impose stricter

conditions on official development assistance (ODA), including for Africa (section 1.7).

Responses to these twin challenges include strengthening economic and social development ties with new development partners from emerging economies—as well as their traditional donors—and mobilizing domestic development resources (chapter 5), especially as such strengthening may reduce African economies' over-reliance on aid flows from abroad in the long run.

In 2012, world commodity prices are expected to moderate with better supply-demand balance, mainly reflecting slower global economic activity.

1.4 World commodity prices remained high

THE INDEX FOR world commodity prices approached a historical high in April 2011, and apart from crude oil, all major commodity category price indices registered record highs in the first half of 2011. The trajectories of commodity prices divide roughly into two phases: most kept their upward trend in the first quarter; in April, however, they began to decline, but still hovered at relatively high levels (figure 1.4).

Movements in 2011 stem from both the demand and supply sides. First, demand from emerging economies continued to present strong support to high commodity prices, though this effect weakened as economies cooled in the fourth quarter. Second, political unrest in the MENA region severely disrupted that region's oil supply, pushing up energy prices on the global market. And third, increasing concerns over global growth prospects and risk aversion re-emerged in the second quarter of 2011, becoming the major downward driver of prices.

In 2012, world commodity prices are expected to moderate with a better supply–demand balance, mainly reflecting slower global economic activity. However, worldwide low interest rates and growth concerns may drive global investors into commodity markets to seek higher returns, adding volatility to prices. Risks are mainly on the downside, with possible price slumps in the worst-case scenario of global recession.

Figure 1.4

Index of primary commodity prices, Jan 2005–Nov 2011 (2005=100)

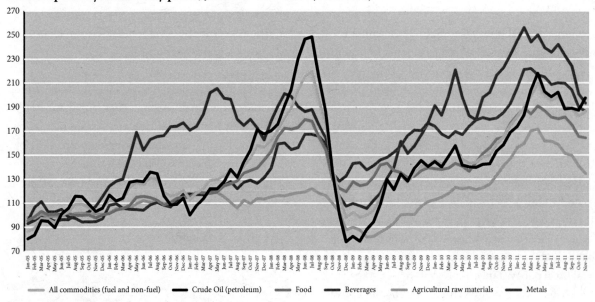

Source: IMF (2011b).

Global energy markets, especially for oil, are projected to face higher nominal prices in the long run.

Crude oil and the global energy market

After a 15-month fluctuation within a narrow upward channel, the world crude oil price picked up another major notch from September 2010, and after falling at the beginning of May, it has since fluctuated at $100–120 per barrel (see figure 1.4). In April, the Brent spot oil price hit $126.99 per barrel, more than one third higher than its 2010 closing price and only 14 per cent below its 2008 all-time high (BP, 2011). Crude oil in general showed higher volatility than other primary commodities.

Volatility in the oil price is expected to continue in 2012 and beyond. Global oil demand continued to firm in 2011, but at only 1.1 per cent after 3.2 per cent in 2010, reaching 89.2 million barrels per day (mb/d) (IEA, 2011). [5] Faltering developed economies and cooling emerging economies contributed to this moderation. In 2012, global demand is forecast at 90.5 mb/d, a 1.4 per cent rise from 2011.

Global oil supply was about 88.2 mb/d in the first three quarters of 2011, 0.9 per cent higher than the 2010 average. [6] The absence of Libya was largely made up by increased supply from Saudi Arabia. In 2012, total non-OPEC oil production is seen reaching 53.65 mb/d, up 1.7 per cent from 2011, and meeting 59.3 per cent of global demand. Still, the tight demand–supply equilibrium is unlikely to ease any time soon, even with the discovery of new sources around the world.

Despite cautious optimism for a lower oil price in 2012, global energy markets, especially for oil, are projected to face higher nominal prices in the long run, not only because of the possible further depreciation of the US dollar (in which oil is denominated), but more important, the evolution of global energy supply and demand. The Japanese nuclear power station disaster renewed anxieties around the globe over the safety of nuclear power, which in recent years has become more acceptable as a replacement for traditional fossil-fuel energy. Other main challenges for global energy use include expanding global energy access, increasing energy investments and mitigating the impact of global climate change (IEA, 2011b). [7]

Food and beverages

The world food price index recorded a historical high in April 2011, after which it showed a gently declining trend, but with increased volatility (see figure 1.4). Explanations for the food price surge included bad weather in most major agriculture-exporting countries in the later months of 2010, increased biofuel use owing to increased global energy prices, US dollar depreciation and market speculation.

Among particular commodities, the price of rice was up more than 20 per cent since May 2011, at odds with wheat and maize prices. Severe floods in Thailand, which disrupted production, and speculative sentiment in the market were responsible for the dramatic increase in the price.

The outlook for the world food price is a slight downtrend in 2012. On the supply side, high prices in 2011 are expected to have induced more agricultural investment, and the weather may also turn out to be more favourable, both of which point to rising food output in 2012. On the demand side, the stuttering world economy is likely to reduce global food imports and dampen biofuel transformation as energy prices decline. Even so, the food price is expected to remain volatile and sensitive to demand or supply shocks, partly owing to low inventories.

Despite the forecast short-term fall, however, global food prices should remain on a plateau in the long run. Food

The food price is expected to remain volatile and sensitive to demand or supply shocks, partly owing to low inventories.

> *Increased volatility of world commodity prices presents new challenges for African countries over the re-emerging issue of food security.*

supply is restricted by a shortage of arable land, rising agricultural production costs and decreasing agricultural productivity, while food demand is stimulated by increasing incomes of the emerging economies and more use in biofuel production by developed economies owing to high energy prices (OECD and FAO, 2011). The high food price

Agricultural raw materials

From April 2009, the index for agricultural raw materials kept on rising and more than doubled by its peak in April 2011, but declined modestly thereafter (see figure 1.4). Strong demand from emerging economies and adverse weather drove up prices. The natural rubber price attained its highest ever level in the first quarter of 2011 owing to

Metals

The metals index hit a record in February 2011, and then fluctuated downward within a narrow range in the following months. Copper prices remained relatively high throughout 2011, reflecting an imbalance between global consumption and production.

The outlook for metal prices in 2012 is closely linked to global economic activity. As China accounts for about 40 per cent of global demand, the country's macroeconomic policy and its stocks have a huge impact. With the world economy likely to show lower than initially projected growth, metal consumption could fall in 2012, taking prices down with it.

Once the global crisis of 2007–2009 ended, prices of precious metals, such as gold and silver, surged. Speculative forces were believed to be the major factor. However,

and increasing volatility could pose serious challenges to food security and poverty reduction efforts, especially in least developed countries.

The world beverages price index was up 73 per cent from its trough in January 2009 and peaked in March 2011. Coffee topped at about $2.45 per pound in May 2011, with increased volatility after September. Global coffee production fell 4.3 per cent in 2010/11 (ICO, 2011). Only Africa as a region raised its coffee output, by about 20 per cent; elsewhere it declined owing to bad weather. Similarly, the price of cocoa peaked at more than $3,450 per tonne in February 2011, but then fell more than 20 per cent by October. The combination of a weaker world economy and favourable weather conditions contributed to the decline (ICCO, 2011).

high demand from emerging economies and insufficient supply in rubber-producing countries. The price of cotton peaked in March 2011 with a steep rise of more than 170 per cent from the second half of 2010, and then fell during the rest of 2011.

the continued depreciation of the US dollar, global low interest rates, and, more important, risk aversion among global investors (given the downbeat global prognosis and volatile financial markets) propped them up.[8]

On the back of increased commodity demand and prices, Africa's merchandise exports increased to 31.5 per cent of GDP on average in 2006–2010. The continent's closer trade relationship with other regions, combined with its over-reliance on primary commodity exports, has made its trade even more vulnerable to global shocks in recent years (see section 1.7). Although Africa has diversified its export destinations a little, many countries still rely heavily on developed economies. Moreover, the increased volatility of world commodity prices, especially food, presents new challenges for African countries over the re-emerging issue of food security.

1.5 World trade growth moderated and current account balances stayed largely stable

THE WORLD TRADE value of goods and non-factor services continued to recover at 13.9 per cent in 2011, but lower than the 17.1 per cent of 2010. Deceleration in trade volume was more marked (figure 1.5). Developed and developing economies' exports grew 12.4 per cent and 15.9 per cent in 2011. European export value climbed by 13.8 per cent, but volume by only 6.7 per cent, indicating a shift towards more valuable goods. Among developing regions, Africa's export growth by value fell to 8.3 per cent from 14.3 per cent in 2010, mainly owing to North African political unrest, while its imports rose sharply by 16.9 per cent, largely because of steeper global food prices.

Figure 1.5

Annual average growth of export values by region, 2005–2012 (%)

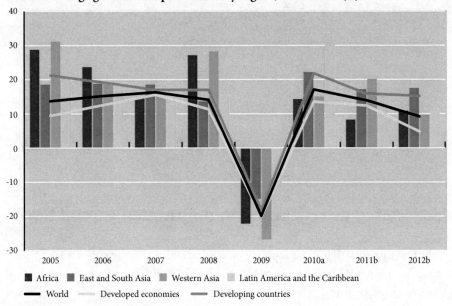

Source: UN-DESA (2012).

Notes: a. Estimated; b. Forecast.

Intraregional trade (that is, within a single global region) increased owing to the rise of emerging countries in recent years, though it still accounted for only 11 per cent of total trade for Africa in 2010, against 65 per cent for the EU (WTO, 2011).[9] Nevertheless, developed economies still dominate world exports' value addition (UNCTAD, 2011b).

The outlook for world trade growth in 2012 at a slower 9.2 per cent is overshadowed by divergent growth prospects. Export growth in developed economies is forecast to fall sharply to 4.8 per cent while the developing countries maintain their momentum at 15.2 per cent. Europe's exports are estimated to rise by only 4.6 per cent. Western Asia's export growth is expected to decline, but to a still-solid 9.7 per cent in 2012. With high unemployment across the globe, intensified protectionism is likely to emerge as the biggest challenge for world trade in 2012.

Trade patterns among the world's major economies and regions determined their largely stable current account balances in 2011 (figure 1.6). The US still ran a huge deficit against China's surplus, while the euro area's current account was in near balance. Japan's surplus narrowed, reflecting the earthquake's impact on its trade and post-disaster reconstruction. The surplus in the Gulf Cooperation Council (GCC) countries rose by more than a third, propelled by high oil prices. Russia's surplus widened only a little, as the non-oil sector deteriorated (EIU, 2011a).

Figure 1.6

Current account balances for selected countries and regions, 2005–2012 (% of GDP)

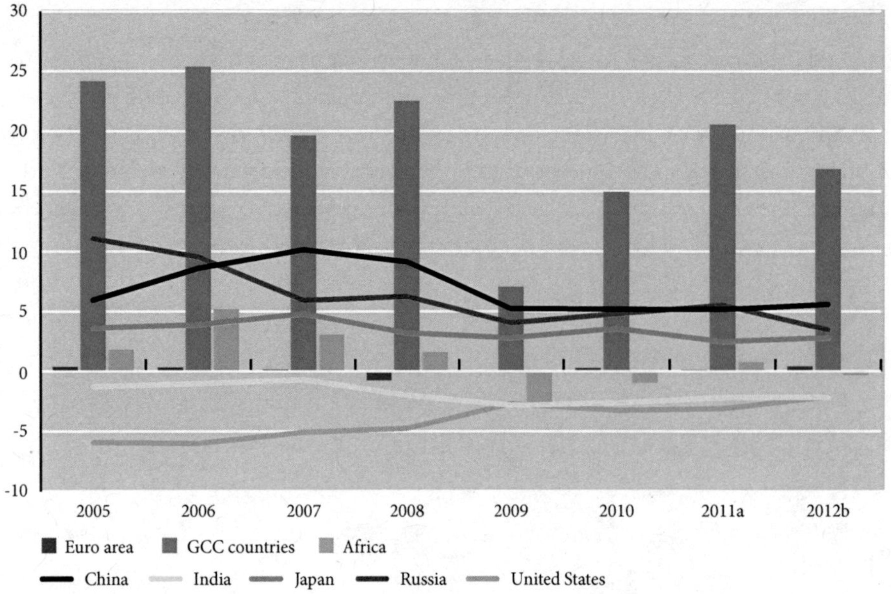

Source: IMF (2011a); authors' calculations.

Notes: a. Estimated; b. Forecast.

1.6 The US dollar depreciated as risk aversion dominated capital flows

THE US DOLLAR depreciated in the first three quarters of 2011 but reversed trend in the last, accompanied by increased real exchange rate volatility of major world currencies that was largely attributable to shifts in US

FDI to Africa recovered only modestly in the first half of 2011.

monetary policy and the worsening euro area debt crisis (figure 1.7). Near zero interest rates in the US and global investors' worries over further quantitative easing by the Federal Reserve kept the dollar weak and many emerging countries' currencies strong. However, growing risk aversion from August as the euro crisis intensified buttressed the dollar and prompted sharp falls in emerging currencies. The Japanese yen and Swiss franc appreciated sharply late in the year, reflecting their safe haven status, when US sovereign debt was downgraded in a historic move and the euro area crisis continued to deepen.

Figure 1.7

Real effective exchange rates for major economies, Jan 2005–Oct 2011, index (2005=100)

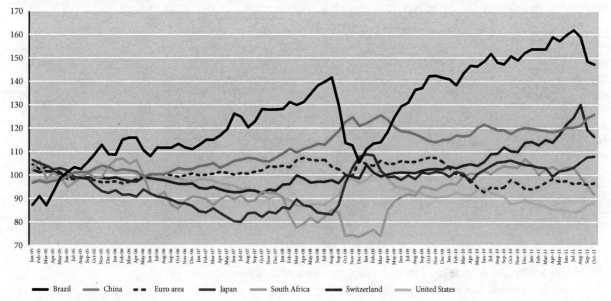

Source: IMF (2011b).

Global foreign direct investment (FDI) flows continued to recover in 2011, but less quickly than in 2010, largely reflecting uninspiring global growth prospects and high investors' greater risk aversion (figure 1.8). In the first half of 2011, they increased by 2 per cent sequentially. Again a divergence appeared between developed and developing economies: FDI flows to the former contracted by 3.9 per cent but to the latter they rose by 7.3 per cent (UNCTAD, 2011a). FDI to South and East Asia remained strong, though to the US and Western Asia it fell by nearly a half and a third, respectively, reflecting investors' concerns over US growth prospects and political uncertainties in the MENA region.

FDI to China surged in the first half of 2011, especially for mergers and acquisitions (M&A). "Green" investment declined worldwide but saw an over 55 per cent rise in the LAC region by September 2011. FDI to Africa recovered only modestly in the first half of 2011, and increased flows to South Africa were largely offset by smaller flows to North Africa.

> *Low global interest rates may boost FDI to Africa as the continent offers expected higher returns than most other developing regions.*

Figure 1.8

FDI inflows by region and selected economies, 2009–2012 ($ billion)

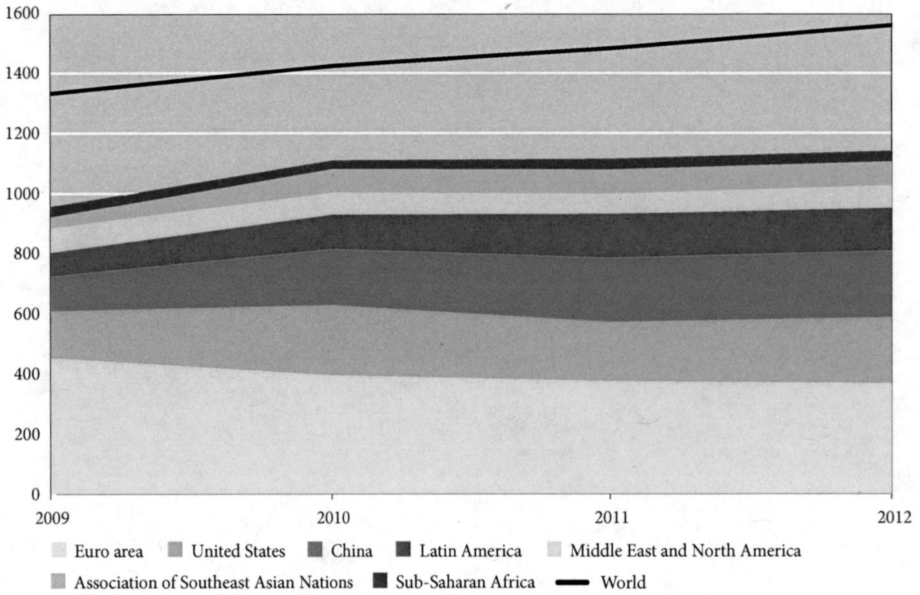

Euro area   United States   China   Latin America   Middle East and North America
Association of Southeast Asian Nations   Sub-Saharan Africa   ▬ World

Source: EIU (2011a).

Uncertainties in the world economy are likely to prevent a strong rebound of global FDI in the immediate future, though developing economies and economies in transition are expected to consolidate their positions as favoured destinations. As emerging economies upgrade their industrial structures, high-tech sectors are likely to receive further FDI inflows.

Low interest rates worldwide may boost FDI to Africa, as the continent offers expected higher returns and far greater investment opportunities than most other developing regions, given the last decade's relatively fast economic growth and improved economic governance.

Portfolio investment saw a steep decline in 2011, mirroring the world's pessimistic growth outlook. The Morgan Stanley Capital International world stock index slumped by 9.2 per cent, while component indices for developed and emerging markets fell by 7.5 and 19.7 per cent in US dollar terms (EIU, 2011b).

Remittances, however, recovered almost to their pre-crisis levels by 2011, even if growth was slow relative to recipient countries' inflation. Volumes varied among developing regions, mainly owing to the political and economic situations of the source countries. Political unrest in MENA curtailed flows to sub-Saharan Africa and South Asia, while the slow US and Japanese economies affected flows to the LAC region and East Asia, respectively. However, high oil prices helped workers in Russia to lift their remittances to Europe and Central Asia, and those in the GCC countries to boost theirs to South Asia. Gloomy global growth prospects weigh on the outlook for 2012 (figure 1.9).

> *For many African countries dependent on aid, a possible decline in aid flows could pose serious challenges in the short term.*

Figure 1.9

Remittance inflows by major recipient region, 2007–2012 ($ billion)

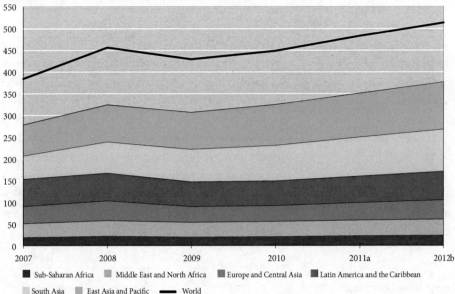

Source: World Bank (2011).

Notes: a. Estimated; b. Forecast

Global ODA climbed 6.5 per cent in 2010, but is expected to grow only 1.3 per cent on average in 2011–2013 because of slower growth prospects in donor countries.[10] Disbursements of ODA in 2010 were still well below commitments and are expected to remain far below the United Nations target of 0.7 per cent of donor countries' gross national income by 2015.

For many African countries dependent on aid, a possible decline in aid flows could pose serious challenges in the short term as many planned projects may have to be abandoned or scaled back. Hence mobilizing, using and distributing financial resources better are key challenges for African economies to sustain or accelerate their growth (chapter 5). Another short-term problem also looms large—the effects on Africa of the debt crisis in the euro area.

1.7 Euro area crisis could seriously affect Africa

THE EURO AREA sovereign debt crisis presents the most severe downside risk for the world and for Africa in 2012 and beyond. Analysis by the Organisation for Economic Co-operation and Development (OECD) suggests that prospects for a quick recovery are dismal and that other regions around the world, including Africa, may feel negative impacts, collectively reflected in decelerating growth.[11]

As Europe has traditionally been Africa's most important export destination and source of capital, the impact of the crisis through the channels of trade, FDI, remittances and aid is now discussed. Beyond these impacts,

The euro area sovereign debt crisis presents the most severe downside risk for global growth in 2012 and beyond.

Africa's banks may feel pressure from globally tightened credit markets and limited liquidity, while some African countries' currencies are expected to depreciate and show greater volatility.

Trade

Trade is expected to be the most prominent channel of the debt crisis's impact on Africa.[12] In 2010, Africa's merchandise exports to the EU represented 10.3 per cent of its GDP and 36.2 per cent of its total exports. North America and Asia took 16.7 and 24.2 per cent of African exports, respectively (WTO, 2011).

Africa's merchandise export composition and destinations can help to gauge the impacts of the crisis on the continent's exports (table 1.2).[13] Fuels and mining products remained Africa's major merchandise export items in 2010, and Europe was the most important destination for all merchandise exports. Asia and North America took large portions of Africa's fuels and mining exports. Intra-African trade had noticeable shares in all product categories except fuels and mining. In recent years, Africa's export destinations have been diversifying with increased engagements with emerging partners, which might provide a cushion for the expected decline in the continent's exports to Europe.

Table 1.2

Africa's exports of merchandise products by region, 2010

	Agriculture		Food		Fuels and mining		Manufactures	
	Value ($ billion)	Share (%)	Value ($ billion)	Share (%)	Value ($ billion)	Share (%)	Value ($ billion)	Share (%)
World	55	100	44	100	333	100	95	100
EU	20	37.1	17	37.9	118	35.3	40	42.3
Africa	11	19.1	9	21.3	24	7.3	23	24.0
Asia	9	15.5	5	10.4	94	28.3	13	14.2
Middle East	6	11.7	6	14.1	3	0.9	5	5.8
North America	3	5.0	2	5.3	73	22.0	9	9.1
Commonwealth of Independent States	1	2.4	1	2.9	0	0.1	0	0.2
South and Central America	0	0.9	0	0.7	11	3.3	2	2.2

Source: WTO (2011).

> *The euro area crisis is expected to weigh heavily on ODA to Africa because the EU is the largest aid provider to the continent.*

A knock-on effect on trade may worsen various African countries' fiscal positions. Oil revenues are a major source of financing for primary fiscal deficits in some countries on the continent. Also, African countries that are heavily reliant on trade and resource tax revenues may suffer from lower commodity demand from the EU (and the world), especially those running high fiscal deficits.

FDI

FDI flows from the EU to Africa are relatively stable compared with those from other parts of the world, and have generally kept on rising over the past few years. However, Africa may face decreased FDI from both the EU and other parts of the world in the short term because of the sovereign debt crisis and resultant slowdown in global growth.

FDI flows to Africa accounted for 3.9 per cent of the world total in 2006–2010. Africa has recently diversified its sources of FDI to emerging economies more, and this may mitigate the worst effects of the euro area debt crisis. For example, China's FDI to Africa reached about 7.5 per cent of the continent's total receipts in 2008 (AfDB et al., 2011).

The baseline scenario foresees no severe deterioration of world FDI to Africa. Africa's relatively high growth and its investment returns support the continent's attraction to global investors—assuming that the crisis does not greatly increase risk aversion globally.

Remittances

Remittances are the second-largest type of capital flows to Africa, and the euro area crisis has already taken a toll—remittances to MENA countries increased the least among regions of the world in 2011, though the situation was still favourable for sub-Saharan Africa in 2011. Western Europe had the largest proportion of remittances to Africa among global regions, with 41 per cent and 39 per cent for sub-Saharan Africa and MENA, respectively, in 2010 (World Bank, 2011).

The baseline scenario foresees subdued remittance growth to Africa in the near future, reflecting the process of economic adjustment and reform in the euro area, which will push down wages and keep unemployment high. As a result, Africa's private consumption is likely to decline and its current account balances to deteriorate generally.

Aid

Another important source of capital to Africa, ODA, is essential for development programmes in some African countries. In 2000–2009, Africa on average received 42 per cent of the ODA disbursed by OECD Development Assistance Committee (DAC) countries, and 49 per cent of that from EU institutions (OECD, 2011b). In 2008, ODA net disbursements accounted for 2.8 per cent of Africa's GDP. Although the ratio of ODA to African GDP overall is small, ODA is critical to some African economies. Indeed, about two thirds of African countries depend on ODA to some extent, and many African countries are heavily reliant on ODA to finance their public spending and capital budgets.

The euro area crisis is expected to weigh heavily on ODA to Africa because the EU is the largest aid provider to the continent. Among the most severely affected EU countries in the crisis, Ireland and Portugal had over 80 per cent and 60 per cent of their ODA channelled to Africa in 2007–2009, respectively. France also directed 63 per cent of its ODA to Africa in the same period. A handful of countries, such as France and Italy, had already reduced bilateral assistance to Africa because of the global economic crisis.

> *Africa may face decreased FDI from both the EU and other parts of the world because of the sovereign debt crisis in Europe.*

> *Global rebalancing presents opportunities and challenges to Africa.*

The expected slowdown of ODA to Africa could pressure social sectors, especially health, education and population programmes as well as water and sanitation, undermining poverty reduction efforts especially in low-income and fragile States.

1.8 Global rebalancing remains a major policy concern

GLOBAL IMBALANCES ARE seen in current account deficits or surpluses of the major economies and regions of the world, which since the "great recession" of 2009 have narrowed substantially, but they remain a serious threat to sustaining global economic growth over the long run (figure 1.10 and box 1.1). In an open world economy, imbalances are a natural phenomenon as capital tends to flow to countries with the highest expected returns.[14] But running persistent large current account surpluses or deficits is unsustainable for an economy, as a deficit economy will finally be unable to finance its consumption or investment through capital inflows at the yield that global investors demand. In 2011, the US still ran the world's largest current account deficit—$467.6 billion, against a maximum of $800.6 billion in 2006—while China, Japan, Germany and oil-exporting countries constituted its major surplus counterparts.

Figure 1.10

Global imbalances, 1996–2016 (% of world GDP)

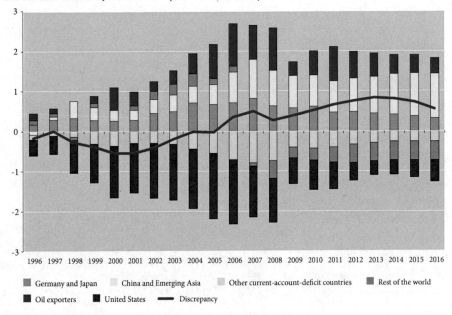

Legend: Germany and Japan · China and Emerging Asia · Other current-account-deficit countries · Rest of the world · Oil exporters · United States · Discrepancy

Source: IMF (2011d).

Box 1.1 Do global imbalances matter?

The current account balance is the difference between national saving and investment (public and private), and there are "good" and "bad" imbalances (Blanchard and Milesi-Ferretti, 2009).

In the good cases, countries with ageing populations tend to record a high savings rate and thus a current account surplus, while those with high investment returns, often coming under the term "deeper and more liquid financial markets", run deficits.

Domestic or systemic distortions or risks result in bad imbalances, which must be addressed. High precautionary saving causes domestic distortion. For example, an over-reliance on export-led growth and an undervalued currency are systemic distortions.

Good imbalances can interact with distortions to create risks, however. The evolution of global imbalances during 1996–2009 illustrated the combined effects of good and bad factors. Although global imbalances were not the cause of the 2007–2009 global crisis, they were "a critically important co-determinant" (Obstfeld and Rogoff, 2009).

Long-run large global imbalances have been a major policy concern in G-20 meetings since the global crisis. Global rebalancing needs close and effective economic coordination among countries and regions. For example, during its April 2011 meeting in Washington, DC, the G-20 agreed to "promote external sustainability" and encourage its member countries to implement policies to "reduce excessive imbalances and maintain current account imbalances at sustainable levels". The G-20 indicators to evaluate key imbalances include public debt and fiscal deficit, private saving and private debt, and the external position.

The first sustainability assessment report advised that major advanced economies should shift "from public-to private-demand-led growth", and emerging economies from "external-to domestic-demand-driven growth" (IMF, 2011g). It also advised that, individually, economies with large deficits should adopt fiscal consolidation, raise their private savings rate and encourage exports, and those with corresponding surpluses should try to eliminate distortions (to lower their national savings rates) or to boost investment (to reduce corporate savings).

Global rebalancing is likely to have significant implications for low-income countries (LICs), which include around half of African economies. Rebalancing tends to increase global manufacturing product prices, while worsening terms of trade for most LICs. This is expected to lower domestic consumption and investment while raising net exports in LICs. Labour-intensive products by LICs are expected to expand, which may help them to diversify their economic base and to benefit from technology and skills spillovers in a longer term (IMF, 2011c).

Rebalancing presents certain risks to LICs, however. Inflexibilities in major economies' markets may redistribute global welfare, to the detriment of LICs. Moreover, to benefit from the process, LICs need to invest more in their infrastructure and improve economic policy design and regulation, so as to enhance their investment environment and attract FDI inflows (Yang, 2011).

Hence global rebalancing presents opportunities and challenges to Africa. As an essential element of the long-run solution to the global crisis, rebalancing has suffered

African countries need to pursue economic diversification and structural transformation vigorously in order to reduce vulnerability to external shocks.

some setbacks with divergent short-term policy objectives among the major world economies recently, pointing to the benefits of injecting a development dimension to global rebalancing. This implies an important role for Africa, complementary to its ambition to become a global growth pole.

Before it can realize this ambition, however, Africa needs to meet growth and structural transformation imperatives (chapter 3), address constraints in infrastructure, technology, human resources and governance (chapter 4), and mobilize and apply financial resources more effectively (chapter 5).

1.9 Conclusions and policy recommendations

THE WORLD ECONOMY is entering a period full of uncertainties and challenges. In the short term, the euro area sovereign debt crisis might push the global economy into another prolonged and deep recession or slow global growth, at steep social cost. High unemployment and rising food and energy prices have already widened income inequality and stirred up widespread discontent and social instability around the planet. The failure of developed-country governments to provide long-lasting solutions to correct global imbalances deepens the malaise.

Africa is not immune to the global crisis, though it is now in a much better position to deal with external shocks. The expected global economic slowdown may well cut demand for its commodity exports, reduce prices and thus hurt its export revenues, but increased output alongside its gradual moves to diversify its exports—as well as recently improved intraregional trade—can help the continent to better weather adverse global developments. ODA shortfalls could threaten many aid-dependent African countries' social development programmes, but could also encourage the continent to mobilize more domestic resources and reduce over-dependence on foreign financial assistance.

In view of these risks and challenges, African governments should implement growth-supportive macroeconomic policies in the short run, while adopting long-term development perspectives. To be more specific, they should increase their investments in programmes such as education, health and infrastructure that can enhance their economies' long-term growth potential in the bounds of their fiscal space. Monetary policy needs to be accommodative to support growth, but must be combined with income policies to provide a minimum social security cushion for the weakest groups in society, so as to consolidate the achievements in reducing poverty over the last decade.

In the long term, Africa's governments need to pursue economic diversification and structural transformation vigorously in order to reduce vulnerability to external shocks, such as the euro debt crisis or volatility in commodity prices. Moreover, African countries must continue to diversify their export destinations and expand economic partnerships, including those with new development partners, while deepening intra-African trade and investment.

Crucially, African countries can grow faster by unleashing their productive potential—by aggressively investing in infrastructure and human capital, and by promoting good governance (chapter 4). This will require strong political leadership and a firm institutional framework to fulfil the broad, transformative long-term agenda.

References

AfDB (African Development Bank), OECD (Organisation for Economic Co-operation and Development), UNDP (United Nations Development Programme), and UNECA (United Nations Economic Commission for Africa). 2011. *African Economic Outlook 2011*. Paris: OECD Publishing.

Blanchard, O. and G.M. Milesi-Ferretti. 2009. "Global imbalances: in midstream?" *IMF Staff Position Note*, December 22.

BP (British Petroleum). 2011. "Brent oil price history." December.

EIU (Economist Intelligence Unit). 2011a. Country forecast database.

_____, 2011b. Country database, December.

_____, 2011c. *The Economist*, December 31.

Eurostat. 2011. Database, December.

ICO (International Coffee Organization). 2011. "Monthly coffee market report, October." London.

ICCO (International Cocoa Organization). 2011. "Cocoa market review, October." London.

IEA (International Energy Agency). 2011. *Oil market report*, October.

IMF (International Monetary Fund). 2007. *World Economic Outlook 2007*. Washington, DC.

_____. 2009. *Regional Economic Outlook: sub-Saharan Africa*. Washington, DC.

_____. 2011a. *Regional Economic Outlook: Western Hemisphere*. Washington, DC.

_____. 2011b. IFS database, December.

_____. 2011c. *New growth drivers for low-income countries: the role of BRICs*. Washington, DC.

_____. 2011d. *World Economic Outlook 2011*. Washington, DC.

_____. 2011e. *Fiscal monitor: addressing fiscal challenges to reduce economic risks*. Washington, DC.

_____. 2011f. "People's Republic of China: financial system stability assessment." Washington, DC.

ILO (International Labour Organization). 2011a. *Global Employment Trends 2011: the challenge of a jobs recovery*. Geneva: International Labour Office.

_____. 2011b. "Global trends: unemployment rate." Geneva.

_____. 2011c. "Report and conclusions of the 12th African Regional Meeting." Geneva.

Obstfeld, M. and K. Rogoff, 2009. "Global imbalances and the financial crisis: products of common causes."

OECD (Organisation for Economic Co-operation and Development). 2011a. "OECD Economic Outlook, Preliminary Version." Paris.

_____. 2011b. "Development aid at a glance, statistics by region, Africa." www.oecd.org/dataoecd/40/27/42139250.pdf.

UN (United Nations). 2010. "Objective and themes of the United Nations Conference on Sustainable Development." New York.

UNCTAD (United Nations Conference on Trade and Development). 2011a. "FDI recovery continued in the first half of 2011, but second-half prospects are bleaker." Global Investment Trends Monitor 7. Geneva.

_____, 2011b. "Trade policy developments, unpublished draft contribution to WESP." Geneva.

UN-DESA (United Nations Department of Economic and Social Affairs). 2011. *LINK Global Economic Outlook*. New York.

_____, 2012. *World Economic Situation and Prospects*, January. United Nations, New York.

Notes

1   The appreciation trend reversed in the last quarter of 2011 and currencies depreciated against the dollar in most LAC countries.

2   The 12th ILO African Regional Meeting stressed the urgency of the high youth unemployment problem in Africa and emphasized that it should be addressed through demand and supply measures.

3   In the first quarter of 2011, the euro area government debt ratio was 86.7 per cent of GDP, with Greece, Italy, Ireland, Portugal, Germany and France at 149.6 per cent, 119.9 per cent, 102.7 per cent, 94.0 per cent, 82.5 per cent and 84.4 per cent, respectively (Eurostat, 2011). Italy's government bond yield went over 7 per cent in November 2011, a dangerous level for fiscal sustainability.

4   China revised its end-2010 gross general government debt ratio up to 34 per cent in 2011. China had earlier been thought of as among those with the lowest government debt, but approached group average after this revision (IMF, 2011e). The asset bubble in China aroused concerns over its local government debt, and the huge fiscal stimulus introduced to counter the crisis may have increased State-owned banks' vulnerability (IMF, 2011f).

5   The figure was under the assumption of 3.8 per cent global growth. In another IEA scenario of 2.6 per cent 2011–2012 global growth, which is close to ours, the global oil demand in 2011 was 89.0 mb/d. In 2012, it is expected to arrive at 89.3 mb/d.

6   Authors' calculations based on IEA (2011a).

7   The Rio+20 Summit scheduled for mid-2012 will shed light on energy investments in developing countries in the context of the green economy (United Nations, 2010).

8   The Chicago Board Options Exchange Gold ETF Volatility Index went up sharply in August 2011 and remained high, suggesting concerns over global growth prospects.

9   Africa's intraregional trade has improved a little (section 2.3).

10   ODA figures and discussion in this paragraph are mainly from UN-DESA (2011).

11   OECD (2011a) presents four scenarios in resolving the sovereign debt crisis. The baseline scenario outlines an orderly default. In the downside scenario, disorderly defaults could happen, but do not mean the breakup of the euro area (the worst-case scenario, not shown). The upside scenario relies on major compromises and political breakthroughs among euro area countries, but has a relatively low probability.

12   The following trade analysis relates to Africa's merchandise trade only, as exports of commercial services were no more than 14 per cent of merchandise exports (by value) in 2010.

13   Section 2.3 discusses Africa's export composition by period.

14   The current and capital accounts are the two sides of a country's balance of payments, which by definition must balance. A current account deficit, for example, means that the country must sell its assets or borrow to buy goods and services abroad.

Economic and Social Developments in Africa and Prospects for 2012

AFTER A DECADE of impressive economic growth, Africa's momentum slowed in 2011, weighed down by contraction of economic activity in North Africa due to political unrest there, and the lingering indirect effects of the 2007-2009 global economic and financial crises in developed countries.

Many African countries are, though, sustaining strong impetus, supported by rising commodity prices and by strong domestic demand (owing to growing incomes and improving economic and political governance). Growth prospects remain optimistic, with output for the continent as a whole expected to recover strongly in 2012. The growth momentum is expected to continue in the medium term.

African economies might, however, be affected by the EU debt crisis and any subsequent deterioration in the global economic environment on several fronts, particularly through trade and capital flows. Africa is nevertheless poised to weather such risks and uncertainties. For more than a decade, the continent has deepened domestic sources of growth, and has strengthened both intra-trade and trade with faster growing economies in Asia and Latin America – away from Europe. This would help Africa mitigate the growth impact of a possible decline in trade with, and capital inflows from, the euro area.

Despite the acceleration of economic growth in Africa over the past decade, however, Africans' welfare has generally failed to improve. Social indicators have picked up only modestly, but with unemployment, particularly among youth, remaining stubbornly high, while income inequalities have widened. This disconnect between growth and social welfare requires policy actions on many fronts, including a focus on accelerating economic transformation in the key sectors that hold the greatest potential for jobs—such as agriculture, services and manufacturing.

This chapter, after discussing the trends and sources of Africa's recent economic performance, reviews developments in the continent's international trade and the impact of growth on poverty. It then presents recent social developments and discusses why economic growth has not been associated with commensurate progress towards the MDGs. It ends by looking at Africa's growth prospects for 2012.

Despite accelerated growth in Africa over the past decade, progress in social development remains slow.

2.1 Economic performance in 2011

Weakened recovery amid social and political unrest

PRIMARILY BECAUSE OF political unrest in North Africa and the continued slump in the developed economies, Africa's economic growth fell by nearly half in 2011, to 2.7 per cent from 4.6 per cent in 2010 (figure 2.1). This rate was far lower than seen before the global crisis.

The intensity and persistence of the social and political turmoil in North Africa increased investor risk aversion sharply, prompting capital inflows to reverse and private investment to decline. Production and exports of oil—the mainstays of North Africa—were also disrupted (notably in Libya), and tourism collapsed (IMF, 2011a). North Africa recorded zero growth in 2011, down from 4.2 per cent in 2010, as the Libya contracted by 22 per cent and Tunisia by 0.6 per cent.

Figure 2.1

Africa's economic growth, 2007–2012 (change in real GDP, %)

North Africa dragged down Africa's growth

A slowdown in sync with global trends, but below the developing country average

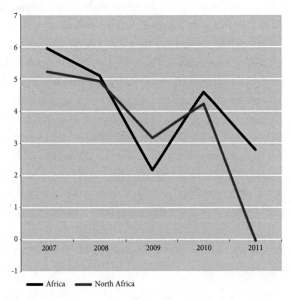
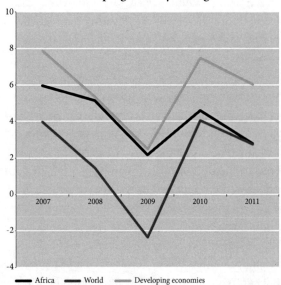

Source: UNECA calculations, based on UN-DESA (2011a).

Still an optimistic picture

Outside North Africa, growth was solid at 4.5 per cent in 2011 (figure 2.2), reinforcing the recovery of 4.8 per cent in 2010. Per capita GDP increased by 2.2 per cent outside North Africa, similar to the growth rate of 2.5 per cent in 2010 (table 2.1). Real income per capita rose by 4.7 per cent in 2011.

Growth continues to depend on commodity exports as one of its key drivers.

Growth was largely driven by increased receipts from commodity exports, stemming from higher prices on international markets (see figure 1.4) and rising demand for commodities, particularly from emerging markets in Asia (IMF, 2011b). Improved terms of trade and higher returns from commodity exports allowed many of Africa's resource exporters to build much-needed buffers in foreign exchange reserves. Several countries also continued to diversify their export production by building local capacity in processing and value addition, helping them to capture new markets for high-valued products in the fast-growing emerging markets of East Asia and Latin America (IMF, 2011b).

Figure 2.2

Africa's economic growth, 2007–2011 (change in real GDP, %)

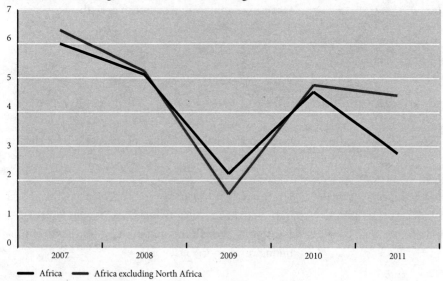

— Africa   — Africa excluding North Africa

Source: UNECA calculations, based on UN-DESA (2011a).

Table 2.1

Economic growth in Africa by country group, 2009–2011 (%)

	Real GDP growth			Real per capita GDP growth		
	2009	2010	2011	2009	2010	2011
Africa	2.2	4.6	2.7	0.0	2.4	0.7
Africa excluding North Africa	1.6	4.8	4.5	−0.7	2.5	2.2
North Africa	3.2	4.2	0.0	1.4	2.4	−1.5
West Africa	4.6	6.9	5.6	2.0	4.3	3.1
Central Africa	1.8	5.2	4.2	−0.8	2.6	1.8
East Africa	3.8	5.8	5.8	1.2	3.1	3.2
Southern Africa	-0.8	3.2	3.5	−2.5	1.6	1.7
Oil-exporting countries	3.3	5.1	1.5	1.2	3.0	−0.5
Oil-importing countries	0.9	4.0	4.2	−1.2	1.8	2.1
Mineral-rich countries	−0.5	3.8	4.1	−2.7	1.6	1.8
Non-mineral, non-oil countries	4.1	4.5	4.5	1.7	2.1	2.3

Source: UNECA calculations, based on UN-DESA (2011a and 2011b).

Note: Real per capita GDP is weighted by population for each country.

Higher commodity prices have benefited commodity-exporting African countries, but rising food and energy prices have hurt countries that are not commodity exporters.

As in previous years, domestic demand supported growth in many countries, and is becoming as important as the export market in some countries. This growth in domestic demand stems from greater public spending on major infrastructure projects, which has also helped boost Africa's productive capacity, particularly in agriculture and extractive industries. Growth also benefited from increased FDI inflows, in response to an improved economic management and business climate. And with rising incomes and urbanization, the domestic consumer market is growing, becoming an important source of growth.

Commodity prices impacted African economies differently

Higher commodity prices have benefited commodity-exporting African countries, but—rising food and energy prices especially—have hurt African countries that are not commodity exporters, with heavy impacts on their balance of payments. Steeper food and fuel prices have hit hard low-income households (especially the urban poor),

exacerbating social tensions and sparking food riots in some countries.

Severe drought in parts of the continent—Chad, Niger and countries in the Horn of Africa (notably Somalia) — devastating agricultural output there, leading to famine among rural poor households.

Varied economic performance

As in previous years, growth in 2011 was highly uneven among countries and groupings (figures 2.3 and 2.4 and see table 2.1). For the first time in five years, growth of the continent's oil exporters lagged behind that of oil importers. Growth in the former group decelerated from 5.1 per cent in 2010 to 1.5 per cent in 2011, despite large windfall oil-export gains from rising global oil prices (figure 2.3). The slowdown stemmed from political instability in oil-rich North African countries, particularly in Libya.

Economic growth in the oil-importing countries picked up, helped by solid domestic demand, a boom in public infrastructure spending and increased agricultural production. Growth rose to 4.2 per cent in 2011 from 4.0 per cent in 2010, consolidating the recovery from the slump induced by the global financial crisis.

Figure 2.3

Growth performance by country group, 2007–2011 (change in real GDP, %)

Oil-exporting versus oil-importing countries:
A divergent recovery

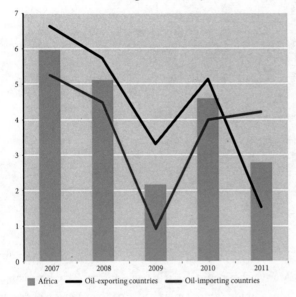

Mineral-rich versus non-mineral-, non-oil-rich:
A uniform recovery

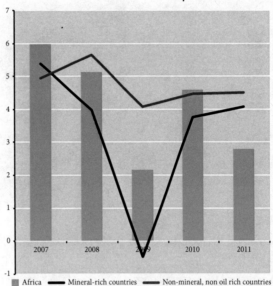

Source: UNECA calculations, based on UN-DESA (2011a) and EIU (2011).

By subregion, growth also showed dissimilarities (figure 2.4). In *East Africa*, most countries maintained their faster growth trajectory despite experiencing severe drought and famine. The subregion registered 5.8 per cent growth in 2011, close to the 6 per cent of 2010. The higher growth was mainly due to Eritrea (17.2 per cent), Ethiopia (7.4 per cent), Rwanda (7.2 per cent), Tanzania (6.4 per cent), Uganda (5.6 per cent) and Djibouti (4.6 per cent). In most of these countries, faster economic activity benefited from sustained public investment in infrastructure (Ethiopia and Tanzania), rising mining output (Tanzania), strengthening FDI in energy (Uganda) and higher agricultural output (Ethiopia).

In *West Africa*, conversely, economic activity moderated in 2011, affected by contraction in Côte d'Ivoire. Subregional growth fell to 5.6 per cent from 6.9 per cent, weighed down by that country's 0.4 per cent contraction, due to

post-election violence and a collapse of exports and the financial sector. Lower oil production by Nigeria also contributed. These factors were, however, largely counterbalanced by faster growth in Ghana (12.2 per cent), boosted by the resumption of commercial oil exploitation. Agriculture, mining and services also grew strongly in 2011.

Central Africa's economic activity remained fairly robust, although output declined from 5.2 per cent in 2010 to 4.2 per cent in 2011. Growth was underpinned by a combination of large public investment in infrastructure, strong performance of services, and increased timber exports. The overall performance covered a lacklustre performance by Chad, which saw a decline in oil production due to labour disputes in the oil sector, and a decline in remittances when many Chadians working in Libya lost their jobs at the outbreak of conflict.

Figure 2.4

Growth in Africa, 2007–2011 (change in real GDP, %)

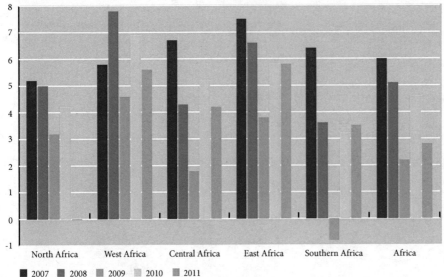

■ 2007   ■ 2008   ■ 2009   ■ 2010   ■ 2011

Source: UNECA calculations, based on UN-DESA (2011a) and EIU (2011).

In *Southern Africa*, overall output expanded by 3.8 per cent in 2011, up from 3.5 per cent in 2010, with considerable variations in the subregion. South Africa, whose greater integration with global markets makes it more vulnerable to external shocks, recovered rather slowly, growing by only 3.1 per cent in 2011 from 2.8 per cent in 2010. Its growth was lifted by recovery of consumer spending, in turn fuelled by cheap credit and low inflation. Prospects for a speedy recovery of private investment and consumer spending were undermined by slow global growth, while concerns of persistent unemployment reduced fiscal space as the government sought to raise the labour intensity of economic growth through a stimulus package.

> *Continental growth has rarely translated into strong jobs growth and unemployment rates remain high, especially among the youth.*

Many other countries achieved solid growth. Botswana, Mozambique and Zambia had growth of above 6 per cent, reflecting rising mining output and strong global demand for minerals (as well as a bumper harvest in Zambia). Growth in Angola and Zimbabwe surpassed 4.0 per cent, driven by increased oil output and investment (Angola) and by an improved political and economic climate (Zimbabwe). Only Swaziland bucked the trend somewhat: its output expanded by only 2.5 per cent in 2011, up from 2.0 per cent in 2010, on account of severe cutbacks in private and public spending in response to a deep fiscal crisis.

North Africa performed poorly as economic activity suffered from political and social strife that erupted in most countries. Output was flat in 2011, after expansion of 4.2 per cent in 2010. Libya led the contraction, with economic activity collapsing by 22 per cent, following disruptions to production of oil and exports of hydrocarbons. Egypt's growth fell sharply to 1.3 per cent from 5.1 per cent in 2010, and Tunisia's output contracted by 0.3 per cent. Disruptions to tourism—a major source of foreign exchange and employment—were heavy in those two countries.

Not enough jobs created, but quality of growth has improved

Continental growth has too rarely translated into strong jobs growth. High levels of unemployment, particularly among youth, remain. North Africa seems the most affected, with unemployment estimated at 9.8 per cent in 2011, versus 7.9 per cent for the rest of Africa (ILO, 2011). These figures understate the severity of the jobs crisis, however: women face twice the unemployment rate of men (15 per cent versus 7.8 per cent). Moreover, of those employed, the vast majority are in vulnerable work, mostly in low-productive informal activities. The poor productivity of these micro-enterprises undermines their ability to generate decent jobs and reduce underemployment.

The failure of economies to generate adequate employment is partly because recent growth has been driven by the capital-intensive extractive industries (mining and oil exploration). These activities also have limited forward and backward linkages with the rest of the economy. African countries therefore need to diversify their sources of growth towards developing pro-poor sectors if they are to make inroads into reducing high unemployment and poverty rates.

Nevertheless, evidence from household surveys indicates that the average living standards of relatively poor households in some of the fast-growing economies have risen strongly since the beginning of 2000 (IMF, 2011b). The poorest 25 per cent of households have fared best in countries where output grew the fastest. This welfare improvement is explained in large measure by cross-country differences in the pace and extent of growth in agricultural employment, which in turn has helped to lift household consumption among the poor. This evidence points to the importance of investing in agricultural productivity.

Inflationary pressure increased in Africa

Inflation rose across most of the continent in 2011, sparked initially by higher food and fuel prices. Continent-wide, consumer price inflation rose to 8.4 per cent in 2011, from 7.7 per cent in 2010 (figure 2.5). In the Horn of Africa, severe drought contributed to much sharper increases in inflation, mainly for food. In Ethiopia, for example, inflation rose to nearly 40 per cent, and in Guinea and Uganda, about 20 per cent. Non-food inflation also picked up in some countries: about 10 had non-food inflation above 10 per cent, including Ethiopia, Uganda, and Guinea (IMF, 2011b). In other countries, such as Ghana, Malawi, Rwanda and Zambia, good harvests kept food inflation low, and overall inflation stayed in single digits.

Promoting pro-poor growth is essential for African countries to reduce high unemployment and poverty rates.

Figure 2.5

Trends in African inflation, 2006–2011 (annual change in consumer price index, %)

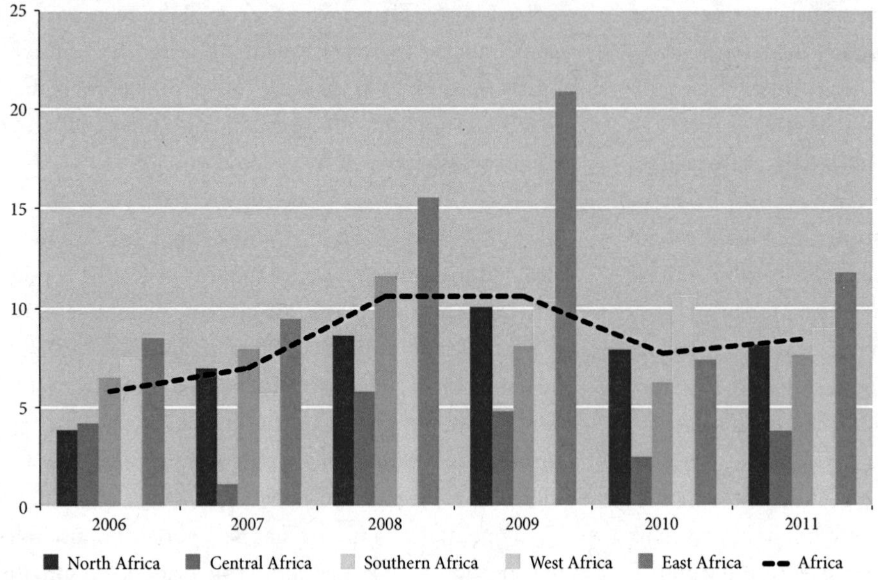

Legend: ■ North Africa ■ Central Africa ■ Southern Africa ■ West Africa ■ East Africa ▪▪ Africa

Source: UNECA calculations, based on IMF (2011c) for 2006-2010 and estimates for 2011.

Economic policy shifted to neutral—but still accommodative

Monetary policy in most African countries was largely supportive of growth. It turned from accommodative to neutral in 2011, as central banks faced the difficult task of containing imported inflation while bolstering recovery. A gradual tightening occurred in only a handful of countries, and, even then, not decisively. In most cases, policy instruments (such as interest rates) were kept unchanged from the levels to which they were lowered during the global crisis.

Fiscal policy remained supportive in 2011, as most countries sought to stimulate growth by raising spending on infrastructure and social protection programmes.

The two central banks in the CFA zone,[1] for example, maintained low interest rates in 2011 despite the European Central Bank's actions towards policy tightening earlier in the year. Similarly, the South African Reserve Bank kept its policy interest rate low for most of 2011. Notable exceptions were Nigeria and countries in the East African region (Kenya, Rwanda and Uganda) where policy rates were raised several times to curb inflationary pressures. For 2012, East African monetary authorities have decided to keep policy tight to curb lingering inflationary pressures.

It is too early to tell whether tight monetary policy is the best instrument to curb inflation and stimulate growth. Many countries are most likely to keep monetary policy accommodative because a solid global recovery is unlikely to materialize soon—and will not until the euro area sovereign debt crisis is definitively resolved.

Fiscal policy also remained supportive in 2011, as most countries sought to stimulate growth by raising spending on infrastructure and social protection programmes—such as through price subsidies and service delivery—to protect the poor from the economic crisis. Elections in some 20 countries also stimulated public spending in

2011. As a result, Africa's aggregate fiscal deficit widened to 4.4 per cent of GDP in 2011, from 3.7 per cent in 2010 (figure 2.6). In North Africa, some increases in public spending were directed at promoting social stability through price subsidies.

Figure 2.6
Africa's fiscal balances, 2007–2011 (% of GDP)

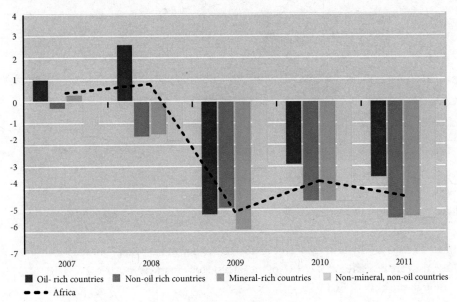

■ Oil- rich countries ■ Non-oil rich countries ■ Mineral-rich countries ■ Non-mineral, non-oil countries
● ● ● Africa

Source: *UNECA calculations, based on EIU (2011) and IMF (2011c).*

Largely benign external positions

Africa's aggregate external balance improved slightly in 2011, on the back of growing shipments from commodity exporters (figure 2.7). The current account balance turned to a small surplus (0.8 per cent of GDP), from an equally small deficit in 2010. Within country groups, however, the outcomes remained diverse, notably between oil-exporting and oil-importing countries. External surpluses increased in most oil and mineral exporters, while the current account deficits of oil-importing countries widened. The improvement in the current account balances of exporting countries enabled them to build foreign exchange reserve buffers and reduce their reliance on ODA as a source of current account financing, although ODA remained important to several countries with larger deficits.

ODA flows to Africa remained stagnant in 2011, partly because of pessimistic growth prospects and fiscal difficulties among many donor countries. Humanitarian assistance flows also declined, before rising in the latter part of 2011, in response to the severe drought and famine in the Horn of Africa. Debt relief flows, by contrast, continued to rise in 2011.

ODA flows to Africa stagnated in 2011 because of pessimistic growth prospects and fiscal difficulties in many donor countries.

Figure 2.7

Current account balances in Africa, 2007–2011 (% of GDP)

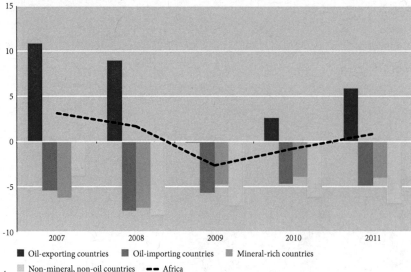

Source: UNECA calculations, based on IMF (2011c).

FDI inflows into Africa are estimated at $52.4 billion in 2011, close to the 2010 level. In 2012, they are projected to reach $55 billion (EIU, 2011).[2] Although the bulk of FDI still went to the extractive industries, there is evidence that it is becoming more diversified (AfDB, OECD, UNDP and UNECA, 2011), by source and destination. Portfolio inflows were generally weak, however, pacing the decline of African stock markets (25 per cent in the first half of 2011) because of the political transition in Egypt and Tunisia, which house two of the largest stock markets in Africa.

Despite sustained increases in capital inflows over the last decade, Africa's domestic resource gap and financing needs for achieving the MDGs by 2015 appear as high today as they were estimated in the late 1990s (Chapter 5 discusses constraints to Africa's development financing and ways to tackle them.)

2.2 Recent trends in international and intra-African trade

Shifting patterns of international trade

TRADE IS INCREASINGLY an engine of growth and Africa has continued to expand strongly since the global crisis. After a large contraction in 2009, African exports rebounded by 25 per cent in dollar terms in 2010, outstripping world export growth of 21 per cent. Africa's imports increased by 15.6 per cent in 2010, allowing the continent to return to a modest merchandise trade surplus of $5 billion. Africa's share of global trade increased marginally to 3.2 per cent (to be seen against its 2.6 per cent of global output and 14.8 per cent of the world's population).

Given the continuing dominance of primary commodities—fuels in particular—in Africa's export composition (figure 2.8), export fortunes mirror the international commodity price trends described in chapter 1. To illustrate: the value of African exports fell by 31 per cent in 2009 and grew by 25 per cent in 2010—but in volume terms, these figures equate to only 11 per cent and 9 per cent of exports in these two years. In other words, price accounts for almost two thirds of the growth or contraction in the value of trade.[3] The high receipts from the export of fuels are then used to finance Africa's import of manufactured goods (figure 2.9). This imbalance in the trade pattern underscores the case for building productive capacities for structural transformation.

Figure 2.8

African exports by broad category, 2000–2010 (current $ billion)

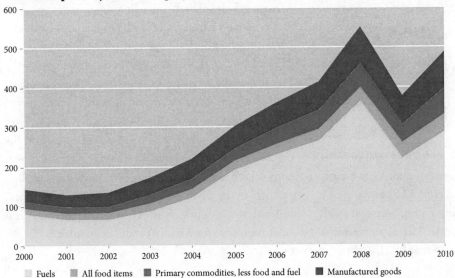

☐ Fuels ▨ All food items ■ Primary commodities, less food and fuel ■ Manufactured goods

Source: UNCTAD (2011), accessed 19 October 2011.

Figure 2.9

African merchandise trade balance by broad category (current $ billion)

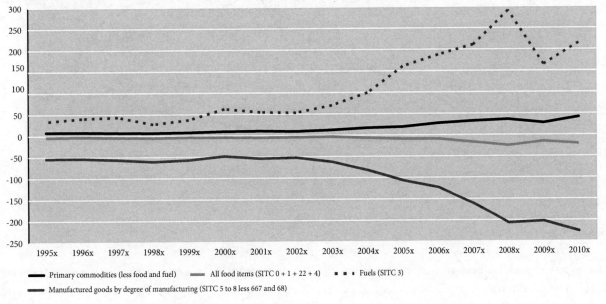

—— Primary commodities (less food and fuel) —— All food items (SITC 0 + 1 + 22 + 4) ▪ ▪ ▪ Fuels (SITC 3)

—— Manufactured goods by degree of manufacturing (SITC 5 to 8 less 667 and 68)

Source: UNCTAD.(2011), accessed 19 October 2011.

The lacklustre response of imports relative to exports can be attributed to less pent-up demand in Africa than in the regions most hit by the global crisis (WTO, 2011)— import contraction in 2009 in Africa was less than elsewhere, because African exports have a low import content, implying that increased imports may not necessarily require a matching expansion in exports. On a positive note, the lack of integrated production networks in Africa means that trade is more resilient to crisis than in more integrated regions.

Intra-Africa trade is disappointingly low, at around 11 per cent of Africa's total trade in 2010.

Africa is increasingly diversifying trading relationships towards emerging economic powers (figure 2.10). For example, China and India now consume 12.5 per cent and 4 per cent of Africa's exports—representing 5 per cent and 8 per cent of these countries' imports. Africa's engagement with China has in particular been fruitful. The share of

Chinese mineral and fuel imports from Africa grew from less than 5 per cent in 1995 to almost 25 per cent in 2010. African exports of high-valued products to the Group of Five (Indonesia, Malaysia, Saudi Arabia, Thailand, and United Arab Emirates) have also been growing.

Yet to capture more of the Asian market, African countries need to step up their expansion of their manufacturing base and engender productivity gains (IMF, 2011a). With uncertainty surrounding demand from Europe and the US, Africa would gain from diversifying its trading relations. In the medium term, however, traditional trading partners in the developed world will remain important, and a strategic approach is needed to explore new and lucrative niches for African products in Europe.

Figure 2.10

Africa's share of selected import markets, 1995–2010 (%)

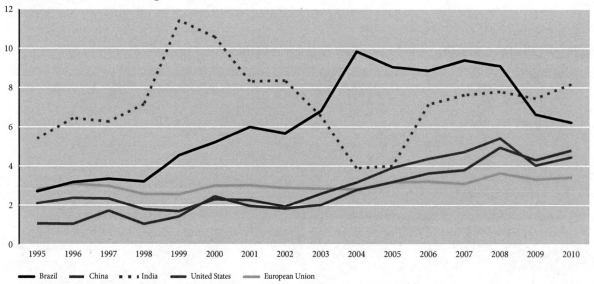

Source: UNCTAD (2011), accessed 26 October 2011.

Africa's service trade has been growing consistently with global trends, indicating its increasing potential. Travel and tourism account for 50 per cent of Africa's service exports. Despite the disruptions to services in North Africa in 2010 and 2011, sub-Saharan Africa continued to exploit its comparative advantage in tourism, recording a 13 per cent increase in 2010, for example. South Africa boosted its travel receipts by 24 per cent owing to the large number of foreign visitors attending the FIFA World Cup (WTO, 2011). In other sectors, Kenya and Ghana in particular

have benefited from exports of business-processing services, taking advantage of improved infrastructure for information and communication technology (ICT) and reasonably well-educated and urbanized workforces (IMF, 2011b).

In global trade, developing countries' average most-favoured-nation applied tariff rates came down to 9.9 per cent in 2009 (world: 8.6 per cent), from 10.5 per cent in 2008 (world: 9.3 per cent) (World Bank, 2010). Yet some

G-20 countries put through modest import controls in 2009 although the World Trade Organization (WTO) recorded no new trade barriers in 2010 (WTO, 2011). Since the G-20 Seoul Summit in November 2010, however, almost 200 protectionist measures have been brought in, with G-20 governments accounting for 80 per cent and the four BRIC countries for one third (Evenett, 2011).[4] Market-closing instruments outweigh market-opening measures by far, though direct border controls are progressively being lowered.

The optimistic proclamations on the prospects for concluding the Doha Round (or an early harvest for LDCs) made in 2010 were not matched by concrete progress in 2011 such that the December Ministerial Meeting in Geneva was limited in scope to exploring the way forward, rather than substantive negotiations. The appropriate balance between emerging and advanced economies commitments remains undecided, and while there is consensus that fresh and credible approaches are required, 2011 ended without any agreement as to their form.

> *Africa's regional economic communities (RECs) are strengthening intra-REC transport infrastructure.*

With respect to Economic Partnership Agreements, the European Commission announced in September 2011 that those countries that have concluded an EPA with the EU but have not taken the necessary steps toward ratification by January 2014 will be withdrawn from the Market Access Regulation (that which permits DFQF access to the EU).[5] The intention is to ensure fairness between those that have implemented their EPA commitments and those which are yet to do so, but many contentious issues remains outstanding. The next 12 months will be instrumental in shaping EU-Africa trading relations, and if the EPA process continues to falter it may catalyse further rebalancing toward South-South avenues of cooperation.

The promise of intra-African trade hindered by high protection

Intra-African trade is disappointingly low, at some 11 per cent of Africa's total trade in 2010. This is despite the myriad opportunities for intra-African trade, as demonstrated by a six-fold increase in trade within the Common Market for Eastern and Southern Africa (COMESA) over the past decade (figure 2.11). The East African Community (EAC) has also enjoyed success in recent years in diversifying production and moving up the value chain, and in enhancing resilience to economic crisis. Firms in Rwanda and Uganda have succeeded in capturing much of the value chain for coffee exports, selling branded coffee directly to the US. Kenya has expanded its presence in telecommunications and tourism—driven by a good infrastructure base, an active government and low levels of initial export concentration (OECD and OSAA, 2010; WEF, 2011). Conversely, homogeneity of exports and poor transport infrastructure hinder trade integration in the Economic Community of Central African States (ECCAS).

Figure 2.11

Indices of export values within African regional economic communities (2000=100)

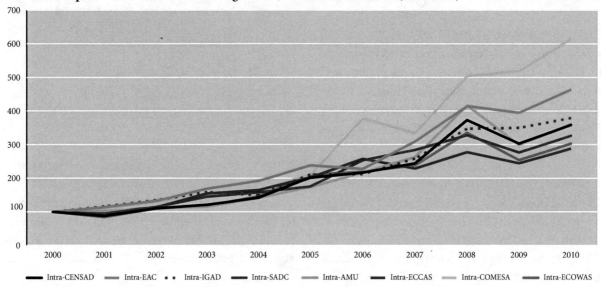

Source: UNECA calculations, based on UNCTAD (2011), accessed 19 October 2011.

Note: Eight Regional Economic Communities (RECs) are recognized by the African Union, namely: the Community of Sahel-Saharan States (CENSAD), the East African Community (EAC), the Intergovernmental Authority on Development (IGAD), the Southern African Development Community (SADC), the Arab Maghreb Union (AMU), the Economic Community of Central African States (ECCAS), the Common Market for Eastern and Southern Africa (COMESA), and the Economic Community Of West African States (ECOWAS).

Estimates of export sophistication in Africa are generally low, which inhibits countries from capturing future growth (Spence and Karingi, 2011), although goods traded within Africa—from Ghana and Kenya, for example—are more sophisticated than those traded with the rest of the world (table 2.2). This evidence of a mutually reinforcing relationship between regional integration and export sophistication further boosts the case for expanding intra-African trade as a tool towards realizing Africa's global growth pole ambitions.

Table 2.2

Top five exports by value to Africa and the rest of the world, 2008

Ghana to the world	Ghana to Africa
Gold, semi-manufactured forms	Gold, semi-manufactured forms
Cocoa beans, whole or broken, raw or roasted	Machinery parts, non-electrical
Cashew nuts, fresh or dried	Plywood, all softwood
Gold in unwrought forms	Panels, laminated woods
Lumber, non-coniferous	Aluminium alloy plate, sheet, strips
Kenya to the world	**Kenya to Africa**
Tea, black in packages	Tea, black in packages
Cut flowers and flower buds, fresh	Oils petroleum, bituminous, distillates
Vegetables, fresh or chilled	Portland cement, other than white cement
Cut flowers and flower buds, dried	Cigarettes containing tobacco
Coffee, not roasted, not decaffeinated	Medicaments, in dosage

Source: United Nations (2011a).

Yet, if Africa is to expand its internal trade, it will have to reduce or remove tariffs: intra-African average applied protection remains high at 8.7 per cent.[6] The establishment of a Pan-African Free Trade Area, as agreed by the African Ministers of Trade in Kigali in November 2010, would remove tariffs on internally traded goods and services. When that Free Trade Area (FTA) becomes a reality, the share of intra-African trade would undoubtedly increase. A recent estimate by UNECA, based on Computable General Equilibrium (CGE) modelling of a continental FTA, concludes that the share of intra-African trade would increase from 11 to 15.4 per cent of total trade by 2022 with the removal of all internal tariffs on goods by 2017 (UNECA, AUC, AfDB and UNDP, forthcoming). The gains in industrial goods outstrip those for agricultural products, indicating that the expansion of intra-African trade though a continental FTA can drive structural transformation.

As assumed by the CGE analysis if, beyond these FTA tariff-elimination measures, customs procedures and port handling are made twice as efficient, intra-African trade would double to 21.8 per cent with a continental FTA. At present, the cost of exporting or importing a standardized cargo of a 20-feet container of goods in sub-Saharan Africa is about $2,000, twice the amount in other regions of the world (World Bank, 2011).

Matters have been improving in recent years, however. According to the World Bank Doing Business Report (2012), sub-Saharan Africa even registered a record number of regulatory reforms implemented between June 2010 and May 2011, which aimed, inter alia, to ease trading across borders. Single-window border posts, where traders can file all paperwork for trading in one place, have slashed clearance times. (The African Alliance for e-Commerce provides a platform for sharing experience on these posts.)

Africa's regional economic communities (RECs) are strengthening intra-REC transport infrastructure. The Arab Maghreb Union, for example, is committed to completing the Trans-Saharan and Maghrebian Highways.

> *Access to high-quality education is vital for strengthening the productivity of the labour force and accelerating economic growth.*

Other RECs are promoting regional linkages through initiatives such as the Southern African Development Community (SADC) Multi-country Agricultural Productivity Programme and the Alliance for Common Trade in Eastern and Southern Africa, which focuses on disseminating technologies and building regional networks. Issues to be resolved include easing the movement of people—although the EAC and Economic Community of West African States (ECOWAS) common passports are welcome developments—and strengthening trade finance, which the African Development Bank's $1 billion Trade Finance Initiative in 2009 helped to address (AfDB, 2010).

Aid for Trade is another initiative to promote intra-African trade. Recent research confirms that the initiative helps to increase trade (Helble, Mann and Wilson, 2009), and significantly reduces trade costs in developing countries (Busse, Hoekstra and Koeniger, 2011). However, Busse, Hoekstra and Koeniger (2011) also show that Aid for Trade flows need to be large enough to lower trade costs in the case of LDCs. In Africa, Aid for Trade contributes to diversifying exports and to improving trade competitiveness (Karingi and Leyaro, 2009).

Aid for Trade to Africa increased by 21.2 per cent in 2009 (figure 2.12), continuing its eight-year uptrend, and was the most stable source of trade policy reform in Africa among developing regions. About 37 per cent of total Aid for Trade disbursements (41 per cent of commitments) were destined for Africa in 2009.[7] Variation among African countries was considerable.

Figure 2.12

Aid for Trade flows by region, 2002–2009 ($ million, constant prices)

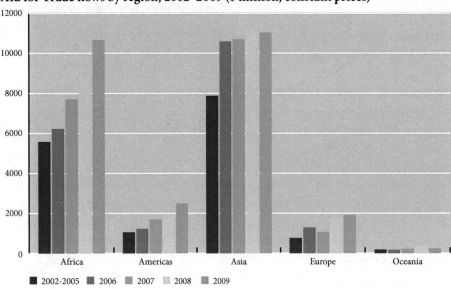

■ 2002-2005 ■ 2006 ■ 2007 ■ 2008 ■ 2009

Source: OECD (2011), accessed 26 October 2011.

2.3 Recent trends in social and human development

TRENDS IN SOCIAL and human development are generally positive, though uneven, among African countries, but are too slow to achieve internationally agreed development goals, particularly the MDGs. The continent has made good progress in increasing primary enrolment (including gender equality), reducing the prevalence of HIV/AIDS and cutting the under-five mortality rate. But progress on health indicators has generally been lacklustre; sanitation has improved only marginally and poverty rates are unlikely to be halved by 2015 (from 2000) in many countries. Nevertheless, the advances in a global context of economic slowdown demonstrate Africa's resilience and commitment towards improving its people's welfare.

Primary school enrolment on the rise but educational quality still a concern

Access to high-quality education is vital for strengthening the productivity of the labour force and accelerating economic growth, and Africa has made good progress in accelerating education enrolment for girls as well as boys, particularly at the primary level. By 2011, most African countries have achieved gender parity in primary schools, and in Malawi, Rwanda, Senegal and Togo, for example, girls outnumber boys.

Africa's economic growth has not yielded commensurate dividends in poverty reduction.

Of the 36 African countries with data for 2008/09, 16 have achieved net primary school enrolment ratios of more than 90 per cent. The rate of increase has been excellent: between 1999 and 2009, primary enrolment rose by 18 percentage points in Central, East, Southern and West Africa, compared with 12 percentage points in South Asia. Benin, Burkina Faso and Mozambique lifted net enrolment by 25 percentage points between 1999 and 2009 (United

Nations, 2011b), and Ethiopia from 50 per cent in 1990 to 86.5 per cent in 2010 (UNECA and AUC, 2011).

Primary completion rates, however, are still too low, partly because of the poor quality of education, and it seems that investments in educational facilities and qualified teachers have lagged behind efforts to increase enrolment. Secondary and tertiary enrolment rates need to improve.

Women's empowerment slowly gaining traction

Women are increasingly taking centre stage in Africa's development process. Sub-Saharan Africa in the last decade saw the largest increase in the representation of women in parliament, a figure that rose from 13 per cent in 2000 to 20 per cent in 2011. Eighty per cent of African countries (with data) increased that proportion between 1990 and 2010. The top three performers in 2010 were Rwanda (56 per cent), South Africa (45 per cent) and Mozambique (39 per cent) (UNECA et al., 2011). Rwanda is especially impressive, and stands as an inspiration to other African countries: women constitute 38 per cent of ministers, 35 per cent of senators, 56 per cent of deputies, 40 per cent of governors and 36 per cent of judges (Groupe Jeune Afrique, 2012).

In addition, the share of wage-earning women in non-agricultural sectors increased slightly from 24 per cent to 33 per cent between 1990 and 2009 (United Nations, 2011b).

Large steps in preventing new HIV/AIDS infections

Addressing the scourge of HIV/AIDs, malaria and other diseases that deprive the continent of its productive labour force is critical if Africa is to realize its growth potential. Although sub-Saharan Africa is the global region most heavily affected by HIV,[8] the rate of new infections has shown a notable decline, from 2.2 million in 2001 to 1.9 million in 2010. The epidemic remains most severe in Southern Africa, which accounted for almost half the deaths from AIDS-related illnesses in 2010; it is less prevalent in North Africa. Heightened awareness campaigns on behavioural change, and the promotion and use of condoms and antiretroviral treatment, have curbed the numbers of new infections and AIDS-related deaths.

Progress in malaria treatment

The estimated number of global malaria cases fell from 233 million in 2000 to 225 million in 2009 (ILO, 2010). Since 2000, 11 countries in Africa have shown steeper than half reductions in the number of confirmed malaria cases (and/or reported hospital admissions for malaria) and deaths (United Nations, 2011b).[9] Likely reasons include increased use of insecticide-treated bed nets, particularly in rural areas; improved diagnostic testing and surveillance; and wider access to anti-malaria drugs. Collectively, these measures have helped to save an estimated 1.1 million lives in Africa over the past 10 years. Yet malaria is still a leading cause of mortality and morbidity in Africa: of estimated global malaria deaths in 2011, 91 per cent were in Africa, and 86 per cent of this group were children under age 5 (WHO, 2011).

Child and maternal mortality improving but still too high

Africa has some of the world's highest under-five mortality rates and maternal mortality ratios, but has registered modest declines in recent years. Only two countries in Africa—Egypt and Tunisia—have achieved a two-thirds reduction in child mortality since 1990. Across sub-Saharan Africa, under-five mortality fell from 174 per 1,000 live births to 121 between 1990 and 2009. Better still, the average rate of reduction in under-five mortality rose from 1.2 per cent in 1990–2000 to 2.4 per cent in 2000–2010.

At 620 deaths per 100,000 live births in 2008, the maternal mortality ratio in sub-Saharan Africa is not only among the highest in the world but is declining very slowly relative to other global regions (WHO, 2011). Of the sub-Saharan countries with data for 2008, 24 registered a ratio of more than 500 deaths per 100,000 live births.[10] Progress has been faster in North Africa, which recorded a 69 per cent decline between 1990 and 2010, compared with a 1 per cent decline in the rest of Africa. North Africa's success was driven by a sharp increase in the number of deliveries attended by skilled health personnel (United Nations, 2011b).

Growth's modest effects on reducing poverty

Africa's economic growth has not yielded commensurate dividends in poverty reduction. The proportion of people in Central, Eastern, Southern and Western Africa living on less than $1.25 a day declined in 1990–2005, but only from 58 per cent to 51 per cent. On recent and forecast growth trends, Africa is unlikely to halve the rate of extreme poverty by 2015 (United Nations, 2011b).

The limited impact of growth on poverty reduction in Africa stems from the narrow base of the sources of growth. As seen earlier and discussed further in chapters 3 and 4, Africa's growth is still largely driven by primary production and exports, the benefits of which accrue to small

> *Wide income inequality in Africa has contributed to Africa's weak growth-poverty elasticity.*

In response to the burden of high maternal mortality, in 2009 African leaders launched the African Union (AU) Campaign on Accelerated Reduction of Maternal Mortality in Africa, which is under way in more than 34 countries. Its success will be vital in improving the health and life expectancy of pregnant women in Africa.

enclaves within the larger economy. Thus the growth–employment nexus in Africa is weak, leading to slow growth in remunerative job opportunities and intensifying vulnerable employment—all in all explaining the modest declines in poverty.

Indeed, recent global estimates show that sub-Saharan Africa has the lowest growth–poverty elasticity in the world (table 2.3): a 1 per cent increase in growth reduces poverty by only 1.6 per cent, but by 3.2 per cent in North Africa (and 4.2 per cent in Eastern Europe and Western Asia, which has the highest elasticity).

Table 2.3

Elasticity of poverty in relation to growth and inequality in Africa and some selected regions

Region/subregion	Growth	Inequality
East Asia and Pacific	−2.47	3.49
Eastern Europe and Western Asia	−4.22	6.85
Latin America and Caribbean	−3.08	5.00
Middle East and Central Asia	−2.75	3.91
South Asia	−2.10	2.68
Sub-Saharan Africa	−1.57	1.68
North Africa	−3.17	4.82
West Africa	−1.80	2.02
Central Africa	−1.35	1.31
East Africa	−1.40	1.32
Southern Africa	−1.65	2.18

Source: Fosu (2011).

Around three in every five workers in sub-Saharan Africa are poor. Although matters improved in 1999–2003, this ratio has been stagnant at 58 per cent since 2008. North Africa has also experienced a levelling in the share of working poor since 2008, albeit at better levels.

In total employment, the share of the working poor remained constant at around 16 per cent in 2008 and 2009 (table 2.4). The relatively high incidence of poor workers in Africa is linked to the precarious nature of their jobs— three in four workers are in vulnerable employment. And, despite a decline in such employment in 2000–2009 in sub-Saharan Africa (from 79.5 per cent to 75.8 per cent), the figures are still very high and represent a serious challenge for African governments.

Table 2.4

The working poor in Africa

	(million)				(% of total employment)			
	1999	2003	2008	2009	1999	2003	2008	2009
North Africa	10.5	11.1	10.5	10.7	21.4	20.2	16.2	16.1
Africa excluding North Africa	147.5	156.2	170.2	174.6	66.9	63.0	58.5	58.5

Source: ILO (2011).

High inequalities undermining poverty reduction efforts

Wide income inequality in Africa, the second-most unequal grouping after Latin America (World Bank, 2009), has contributed to Africa's weak growth–poverty elasticity. Inelasticities in poverty inequality are particularly high (4.8) in North Africa, suggesting that a unit increase in inequality increases poverty by almost 5 per cent (see table 2.3). Such inequality, coupled with the lack of pro-poor or inclusive economic growth, is reflected in large spatial and group disparities in access to and use of social services.

For example, in sub-Saharan Africa, an urban dweller is 1.8 times more likely to use an improved drinking water source than a rural dweller. Further, the poorest 20 per cent of the population in urban areas are almost six times more likely to rely on an unimproved drinking water source than the richest 20 per cent. In urban areas, the poorest households are 12 times less likely than the richest to have piped drinking water supply on the premises (UNECA, 2009).

Meeting the challenges

An integrated approach

Achieving the MDGs by 2015 will require an integrated approach that takes in the interrelatedness of social and human development. By focusing efforts on interventions that have the greatest knock-on effects on other social and human indicators, policymakers can leverage the developmental impact of scarce human and financial resources.

Empirical evidence of the linkage among such indicators is abundant. Several studies have demonstrated, for instance, the impact of female education on child mortality rates and under-nutrition (such as Summers, 1994; Murthi et al., 1995; and Drèze and Murthi, 2001). Using micro data, Summers (1994) reports that the under-five mortality rates for women with more than seven years of education are 80–120 per 100,000 lower than rates for women with no education.

Better female education also reduces child under-nutrition, which is closely linked to child mortality. Smith and Haddad (1999), for instance, show that a 1 percentage point increase in female secondary enrolment reduces the share of underweight children by 0.17 percentage points. Klasen and Lamanna (2003) generate similar findings for the impact of female literacy on child under-nutrition.

Equity in access through social protection

Fiscally sustainable social protection programmes that not only provide income support but strengthen the productive capacities of vulnerable groups can reduce income inequality while promoting inclusive growth.[11] Sub-Saharan Africa only spends 8.7 per cent of GDP on social services, the lowest of all the world's regions, and merely 5.6 per cent without public health spending. This low expenditure undoubtedly translates into poor provision of social services to neglected population groups. Some studies (such as ILO, 2010) have shown that countries with the highest investments in social security tend to exhibit low poverty rates and low labour market informality (box 2.1).

> *Successful social protection programmes are well targeted, anchored by strong political support, effectively coordinated and not overly dependent on external funding.*

Box 2.1: Political consensus on social protection

The political commitment to social protection as a way to tackle inequitable progress towards the MDGs has found fertile ground at international and regional levels.

Internationally, recognizing the necessity of ensuring universal social protection, the United Nations System Chief Executives Board adopted in April 2009 a Universal Social Protection Floor (SPF-I) as one of nine initiatives to respond to the food, fuel, economic and financial crises.

The potential of social protection in reducing poverty and achieving the MDGs had been previously recognized by the African Union (AU), which made social protection a priority by adopting the Social Policy Framework for Africa at the AU Conference of Ministers of Social Development in 2008, endorsed by the AU Executive Council in January 2009.

The framework states that "social protection has multiple beneficial impacts on national economies and is essential to build human capital, break the intergenerational poverty cycle and reduce the growing inequalities that constrain Africa's economic and social development". It recommends that governments should provide for national legislation on social protection; develop national development plans and poverty reduction strategies with links to MDG processes and outcomes; and review and reform social protection programmes.

Source: UNECA compilation.

Latin America's experience with conditional cash transfers demonstrates the potential impact of social protection programmes on social and human development indicators. Brazil's and Mexico's cash transfer programmes, for example, which link child income support to attendance at school and immunization, have greatly lifted enrolment and nutritional levels of children.

A UNECA study of social protection programmes in nine African countries in 2010 also confirmed the benefit of social protection instruments as they relate to six MDGs (table 2.5). All intervention types have a high impact on poverty, and most have a strong effect on child health. Cash transfers, school feeding programmes, productive safety nets and non-contributory pensions have the most widespread effects for attaining the MDGs.

Table 2.5

Impact of social protection interventions on MDGs 1–6

Intervention	MDG 1	MDG 2	MDG 3	MDG 4	MDG 5	MDG 6
Cash transfers	High	High	Medium	Medium	Low	Medium
School feeding	High	High	High	High	Low	High
Public works	High	Low	Low	Medium	Low	Low
Farm subsidy	High	Low	Low	High	Low	Medium
Productive safety net	High	High	Medium	Medium	Medium	Medium
Non-contributory pensions	High	Medium	Medium	High	High	High

Source: UNECA (2010).

The interventions with the strongest impact are those that rebuild the productive capacities of vulnerable groups. Cash transfers, for example, provide protection to the poorest groups, families with children in school, pregnant mothers and those with HIV/AIDS.

In Ethiopia, a productive safety net programme supports vulnerable populations while enhancing their productive capacity. It has three core components: labour-intensive public works for the actively productive population, conditional transfers for very poor people who cannot participate in productive work and unconditional transfers for people with no assets (UNECA, 2010).

Successful social protection programmes are well targeted, anchored by strong political support, effectively coordinated and not overly dependent on external funding. Other important conditions for success are institutional frameworks—to increase the likelihood of predictable and adequate funding—national guidelines and budget provisions, and close attention to the programmes' fiscal sustainability.

On this last point, African countries must plan for sustainable social protection by efficiently mobilizing domestic resources, reallocating budgets and cautiously using external support. When governments adopt specific social protection instruments (such as cash transfers) without complementary interventions that support livelihoods (such as skills acquisition), they make it hard for people to exit the poverty trap and undermine fiscal sustainability.

Lastly, for social protection to strengthen social development, authorities should manage schemes holistically, considering both life-cycle risks (such as early childhood and old age) and livelihood risks (such as unemployment or food production shocks). Run this way, programmes tend to generate maximum benefits for reaching the MDGs and other human development indicators (UNECA, 2010).

2.4 Africa's outlook set fair

AFRICAN ECONOMIES ARE poised to continue growing reasonably well in the medium term. Growth is expected to recover to 5.1 per cent in 2012 and 5.2 per cent in 2013, underpinned by strong export demand, rising commodity prices and firm domestic demand (buttressed by government infrastructure spending).

North Africa is set on a recovery path as political stability returns, and is projected to grow by 4.7 per cent and 5.4 per cent in 2012 and 2013, respectively. Growth in West Africa is forecast to pick up to 6.3 per cent and 6.5 per cent in these two years, while growth in Central Africa is projected at 4.7 per cent in 2012 and 3.7 per cent in 2013. East Africa is expected to post somewhat stronger growth of 6.3 per cent in 2012, and 5.8 per cent in 2013. Growth in Southern Africa is projected to be a strong 4.5 per cent in 2012 and 4.2 per cent in 2013 (UN-DESA, 2011).

This positive outlook largely depends on the health of the global economy. Failure by euro area governments to resolve their sovereign debt crisis will obviously affect Africa on many fronts, while emerging economies—the main driver of Africa's exports—face some risks of overheating. If demand falls for African commodities, the external sector could contract sharply. Further, a global downturn would hit Africa's service sector, particularly tourism, and could reverse capital flows to Africa, including ODA, FDI and remittances, undermining Africa's financial markets.

But Africa, ultimately, decides its own destiny: economic recovery is likely to take place in an environment of persistent high unemployment and increasing global economic vulnerability, challenging African leaders in 2012 and beyond—to harvest and then distribute the fruits of growth more equitably, to bring down unemployment and to resolve persistent food-price inflation.

These are all difficult issues that require a combination of well-designed macroeconomic, structural and social policy interventions that track each country's circumstances and that unleash Africa's productive potential—the subject of the next two chapters.

References

AfDB (African Development Bank). 2010. "Africa in the wake of the global financial crisis: challenges ahead and the role of the Bank". Policy Briefs on the Financial Crisis 1. Tunis.

_____. OECD, UNDP and UNECA (Organization for Economic Cooperation and Development, United Nations Development Programme, and United Nations Economic Commission for Africa). 2011. *African Economic Outlook 2011*. Paris, OECD Publishing.

Boumellassa, H., D. Laborde, and C. Mitaritonna. 2009. "A picture of tariff protection across the world in 2004, MAcMap-HS6, version 2." Discussion Paper 00903. International Food Policy Research Institute, Washington, DC.

Busse, M., R. Hoekstra, and J. Koeniger. 2011. "The impact of aid for trade facilitation on the costs of trading." Working Paper.

Deninger, K., and L. Squire. 1998. "New ways of looking at old issues: inequality and growth." *Journal of Development Economics* 57 (2): 259–87

EIU (Economist Intelligence Unit). 2011a. "Online country data." www.eiu.com/.

European Commission, 2011. "Proposal for a Regulation of the European Parliament and of the Council amending Annex I to Council Regulation (EC) No 1528/2007 as regards the exclusion of a number of countries from the list of regions or states which have concluded negotiations. COM(2011) 598 final, 2011/0260 (COD)." EC, Brussels, Belgium

Evenett, S.J., ed. 2011. "Resolve falters as global prospects worsen: the 9th GTA report." Centre for Economic Policy Research, London. www.globaltradealert.org/sites/default/files/GTA9.pdf.

Fosu, A. 2011. "Growth inequality and poverty reduction in developing countries: recent global evidence."

Working Paper 2011/01. United Nations University World Institute for Development Economics Research, Helsinki

Groupe Jeune Afrique. 2012. *The Africa report: investing Rwanda*. Paris.

IMF (International Monetary Fund). 2011a. Regional Economic Outlook: Middle East and Central Asia. Washington DC.

_____. 2011b. Regional Economic Outlook: Sub-Saharan Africa. Washington, DC.

_____. 2011c. "World Economic Outlook Database." www.imf.org/external/pubs/ft/weo/2011/02/weo-data/index.aspx.

ILO (International Labour Organization). 2010. *World Social Security Report 2010/2011: providing coverage in times of crisis and beyond*. Geneva.

_____. 2011. Global employment trends 2011: the challenge of jobs recovery. Geneva.

International Centre for Trade and Sustainable Development (ICTSD) and European Centre for Development Policy Management (ECDPM), 2011. "Special Update: European Commission puts renewed pressure on EPA negotiations." *Trade Negotiations Insights* 7(10), 2-20 (ictsd.org/downloads/tni/tni_en_10-7.pdf).

Karingi, S.N., and V. Leyaro. 2009. "Monitoring aid for trade in Africa: an assessment of the effectiveness of aid for trade." African Trade Policy Centre 83. United Nations Economic Commission for Africa, Addis Ababa.

Karingi, S.N., and M.D. Spence. Forthcoming. "Impact of trade facilitation mechanisms on export competitiveness in Africa." African Trade Policy Centre. United Nations Economic Commission for Africa,

Addis Ababa. (www.gtap.agecon.purdue.edu/resources/download/5262.pdf).

Klasen, S., and F. Lamanna. 2003. "The impact of gender inequality in education and employment on economic growth in the Middle East and North Africa." Mimeo. University of Göttingen, Göttingen, Germany.

Murthi, M., A-C. Guio, and J. Drèze. 1995. "Mortality, fertility, and gender bias in India: a district-level analysis." *Population and Development Review* 21: 745–82.

Drèze, J., and M. Murthi. 2001. "Fertility, education, and development: evidence from India." *Population and Development Review* 27: 33–63.

OECD (Organisation for Economic Co-operation and Development). 2011. "Creditor reporting system." http://stats.oecd.org/Index.aspx?DataSetCode=CRSNEW.

_____ and OSAA (United Nations Office of the Special Adviser on Africa). 2010. Economic diversification in Africa: a review of selected countries. Paris and New York.

Smith, L., and L. Haddad. 1999. "Explaining Child Malnutrition in Developing Countries." Research Report 111. International Food Policy Research Institute, Washington, DC.

Spence, M. and S. Karingi. 2011."Impact of Trade Facilitation Mechanisms on Export Competitiveness in Africa." African Trade Policy Centre Work in Progress No.85, UNECA, Addis Ababa, Ethiopia

Summers, L. 1994. *Investing in all the people*. Washington, DC: World Bank.

UN (United Nations). 2011a. "United Nations Commodity Trade Statistics Database." United Nations Statistics Division, New York. http://comtrade.un.org/.

———. 2011b. *The Millennium Development Report*. New York.

UNCTAD (United Nations Conference on Trade and Development). "UNCTADstat." http://unctadstat.unctad.org/ReportFolders/reportFolders.aspx.

UN-DESA (United Nations Department of Economic and Social Affairs). 2011a. Global Economic Outlook database. www.un.org/en/development/desa/policy/proj_link/global_economic_outlook.shtml.

_____. 2011b. World population prospects: the 2010 revision, CD-ROM edition. Population Division. United Nations.

UNECA (United Nations Economic Commission for Africa). 2010. "The scope for social safety nets and social protection schemes to advance progress on the MDGs: Algeria, Ethiopia, Kenya, Mauritius, Malawi, Namibia, Nigeria, Tunisia, South Africa. UNECA. Addis Ababa. Ethiopia.

_____. 2009. Equal access to basic services in African LDCs: The need for coherent, inclusive, and effective policy frameworks, Addis Ababa

_____. and AUC (African Union Commission). 2011. *Economic report on Africa 2011: governing development in Africa—the role of the state in economic transformation.* Addis Ababa.

_____. AUC, and UNDP (United Nations Development Programme). 2011. Assessing progress towards the Millennium Development Goals, Addis Ababa, UNECA

_____. AUC, AfDB and UNDP. (*forthcoming*). Assessing Regional Integration in Africa V. UNECA, Addis Ababa, UNECA

WEF (World Economic Forum). 2009. *The Africa Competitiveness Report 2009*. Geneva. www3.weforum.org/docs/WEF_GlobalCompetitiveness_AF09_Report.pdf.

———. 2011. *The Africa Competitiveness Report 2011*. Geneva. www3.weforum.org/docs/WEF_GCR_Africa_Report_2011.pdf.

WHO (World Health Organization). 2011. *World Health Statistics*. Geneva.

World Bank. 2012. Doing Business 2012: Doing Business in a More Transparent World.

_____. 2011. Doing Business: Trading Across Borders Database. (http://www.doingbusiness.org/data/exploretopics/trading-across-borders)

_____. 2010. Trends in average MFN applied tariff rates in developing and industrial countries", 1981–2009. (http://siteresources.worldbank.org/INTRES/Resources/469232-1107749512766/tar2009.xls).

WTO (World Trade Organization). 2011. *World Trade Report 2011: the WTO and preferential trade agreements: from co-existence to coherence*. Geneva. www.wto.org/english/res_e/booksp_e/anrep_e/world_trade_report11_e.pdf.

Notes

1 African Financial Community.

2 FDI data are available for only 38 countries.

3 Primary commodities typically adjust through prices rather than volume owing to extremely slow supply responses.

4 They overlap.

5 LDCs will still enjoy DFQF access under the Everything but Arms Scheme, LICs and LMICs will have the option of the generalized System of Preferences, but Botswana and Namibia, as upper middle income countries, will have neither option available if they choose not to work towards ratification (ICTSD and ECDPM 2011).

6 See Boumellassa et al. (2009) for more details.

7 The top 10 recipients (accounting for more than half the total) were Ethiopia, Egypt, Tanzania, Morocco, Uganda, Mozambique, Ghana, Kenya, the Democratic Republic of the Congo and Mali.

8 Africa, excluding North Africa, accounted for about 68 per cent of all people living with HIV and 70 per cent of new HIV infections.

9 Algeria, Botswana, Cape Verde, Eritrea, Madagascar, Namibia, Rwanda, Sao Tome and Principe, South Africa, Swaziland and Zambia.

10 Angola, Burkina Faso, Burundi, Cameroon, Central African Republic, Chad, Congo, Democratic Republic of the Congo, Guinea Bissau, Kenya, Lesotho, Malawi, Liberia, Mali, Mauritania, Mozambique, Niger, Nigeria, Rwanda, Sierra Leone, Somalia, Sudan, Tanzania and Zimbabwe.

11 Social protection may be defined loosely as "a set of measures that support society's poorest and most vulnerable members and help individuals, households and communities to better manage risks" (UNECA et al., 2011).

Africa as a Pole of Global Growth

3

AFTER STAGNATING FOR much of its post-colonial history, Africa has witnessed a remarkable improvement in its economic performance in the last decade, with its GDP growing by an annual average of 5.6 per cent in 2002–2008 (before the global economic crisis), making it the second-fastest growing region in the world, just behind East Asia. And since then, growth has picked up well (chapter 2)—of the world's 15 fastest-growing economies in 2010, 10 were African.

More reassuring, not only have the resource-rich countries seen growth—many African countries that do not boast oil or mineral wealth have done well. This resurgence is giving rise to a growing recognition of Africa as an emerging market and a potential global growth pole.

The analysis in this chapter underscores key policy issues. Since independence, African growth has been driven by primary production and export and only limited economic transformation, against a backdrop of high unemployment and worsening poverty. Even with improvements in the last decade, further economic transformation, job creation and poverty reduction are needed as the region faces development deficits. Still, Africa's recent resurgence has benefited from gains in macroeconomic management, good governance and control of corruption so that manufacturing, modern financial and telecommunications services and tourism are beginning to make real contributions to growth. The resurgence has also benefited from increased capital inflows—especially foreign direct investment (FDI)—aid and debt relief.

This resurgence has prompted African leaders, development partners and others to assert that future world growth will depend on unleashing the productive potential and harnessing the untapped consumer demand of Africa. In essence, the world will benefit greatly from Africa joining the league of global growth poles.

But what are "global growth poles"? In a nutshell, they are economies that help to drive growth elsewhere on the planet, through dynamism and size, and for Africa to become a global growth pole, the continent should sustain the recent growth momentum for at least two more decades—as well as vigorously address the challenges of structural transformation of output and trade, broadening and strengthening the infrastructural and human resource base as well as strengthening and modernizing science and technology capability. It must also capitalize on and manage the opportunities and risks presented by the emerging multipolar world, as well as the gradual shift in economic power from developed regions to emerging and developing regions.

The world will benefit greatly from Africa joining the league of global growth poles.

3.1 Africa's economic performance, 1960–2010

IN THE 1950s and early 1960s, Africa was largely seen as a very promising and prosperous continent, in contrast to Asia mired in seemingly irredeemable poverty and ravaged by wars. Fortunes soon changed, and after a spurt of post-independence economic growth, external shocks, poor policy responses and ineffective development led to economic stagnation in many African countries, slowing even front-runners such as Côte d'Ivoire and Kenya. Asia now accounts for some two fifths of global GDP (at purchasing power parity), over one quarter of global exports and imports, and over one fifth of global inflows of FDI.

In 2008, China and India accounted for about 6.6 per cent and 2 per cent of world GDP, but Africa only 2 per cent.

In the last decade, however, Africa has transformed itself to become the world's second-fastest-growing region after East Asia for most of the period (figure 3.1)—albeit with varied progress among countries.

In what follows, we briefly catalogue Africa's economic performance since independence, focusing on the dominant policy regimes and major growth drivers.

Figure 3.1

Growth performance of different regions of the world, 1971–2011

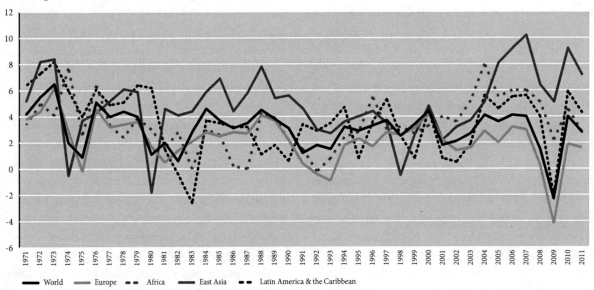

Source: Data for 1971–2004 from United Nations Statistics Division; data for 2005–2011 from UN-DESA (2012). Data on Europe for 2005–2011 includes only the European Union.

> *Africa has transformed itself to become the world's second-fastest growing region after East Asia.*

Post-independence, 1960–1985

Most African nations attained political independence in the 1960s, and saw positive and fairly stable GDP growth in the next one and a half decades of around 4 per cent (figure 3.2). Although this rate was almost comparable to that in Asia and the Americas, high population growth kept per capita annual income growth in Africa to below 2 per cent (figure 3.3).

The import substitution industrialization (ISI) development model was at the heart of Africa's growth and development strategies during this period. The initial focus was on consumer goods, with the expectation that, as industrialization advanced, domestic production of the intermediate and capital goods needed by industry and other sectors would pick up. Another expectation was that the replacement of imported goods with domestically produced goods would, over time, enhance self-reliance and help prevent balance-of-payments problems.[1] Unfortunately, neither expectation was met.

By the late 1970s, it was evident that industrial development through the ISI model and myriad State-owned enterprises (SOEs) could not last, particularly because ISI in most African countries did not lay an emphasis on generating foreign exchange, and its scarcity had become a serious constraint.[2]

Figure 3.2
GDP growth, 1960–1985 (%)

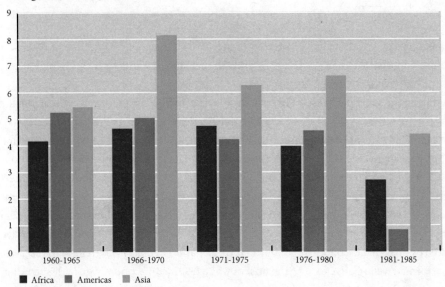

Source: World Bank (2011a).

Figure 3.3

Per capita GDP growth, 1960–1985 (%)

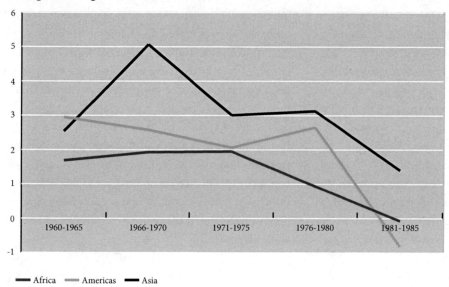

Source: World Bank (2011a).

In the 1970s, imports of goods and services as a share of GDP were consistently higher than exports.[3] Also, primary commodities dominated African exports, except for Mauritius and South Africa, during the same period.

African economies gradually accumulated external debt: as a share of GDP it leaped from 23.5 per cent in 1971–1975 to 42.8 per cent in 1976–1980, peaking at 70.4 per cent in 1981–1985. FDI as a proportion of GDP remained quite low at a meagre 1.9 per cent of GDP in 1976–1980 and declined to only 1.0 per cent in 1981–1985. Domestic investment in the economy, however, measured by gross fixed capital formation as a share of output, performed well relative to other developing regions, although it started declining at

the end of the 1980s. Foreign aid as a share of GDP was consistently higher than in other developing regions.

In sum, the major drivers of economic growth during the early post-independence era were primary production and export. The plan to transform Africa's economies through ISI failed, and by the late 1970s, socio-economic conditions in most African countries had deteriorated considerably. Many countries had trade deficits, worsening terms of trade, rising international indebtedness, huge fiscal deficits, rising subsidies to inefficient and unproductive public enterprises and steep declines in foreign reserves. The upshot was a decline in economic growth such that, by the early 1980s, Africa was one of the world's slowest-growing regions (see figure 3.1).

Structural adjustment, 1985–1995

Structural adjustment programmes (SAPs) in Africa began in the mid-1980s. Their origins can be traced back a few years earlier, when African countries experienced a severe balance-of-payments crisis from the cumulative effects of the oil crisis, the decline in commodity prices and the growing import needs of domestic industries.

In response, many countries sought financial assistance from international financial institutions (IFIs) such as the International Monetary Fund (IMF) and the World Bank. African countries that adopted SAPs were expected to implement certain policy reforms as a condition for receiving financial assistance from the IFIs.[4] As a result, most African countries (supported by the IFIs) formulated and implemented wide-ranging "market-friendly" economic policy reforms in the mid-1980s, including liberalizing their trade and exchange rate regimes.

Even though many African countries vigorously pushed through SAPs, economic growth declined from 3.02 per cent in 1985–1990 to 1.45 per cent in 1991–1995 (figure 3.4). Correspondingly, per capita real GDP improved marginally in 1985–1990 by 0.23 per cent, but declined by 0.89 per cent in 1991–1995 when other developing continents reported growth (figure 3.5).

External debt accumulation during the SAP period assumed alarming proportions in Africa.

Figure 3.4
GDP growth, 1985–1995 (%)

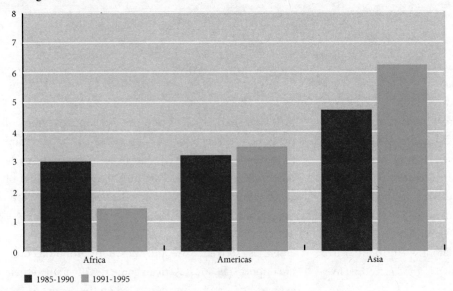

Source: World Bank (2011a).

Figure 3.5

Per capita GDP growth, 1985–1995 (%)

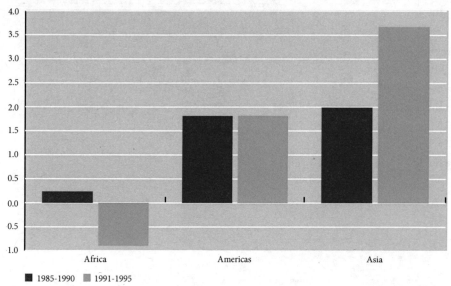

■ 1985-1990 ■ 1991-1995

Source: World Bank (2011a).

The minimal improvement in growth was also reflected in sluggish sectoral performance. Agricultural value added as a proportion of GDP improved slightly in 1985–1990 to 30.5 per cent but declined thereafter to 28.9 per cent in 1991–1995. Similarly, the share of manufacturing in GDP improved slightly to 12.0 per cent in 1985–1990 but fell to 11.6 per cent in 1991–1995. The overall picture is that SAPs improved economic indices—slightly—in the first five years but these gains were reversed in the succeeding five.

External debt accumulation during the adjustment period assumed alarming proportions in Africa, climbing as a share of GDP from 100 per cent in 1985–1990 to 115 per cent in 1991–1995. FDI, however, improved only a

> *Since the second half of the 1990s, growth has greatly improved in Africa.*

little as a share of GDP, and the developing regions of the Americas saw a higher increase. Gross fixed capital formation as a share of GDP was lower than in the early post-independence era. Foreign aid as a proportion of gross national income went up relative to other developing regions.

Openness to trade rose, but was more pronounced on the import side. Most African countries diversified their exports little, and many depended on the export of primary commodities. In essence, growth drivers remained primary production and exports.

The deteriorating economic conditions in African countries implementing SAPs led to severe criticism. Critics argued that such programmes placed Africa on a slow-growth path, undermined efforts to diversify economically and eroded the continent's industrial base (Soludo, Ogbu and Chang, 2004; Stein, 1992). Most United Nations agencies criticized SAPs for their neglect of the human dimension.[5]

Liberalization and market-led development, 1995–2010

The critics were vindicated. By the end of the 1990s, the IFIs started to reconsider their approaches, given many countries' poor performance under the SAPs and worsening poverty. Eventually, a joint initiative launched by the IFIs at the end of 1999 set the fight against poverty at the heart of growth and development policies. In this initiative, low-income countries wanting to apply for financial aid from the IFIs, or for debt relief under the Heavily Indebted Poor Countries (HIPC) Initiative, were required to draw up a poverty reduction programme, known as a Poverty Reduction Strategy Paper (PRSP). Around that time the United Nations system was setting the MDG targets at levels that balanced ambition with feasibility.

Since the second half of the 1990s—following almost two decades of stagnation and decline—growth has greatly improved in Africa. The continent has not only posted notable (if varying) rates of expansion but is also one of the world's fastest-growing regions. Beyond that, growth is not only spread among countries—with about 40 per cent of them growing at 5 per cent or more in 2001–2008, for example—but is also broad-based, covering resources, finance, retail trade, agriculture, transport and telecommunications (Leke et al., 2011).

Some structural transformation is accompanying Africa's impressive performance, even if in only a few countries. For example, while the majority of African countries are still producers and exporters of primary agricultural products, crude petroleum and solid minerals (such as copper, bauxite and iron ore), manufacturing contributed more than 10 per cent of GDP in 12 countries. Moreover, the rapid growth of telecommunications services, banking and other business services and tourism in many African countries during the last decade is gradually reducing the dominance of low-level services, such as wholesale and retail trade, which are largely informal.

Crucially, although exports of agricultural products (food and raw materials), crude petroleum and other mineral products still dominate, many more African countries are now exporters of manufactured goods, inspired by intra-African trade and trade with emerging economies. Although manufactured exports accounted for up to 20 per cent of total exports in 11 African countries, only Mauritius, South Africa, Zimbabwe, Tunisia and Morocco seem to be major exporters of manufactured products. These countries may therefore have achieved some degree of export diversification.

African countries depend heavily on imports of manufactured goods: the share of such goods in total imports ranged from 46.6 per cent in Sao Tome and Principe to about 84 per cent in Nigeria in 2009. Apart from the five countries just mentioned, however, where a reasonable proportion of the imported manufactured goods may be components or industrial intermediates for use in production of other manufactured exports, imports of manufactured goods in most African countries are final consumer goods (annex table 3.1).

In the structure of aggregate demand, the share of household final consumption expenditure in total expenditure is likely to be very high in most African countries. The degrees of export orientation (export-to-GDP ratios) and import penetration (import-to-GDP ratios) are generally high in Africa, implying that most African economies are vulnerable to external shocks.

For most developing countries, including many in Africa, external debt as a share of GDP declined significantly between 1995 and 2010, thanks to debt forgiveness from international creditors, especially after the adoption of the HIPC Initiative.

FDI as a share of GDP averaged an unprecedented 6.2 per cent in 2006–2008. Although higher than Asia's, it was slightly less than developing Americas' regional average. Yet the bulk of Africa's FDI inflows still went to natural resources (mainly crude oil and solid minerals). Gross

The bulk of Africa's FDI inflows still go to the natural resource sector.

capital formation as a share of GDP also followed an upward trend during the period 1995-2010, though the value was below 25 per cent and less than other developing regions' average (chapter 5). ODA was consistently higher for Africa than other developing regions during this period.

Implications for Africa's development paradigm

The foregoing suggests that the major drivers of economic performance in Africa throughout the first 50 years of independence were primary commodity production and exports. Attempts to transform economies either through ISI or SAPs failed to sustain accelerated growth or economic transformation. The growth spurt of the first decade of the twenty-first century, too, was driven largely by primary production and exports, although good macroeconomic management, microeconomic reforms, good governance, fewer armed conflicts and market-friendly policies played a role.

Still, the challenge of economic transformation persists for many countries, raising concerns over how to sustain the current surge, especially in light of poverty, hunger, youth unemployment, low skills, climate change and a high disease burden (especially HIV/AIDS and malaria). Other constraints come from poor infrastructure, low investment in innovation and technological upgrading, political instability, corruption and low productivity. African countries, like others, also have to deal with rising food and energy prices and the ramifications of the global economic and financial crisis.

Before discussing the imperatives for Africa as a global growth pole, we draw some key lessons from the above discussion. First, Africa's growth, especially before 2000, was extremely variable and volatile. Second, low levels of

While Africa is increasingly being recognized as a global growth pole, the continent should not rest on its laurels.

investment appear to explain this variability and volatility. Yet productivity of domestic investment in the continent is still low, which calls for looking beyond creating conditions for attracting new investors to more explicitly pursuing measures that transform the economy and raise the productivity of existing and new investment.[6] Third, Africa is still overly dependent on primary commodities for food, exports and income more broadly, so that productivity lags far behind the phenomenal progress made in Asia and Latin America.[7] Hence the need to manage response to shocks, particularly in resource-rich countries.

Fourth, a major drawback of the liberalization and market-led development strategy is the attempt to use the market to promote poverty reduction and social development. It cannot simply be assumed that conventional market-restructuring and reform policies—which aim to develop competitive and efficient markets and to stimulate economic growth—reduce poverty through "trickle-down". Growth *and* distribution matter in reducing poverty—and that requires deliberate government interventions.

So although Africa seems to have fared better than some regions since the recent global crisis, the risk of similar events reversing its modest gains calls into question the sustainability and reliability of a strategy based on exports of primary commodities (a strategy embedded in SAPs and the neo-liberal development policies of the post-SAP era).

To sustain economic growth, Africa will need to enhance productivity and competitiveness through investing in infrastructure, technology, higher education and health; broadening the range of and adding greater value to exports; and making the necessary investments in productive sectors and trade facilitation.[8] All these measures require collaboration among stakeholders under the leadership of the developmental State—as detailed in the *Economic Report on Africa 2011* (UNECA and AUC, 2011).

3.2 Imperatives for Africa as a pole of global growth

IN AFRICA, THE impressive growth since the beginning of the twenty-first century, its economies' ability to weather the storm of the recent crisis and the resumption of growth by nearly all countries in 2010 suggest that Africa is one of the world's emerging economic powers.

Justifiably, Africa's emergence has attracted the attention of its leaders and institutions, as well as its development partners. For example, The Committee of Ten African Ministers of Finance and Central Bank Governors, AfDB, UNECA and AUC, working with the Korea Institute for International Economic Policy in their presentation at the Korea–Africa Economic Cooperation Ministerial Conference,[9] concluded that "the world needs a new driver of consumer demand, a new market and a new dynamo which can be Africa. Future growth in the world economy and in the developing world will depend on harnessing both the productive potential and the untapped consumer demand of the continent" (AfDB, UNECA and AUC, 2010: 59).

Similarly, several international financial organizations and private think-tanks have underlined the potential of Africa as a global growth pole.[10] Perhaps most instructive is the assertion by the United Nations Under-Secretary General and UNECA Executive Secretary, Mr. Abdoulie Janneh, that,[11] while Africa is increasingly being recognized as a global growth pole, the continent should not rest on its laurels. This chapter represents an attempt to respond to this clarion call.

Global growth poles: what they are and how they work

Following Adam-Kane and Lim (2011) and World Bank (2011b), a growth pole may be defined as an economy that accounts for a significant proportion of global economic activity whose growth has sufficiently large forward and backward linkages, as well as technological and knowledge spillovers in so many other economies (through production, trade, finance and migration) as to have an impact on global growth.

From this definition, we deduce the imperatives for an economy to be regarded as a global growth pole. We also examine the attributes of China, India and the Republic of Korea—three of the recently acclaimed major emerging economic powerhouses and global growth poles in 2000–2010 (World Bank, 2011b)—to provide a basis for proposing the imperatives to make Africa a global growth pole.[12]

This approach allows us to focus on the key issues of economic size and growth (the necessary conditions) and the linkages between the growth pole and the rest of the world through various channels (the sufficient conditions) (figure 3.6).

Figure 3.6

Channels of growth spillovers from a growth pole

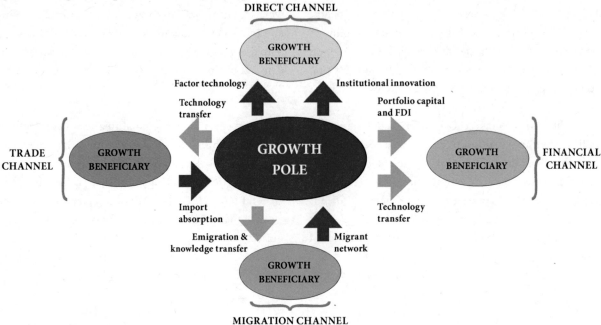

Source: World Bank (2011b).

The global growth polarity index of a country depends on the size of its economy as well as its growth rate.[13] Size and growth constitute the necessary condition that must be met by a global growth pole. The global growth polarity index shows the relative importance of the economy of a country or a region as a driver of global growth and often changes over time with changes in the size of the economy and its growth rate (see figure 3.7). The X-axis is global growth polarity index; the higher the index, the more important the country is as a global growth pole and vice versa. The indication from the figure is that China and India maintained a rising polarity index while Japan and others had declining indices especially between 2006 and 2009. With declining growth in Japan and some other major advanced economies, the indices may decline again while those of China and India may continue to rise. A drawback of this necessary condition is that it does not explicitly reflect the channels through which a global growth pole interacts with, and transmits knowledge and technology to, other economies.

Figure 3.7

Trend of global growth polarity index for top five countries, 2000–2010

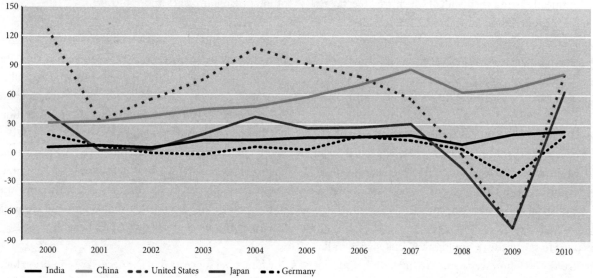

India   China   • • • United States   Japan   • • • Germany

Source: World Bank (2011a).

The first channel is trade (import and export), the second investment (FDI), the third technology and knowledge (R&D) and the fourth is migration. Adam-Kane and Lim (2011) propose empirical measures of these channels. However, for the present purposes, the features of trade and investment activities that indicate the character of the linkages between a growth pole and the other economies with which it interacts are taken to provide a basis for articulating the key attributes of a global growth pole.

Looking at the trade channel, a large part of the imports by a global growth pole from the rest of the world would be manufactured goods, the bulk of which are industrial intermediates and components. Similarly, the bulk of its raw material imports would be processed or semi-processed products. If such imports are efficiently produced in the originating countries, using the best available (ideally, green) technology, and at the lowest possible cost, the producers in the global growth pole will also realize efficiency gains from the imported inputs, thus making its exports more competitive on the international market. A global growth pole whose imports are dominated by these kinds of goods will therefore generate significant forward and backward linkages in the exporting countries, generating significant positive spillovers to the benefit of the peripheral exporting countries.

Equally, the structure of exports by the global growth pole would be dominated by higher-order industrial intermediates and components as well as technology-intensive capital goods. Inevitably, in an efficient producer of finished consumer durable and non-durable goods, this category of manufactured goods can be a significant part of the global growth pole's exports in the short to medium term. In the long term, a global growth pole should have a large domestic market for this category, so that its significance in total exports will decline, gradually.[14]

In the investment channel, a global growth pole should be a major source of investment to the rest of the world. It should also be a major destination for foreign investment. The prospects of interactions with other economies to generate significant forward and backward linkages in the global growth pole as well as in the other economies will be enhanced if foreign investors can find local partners. In this way, the host economies (global growth pole and the periphery) will internalize many of the positive externalities of the investment, especially technology and knowledge spillovers. However, for these economies to realize this potential, they should be able to adapt and apply available technology and knowledge (Ndulu et al. 2007). Conditions that can help emerging economies to do this effectively, aptly put by Juma (2006) include:

> ➤ Investment in basic infrastructure such as roads, schools, water, sanitation, irrigation, clinics, telecommunications and energy, all of which are necessary to lay the foundation for technological learning.

> ➤ Development of small and medium-sized enterprises through developing local operational, repair and maintenance expertise and a pool of local technicians.

> ➤ Government supported, funded and nurtured higher education institutions encompassing academics of engineering and technological sciences, professional engineering and technological associations as well as industrial and trade associations.

Needless to say, as the technology and knowledge spillovers from portfolio investment are likely to be inferior to those from direct investment, emphasis should be on attracting "productive" market-seeking FDI. That said, the benefit (alternatively, damage) from portfolio investment is likely to be higher (alternatively, lower) if such investment is in partnership with a local entity.

Migration is another channel. A global growth pole will support and encourage its citizens to travel to other countries in order to facilitate knowledge and technology transfer—and foreigners in the other direction, for the same purpose. The associated insertion of the global growth pole in such migration networks will be instrumental in reinforcing the trade and investment channels of interaction, linkages and spillovers.

Migrants' remittances are only one aspect of the migration channel of interaction. Perhaps more fundamental are the knowledge and technology transfers, as well as networking. Simply put, a global growth pole will not have many of its unskilled youth emigrating out of desperation. Neither will it encourage emigration of its highly skilled youth and professionals on account of a hostile working environment and living conditions. People who emigrate under these pressures are unlikely to be instrumental in technology and knowledge acquisition and transfer, leaving remittances as the only likely benefit.

The foregoing suggests that the necessary condition for a global growth pole is a reasonably large economy and a high, sustainable economic growth rate. Sufficient conditions include structural transformation—high-quality infrastructure; high-quality human resources; well-developed capacity for development, absorption and adaptation of technology and knowledge; a developed, nurtured and motivated vibrant local entrepreneurial class; and a complementary, innovative financial sector. Key aspects of these two types of imperatives for Africa as a global growth pole are now discussed.

Africa's growth imperative

For Africa to be a global growth pole, its economy should be large and its growth high and sustained for a reasonably long period. If Africa could sustain its 5.6 per cent growth of 2000–2008 for long enough, it would eventually be large enough to be a global growth pole.

In articulating the growth imperative for Africa as a global growth pole, it is thus necessary to build scenarios around growth and size. Several options can be considered. One is to assume that Africa should strive to replicate the experiences of Brazil, Russia, India, Indonesia, China and the Republic of Korea—the BRIICKs, and the new global growth poles. Another is to assume that Africa should strive to maintain its growth of 2000–2008 for long enough to become a global growth pole. We opt for the second option because replicating the experiences of the BRIICKs is less feasible, primarily because the circumstances of today are quite different from those of the last 40 years, when these countries made their huge strides. Also the BRIICKs are single countries, while Africa is made up of 54 countries with different social, cultural, political and economic systems and structures—a one-size-fits-all prescription is neither feasible nor realistic.

We therefore need to make realistic assumptions about the rest of the world, and assume that it will also recover and resume its average 2000–2008 growth by the end of 2012. On this basis, Africa's GDP and that of the rest of the world are projected into the future. For each year, the contribution of Africa to global GDP is computed, until it reaches where China was in 2005 (the midpoint between 2001 and 2010)—when it accounted for 5.1 per cent of world GDP and had become a recognized global growth pole.

From table 3.1, it can be seen that—if Africa can maintain the 2000–2008 average annual growth of 5.6 per cent and the rest of the world does the same at 2.9 per cent—Africa's contribution to world GDP increases from 2.4 per cent in 2012 and reaches 5.1 per cent in 2034. That is, Africa

is likely to meet the growth imperative to be a global growth pole by 2034. Needless to say, other things being equal, the higher the growth rate of Africa, the sooner its share of global GDP hits the 5 per cent mark. If, for example, Africa can maintain an average of 7 per cent growth (specified as the required growth rate to meet the MDGs) while the rest of the world maintains 2.9 per cent, Africa's contribution to global GDP would reach 5 per cent in around two decades.

Table 3.1
Projected Global and African GDP, 2012–2034 ($ billion)

Year	Global GDP (including Africa) [a]	African GDP [b]	African share [c] (%)
2012	42,738.7	1,033.0	2.4
2013	43,995.3	1,088.2	2.5
2014	45,290.2	1,147.2	2.5
2015	46,624.7	1,210.2	2.6
2016	48,000.1	1,277.5	2.7
2017	49,418.0	1,349.6	2.7
2018	50,879.8	1,426.9	2.8
2019	52,387.3	1,510.0	2.9
2020	53,942.2	1,599.5	3.0
2021	55,546.3	1,696.0	3.1
2022	57,201.7	1,800.3	3.1
2023	58,910.5	1,913.3	3.2
2024	60,675.0	2,036.2	3.4
2025	62,497.7	2,169.9	3.5
2026	64,381.5	2,316.0	3.6
2027	66,329.2	2,476.0	3.7
2028	68,344.3	2,651.9	3.9
2029	70,430.3	2,845.7	4.0
2030	72,591.4	3,060.0	4.2
2031	74,832.1	3,297.9	4.4
2032	77,157.5	3,562.7	4.6
2033	79,573.5	3,858.7	4.8
2034	82,086.5	4,190.7	5.1

Source: Projected outputs on the basis of GDP figures obtained from World Bank (2011a).

Notes: a. World GDP (excluding Africa) is projected using the average annual growth rate for 2000–2008, which is 2.9 per cent. Projected global GDP includes Africa. b. African GDP is projected using the average annual growth rate for 2000–2008 for individual African countries before summing to obtain projected African GDP. c. African share is African GDP relative to global GDP (including Africa).

Africa's structural transformation imperatives

Structure of output

The above growth imperative is fundamental to a global growth pole, but the structural imperatives are important as they reflect the potential for the growth pole to drive growth in other economies, hence global growth. It is thus important to propose the structural transformation imperatives for Africa as a global growth pole.

To this end, we examine the structures of China, India and the Republic of Korea in 2005 to benchmark the structural transformation that Africa should strive to attain in order to become a global growth pole in the next two decades. We emphasize at the outset that as total output grows, the contributions of various sectors to total output should change as factors move from lower-productivity to higher-productivity sectors (Lewis, 1954; Kuznets, 1955; Chenery, 1986). In the context of inter-industry linkages, sectors that generate greater forward than backward linkages tend to propagate activities in the other sectors such that over time, the spin-off, higher value-added activities become larger contributors to total output than the sector that generated the spin-off activities in the first instance. In that context, a decline in the contribution of a specific sector to total output does not necessarily imply absolute decline, only relative.

As a starting point, virtually all African countries have articulated national visions that aim to achieve an income status at least one step higher than their current level. It therefore seems reasonable to expect that the economic structures of the African countries will approximate those of countries that are in the targeted income group. Hence the structural transformation imperatives for current high-income and upper middle-income African countries should be that of the Republic of Korea in 2005—a high-income country. For lower middle-income and low-income countries, the structural transformation imperatives should be the average of the structures of China and India, also in 2005.

For agriculture therefore, high-income and upper middle-income African countries should target a share of 3.3 per cent of GDP, and lower middle-income countries and low-income African countries should target 15.5 per cent of GDP, at most. Again, such targeting does not mean that attention should *not* be paid to growth in agricultural productivity and output. On the contrary, even greater attention should be paid to these areas to provide the necessary input for manufacturing and other transformation activities that will add value to primary agricultural commodities as a prelude to structural transformation. Indeed, the hallmark of a successful agricultural revolution is sustained supply of agricultural raw materials to the processing and other transformation industries so that over time, while agriculture maintains a high growth rate, its share in total output will decline as the shares of manufacturing, other industries and sophisticated services increase faster.

For manufacturing, the target for high- and upper middle-income African countries should be 28 per cent of GDP at the minimum, and that for lower middle-income and low-income countries should be 24 per cent of GDP, again at the minimum. For industrial sectors, excluding manufacturing, the targets should be 10 per cent and 14 per cent, respectively, for the two country groups, and for services, 59 per cent and 47 per cent of GDP, respectively.

Percentage changes in the structure of output required to meet these structural imperatives can now be determined. For agriculture, Namibia and Mauritius, among the upper middle-income countries in Southern Africa, should reduce the share of agriculture in total GDP to meet this benchmark (figure 3.8 and annex table 3.1).[15] Again, the implication is that in these countries, manufacturing and other sectors should grow faster as they transform agricultural commodities to higher value-added commodities and services such that their contributions to total output rise relative to that of agriculture. The other countries should strive to preserve the current share, or

> *Africa is likely to meet the growth imperative to be a global growth pole by 2034.*

at least ensure that as the economy grows, the share of agriculture in total GDP does not exceed the 3.3 per cent benchmark. Among the lower middle-income and low-income countries in Southern Africa, Zambia, Mozambique and Malawi should strive to increase the contributions of manufacturing and other sectors to total output; thus the share of agriculture in total GDP should decline significantly as the economy grows.

In East Africa, all the low-income countries should also reduce the share of agriculture in total GDP as the economy grows, and in Central Africa, all countries should seek to do this. In West Africa, all countries should reduce the share of agriculture in GDP substantially, apart from Cape Verde. In North Africa, Algeria, Tunisia, Mauritania and Sudan should strive to reduce the share of agriculture in GDP.

Figure 3.8

Imperatives of agriculture value added for Africa as a global growth pole (% of GDP)

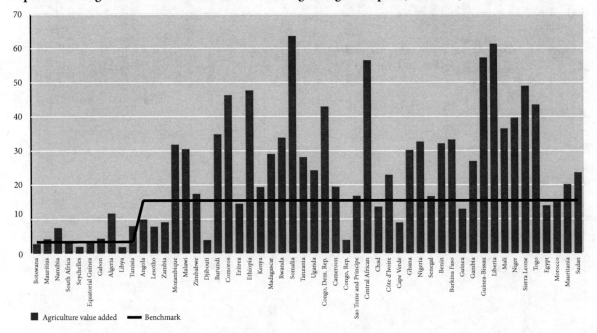

Source: World Bank (2011a).

All African countries should strive to increase the share of manufacturing in GDP over time (figure 3.9). The largest increases are required in Central and East Africa, where most current shares are in low single digits. The challenge of raising the share of manufacturing and sophisticated services, thereby reducing those of agriculture and other industry (excluding manufacturing), is more serious in resource-rich economies such as Botswana, Angola, Equatorial Guinea, Republic of the Congo, Nigeria and Algeria (figure 3.10).

Africa should step up efforts to diversify its economic base away from primary production towards high value added activities.

Figure 3.9

Imperatives of manufacturing value added for Africa as a global growth pole (% of GDP)

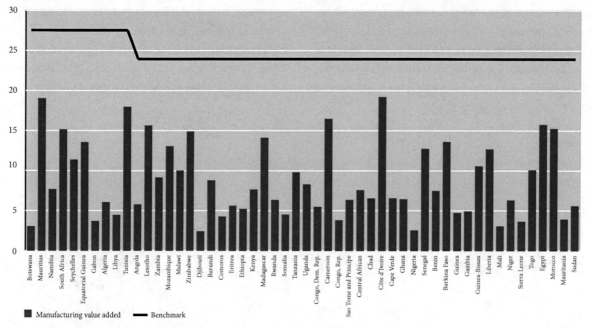

Source: World Bank (2011a).

Figure 3.10

Imperatives of industry value added for Africa as a global growth pole (% of GDP)

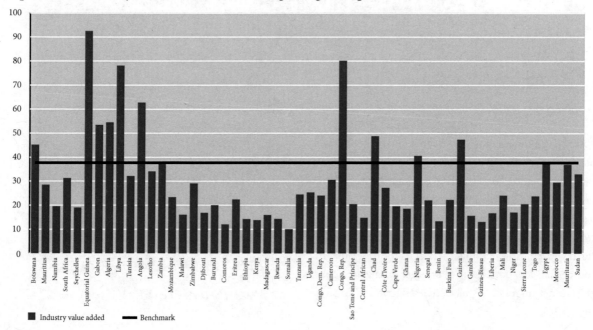

Source: World Bank (2011a).

Services—except for Mauritius and South Africa and, to some extent, most of the North African countries—are dominated by informal, low-productivity distributive trade activities. Virtually all countries should strive to reduce the contribution of this type of services to GDP as a strategy of reducing the preponderance of unproductive informal activities, which are very hard to tax.

In Southern Africa—except for Botswana, Angola and Mozambique—all countries should strive to reduce the share of services in GDP. In East Africa—except for Burundi, Comoros, Democratic Republic of the Congo, Ethiopia and Tanzania—all countries should do this. In Central Africa, only Sao Tome and Principe, and in West Africa, Benin, Cape Verde, Côte d'Ivoire and Gambia, should strive to do so. In North Africa, Tunisia, Egypt and Morocco should endeavour to do the same (figure 3.11).

Figure 3.11

Imperatives of services value added for Africa as a global growth pole (% of GDP)

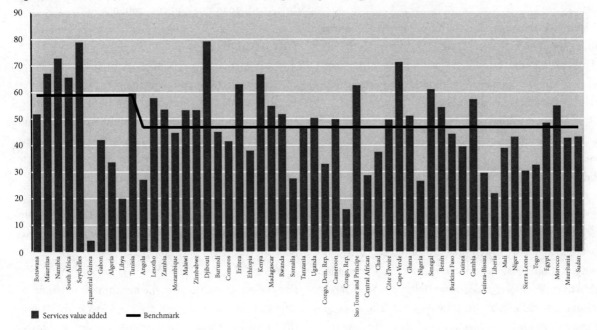

■ Services value added   —— Benchmark

Source: World Bank (2011a).

The general indication is that structural transformation imperatives require the majority of African countries to reduce the share of agriculture in GDP and increase the share of manufacturing and non-manufacturing industry substantially. Also, some countries need to reduce the share of services in GDP. Except for Mauritius and South Africa, all countries should strive to modernize unproductive distributive trade activities and in the process transform them to formal, more productive activities that can also be brought into the tax net.

In sum, Africa should step up efforts to diversify its economic base away from primary production (agriculture and minerals) and distributive trade dominated by informal operators, towards higher value-added production activities in manufacturing and more sophisticated services, together supporting a modern, knowledge-intensive economy.

> *Like infrastructure, a well-educated, enlightened and healthy human resource base is a key imperative for a global growth pole.*

> *African governments should nurture and support an indigenous entrepreneurial class.*

Trade

As elaborated above, perhaps the most important channel of interactions and spillovers between a global growth pole and other economies is trade. Accordingly, the structures of exports and imports are key imperatives of the structural transformation of a global growth pole.

The export benchmark for high- and upper middle-income African countries is the Republic of Korea and for lower middle-income and low-income African countries it is the average of China and India. All African countries should reduce the shares of food and agricultural raw materials in total merchandise exports for the continent to become a global growth pole. Resource-rich African countries should also reduce the share of fuel, ores and metals in total exports and substantially raise the shares of manufactured exports in total exports. The sizes of the reductions and increases vary across countries (annex table 3.2).

On the structure of imports, all African countries should reduce the shares of food in total imports (annex table 3.3), increase the share of agricultural raw materials in total imports and increase the shares of fuel, ores and metals in total imports.[16] For manufactured imports, the size of the change required by African countries is quite small. However, most of the manufactured imports by the benchmark countries are really components used as inputs in the production of other high value-added manufactured goods, some of which are exported and some intended for the domestic market.

For example, imports of ICT goods accounted for over 18 per cent of total imports of the Republic of Korea in 2005. The corresponding figures for China and India were 26.5 per cent and 8.2 per cent (Ajakaiye, 2007). In essence, imports of a global growth pole should largely be to support the production platforms that efficiently produce higher value-added goods for domestic and export markets.

The challenge for African countries in imports of manufactured goods is therefore not only the reduction of their share in total imports, which is relatively small, but a major shift from the imports of finished and final consumer goods (the familiar, fully built-up units) towards industrial intermediate inputs and components.

Infrastructure

The infrastructure imperatives for high- and upper middle-income African countries are benchmarked to Korea in 2005, while those for lower middle-income and low-income African countries are benchmarked to the average of China and India, also in 2005. Key elements are energy, roads and telecommunications. For energy, the indicators are per capita electricity consumption and GDP per unit of energy use; for roads, the share of paved roads in total road length; and for telecommunications, telephone lines per 100 persons, mobile (cellular) phones per 100 persons and Internet users per 100 persons.

For per capita energy use, the benchmark for high- and upper middle-income countries is 4,365 kilowatt-hours (kWh) while that for lower middle-income and low-income countries is 896 kWh. These are changes that the various African countries should secure in two decades to meet the energy use imperative. Only Egypt has met this imperative, while Libya, South Africa, Zimbabwe and Morocco in 2010 were closest to the benchmarks (annex table 3.4). All other countries have to step up energy supply and use significantly in order to meet this imperative. On GDP per unit of energy use, several African countries have met this benchmark, in which case the challenge for them is to maintain momentum. The African countries that are below the benchmark should step up both the volume and efficiency of energy use.

For roads, Mauritius, Seychelles, Comoros, Sao Tome and Principe, Cape Verde, Egypt and Morocco have met the benchmark. All other countries should raise the proportion of paved roads substantially to ensure that Africa meets the global growth pole imperatives in the next two decades (annex table 3.5).

On telecommunications, all African countries are yet to meet the benchmark for telephone lines per 100 persons (annex table 3.5), though quite a number have met the benchmark for Internet users per 100 persons. Similarly, several African countries have met the benchmark for mobile cellular coverage.

In a nutshell, African countries should invest aggressively in infrastructure upgrading to meet the infrastructure imperatives of a global growth pole by the mid-2030s.

Human resources

Like infrastructure, a well-educated, enlightened and healthy human resource base is a key imperative for a global growth pole. Such a human resource base is required for efficient production, knowledge transfer and technological adaptation and innovation. A high-quality human resource base is the foundation for ensuring local capacity to interact, collaborate and partner with foreign investors, maximizing the linkages and spillovers for the domestic economy. Similarly, this human resource base is required to ensure that migration plays its role in knowledge transfer and technological adaptation from the global to the local economy—and vice versa. Indices that represent key imperatives of quality human resources are tertiary, secondary and primary enrolment rates, adult and youth literacy rates, life expectancy, infant mortality rate and survival rate to age 65.

In education, most African countries have met the benchmark for primary enrolment (annex figure 3.1 and annex table 3.6). But only a few African countries have met that for secondary enrolment, and Egypt is the only country to have met the benchmark for tertiary enrolment (annex figures 3.2 and 3.3). As African countries strive to meet these imperatives, the issue of quality of education at all levels should be addressed. Similarly, very few African countries have met the benchmarks for adult and youth literacy rates (annex figures 3.4 and 3.5).

In health, only Cape Verde, Egypt and Morocco have met the benchmark for life expectancy (annex figure 3.6 and annex table 3.7), while no African country has met the benchmark for the infant mortality rate (annex figure 3.7). Only Cape Verde, Egypt and Morocco have met the benchmark for the male survival rate to age 65 (annex figure 3.8).

All African countries should strive to reduce the burden of disease, especially HIV/AIDS and malaria, which undermine the benefits of high-quality health services and higher education. African countries have to invest heavily in these areas in order to prepare its human resource base to become a global growth pole.

An indigenous entrepreneurial class

A global growth pole will interact with the other economies to the advantage of the domestic and global economy if it can organize a strong and efficient domestic production platform that can partner on mutually beneficial terms with counterparts from the rest of the world. In addition to the growth, output structure, trade, infrastructure and human resources imperatives described above, a virile indigenous entrepreneurial class is another imperative for a global growth pole.

Researchers have yet to identify a suitable index to develop a benchmark. Yet there is no doubt that—apart perhaps from Mauritius and to some extent South Africa, Egypt and Tunisia—many African countries have a dearth of local entrepreneurs who can work with foreign counterparts on mutually beneficial terms. African governments should therefore vigorously nurture and support an indigenous entrepreneurial class, so that the continent can become a global growth pole in the next two decades.[17]

3.3 Capitalizing on opportunities and managing risks

THERE IS GENERAL agreement that the world economy has become multipolar, one in which more than one country is helping to drive the growth process in other countries.[18] Since the beginning of the century, the dominance of the US and Europe as drivers of the global economy has declined significantly, especially in the second half of the decade. Indeed, China and India have joined the league of global growth drivers.

This shift in global economic power is associated with a shift in global balance. Of the top 15 global growth drivers, only six have a current account surplus—Germany is the only one in Europe and the rest are Asian (table 3.2).

This suggests that the economic power has shifted to the South, a view expressed by Cilliers, Hughes and Moyer (2011) and the McKinsey Global Institute (2010), among others. Africa has to capitalize on the key opportunities—and manage the risks—of this shift, and of its own recent improvement.

Table 3.2

Polarity indices and current account balance, top 15 growth poles, 2010

Country	Polarity index	Current account balance
China	82.13	2.9
United States	81.98	−3.1
Japan	63.77	2.4
India	23.22	−3.5
Germany	18.50	5.2
Brazil	16.87	−2.2
Korea, Rep.	12.12	2.0
Argentina	9.79	−0.3
Mexico	9.41	−1.9
Turkey	8.55	−9.8
Canada	6.59	−2.7
Singapore	5.78	17.7
France	5.40	−2.4
United Kingdom	5.22	−1.5
Hong Kong SAR, China	4.30	4.2

Source: Polarity indices are computed from World Bank (2011a); current account balances are from The Economist, 17 December 2011.

Macroeconomic management

African countries need to capitalize on their recently improved macroeconomic management and ensure that the associated resource inflows are well invested in the key areas of infrastructure, science and technology, human resources and development of the local entrepreneurial class.

A major macroeconomic risk is managing external reserves and public expenditure, especially controlling corruption and waste. Poorly managed reserves can cause the exchange rate to appreciate, hurting exports. If corruption is not controlled, expenditure on these key areas

will be inefficient. Weak capacity of the State bureaucracy to manage public expenditure in general and in these particular areas will undermine the benefits of the opportunities mentioned.

In order to maximize the opportunities and manage the risks, therefore, it is imperative for African governments to articulate and then effectively carry out medium-term development plans for their long-term visions. They should consider the tenets of the developmental State articulated in the *Economic Report on Africa 2011* (UNECA and AUC, 2011), and control corruption, strengthen macroeconomic management and develop an indigenous entrepreneurial class. Such an approach will speed up structural transformation, residualizing primary production and export as drivers of growth (chapter 4).

Demand for primary resources

One of the major opportunities presented to Africa by the contemporary multipolar world is increased demand for primary commodities. At early stages of development, production in emerging economies tends to be primary product–intensive. This intensity generally declines as development proceeds and as the economy moves towards knowledge-intensive goods.

The preponderance of developing countries among the new global growth drivers presents opportunities for African countries, the majority of which produce and export primary commodities. World prices of these primary commodities are likely to remain high for some time mainly because of the heavy demand from emerging markets but also because of the recovery of Africa's traditional trading partners. Thus resource-rich African countries and producers of primary agricultural commodities are likely to enjoy a favourable balance of trade and comfortable external reserves for some time. Moreover, resource-rich African countries are expected to continue attracting FDI into the extractive industries.

Cheap manufactured imports

International prices of manufactured goods are falling steadily (Kaplinsky, Robinson and Willenbockel, 2007). A major benefit, especially for low-income African countries, is access to affordable imports of manufactured goods, which should help in reducing poverty. With the dominance of finished manufactured goods in Africa's imports, African consumers are at first glance the real beneficiaries of the falling international prices of manufactured goods.

But a major risk is deindustrialization, as local producers lose market shares to cheaper imports. Moreover, in a competitive environment, African manufactured exporters based on small and medium-sized firms are unlikely to be able to compete with increasingly large producers operating complex global production networks based on imported industrial intermediates and components from the most cost-effective sources (Finger and Low, 2012). The associated loss of income and employment is a major concern in an environment already with high unemployment.

Another risk associated with cheap imports is low quality and the consequent health hazards. Low-quality goods are also likely to require frequent and costly maintenance. When such goods are imported for production and export of value added goods, they may not meet increasingly stringent standards, adversely affecting the acceptability and access of products in local and international markets.

Cheap imports also run the risk of Africa's continued specialization in production and export of primary products and excessive economic concentration. Apart from going against the transformation imperatives, such specialization will make Africa more vulnerable to terms-of-trade shocks.

African countries should respond in three ways. To maximize the benefits of falling international prices of manufactured goods, they should restructure their imports

African governments should subject all foreign investment proposals to rigorous value-chain analysis and insist on local processing of primary commodities.

in favour of imports of cheaper capital goods needed to process the primary agricultural and mineral products at lower cost, for the export and domestic markets. To avoid the risk of low-quality imports, they should develop and enforce appropriate standards, and build the necessary quality assurance organizations. Finally, to mitigate the risks of deindustrialization, they should develop and nurture indigenous entrepreneurs capable of partnering with their foreign counterparts. This can help insert African countries in the global production networks at the higher end of the value chain. Such moves should be accompanied by incentives necessary to attract foreign investors.

One attribute of moving to a global growth pole and eventual graduation to a knowledge economy is low and falling reliance on primary commodities as inputs, as efficiency rises and as the benefits of intensive research and development feed through. In essence, African primary producers and exporters benefiting from impressive growth should take full advantage of these—possibly short-term—opportunities.

An industrial policy for diversified FDI

One benefit of the multipolar world is the diversified sources of FDI, which can help countries to avoid the "race to the bottom", given that African countries can now seek particular types of FDI without fear of other collusive foreign investors abandoning them. Consequently, African countries are now in a better position to negotiate favourable terms with foreign investors, including in areas such as joint ventures and outsourcing important operations to local businesses.

One risk is that African leaders may fail to press on with further governance reforms, as most foreign investors may not insist on good governance and control of corruption. This may create opportunities for massive illicit capital flight thus curtailing the benefits of foreign investment (chapter 5).[19] Another risk is continued concentration of foreign investment in resource extraction rather than a shift to manufacturing. Also, some foreign investors may not use the best technology to minimize the environmental impact of operations. In addition, foreign investment—even outside the extractive industries—may target primary production aimed at guaranteeing the supply of agricultural raw materials for processing and adding value in the home country, rather than in Africa. Such FDI may insert Africa into the low end of production networks with limited linkage and spillovers to the rest of the economy.

To offset these risks, African countries have various options. They should capitalize on the enlarged pool of foreign investors by articulating clear industrial policies compatible with economic transformation, and by encouraging FDI that will complement such transformation. (Developing indigenous entrepreneurs is a prerequisite.)

All African governments should subscribe to the African Peer Review Mechanism (APRM) of AU/NEPAD (chapter 4), in order to mitigate the risks of poor governance, corrupt practices and associated illicit capital flight. On environmental damage, they should insist on environmental impact assessments as a condition for licensing all operations by investors, local or foreign. They should also ensure regular monitoring of the environmental impact of operations and that investors use the best technology for minimum environmental impact. Also, they should require all operators to undertake adequate restoration and restitution activities to deal with the inevitable damage to the environment. Licences should be subject to renewal at reasonable intervals, affording an opportunity to check compliance with environmental standards.

Finally, to mitigate the risks associated with inserting Africa into the wrong end of the international production network, Africa's governments should subject all foreign investment proposals to rigorous value-chain analysis and insist on local processing of all primary commodities, including mineral products before export. This way Africa will also export industrial intermediates and not just primary commodities—a move compatible with the transformation imperatives discussed earlier.

Infrastructure development with support of traditional and new partners

As with FDI, the emergence of a multi-polar world also diversified the prospective partners in developing infrastructure. One benefit of this is the falling cost of doing this, though low quality is a risk alongside a preponderance of turnkey systems, which together entail high maintenance costs and hence, possibly, scrapping the project.

To mitigate these risks, African countries should develop local entrepreneurs in infrastructure construction and maintenance, and insist on partnerships between foreign and local firms in infrastructure projects. They should also develop capacity to design such projects and monitor construction. These measures call for a capable developmental State (UNECA and AUC, 2011).

Diasporas

Africa is a source of skilled and unskilled migrants and recipient of unskilled migrants from other regions (Ajakaiye, Lucas and Karugia, 2006). While skilled workers migrate because of a poor working environment and poor living conditions, unskilled migrants do so out of restricted opportunities for employment. Migration is one of the key channels through which a global growth pole can interact with other economies through transfer of knowledge and technology.

African countries benefit from remittances (Ratha et al., 2011), but the apparent neglect of potential spillovers from returning skilled migrants should not continue. Most African leaders try to meet some of their citizens in diasporas when they visit the host countries. Such efforts should be complemented by more carefully targeted incentives to attract skilled emigrants back home, as this will facilitate the imperatives for knowledge and technology transfer.

3.4 Conclusions and recommendations

AFTER STAGNATING FOR much of its post-colonial history, Africa has witnessed a growth resurgence, especially in 2002–2008, making it the second-fastest-growing region in the world which, in 2010, contained 10 of the world's 15 fastest-growing economies. The growth resurgence is not limited to the resource-rich countries.

This resurgence is giving rise to Africa's growing recognition as an emerging market and a potential global growth pole. For Africa to become a global growth pole, this chapter has presented options—or imperatives—for the continent.

Generally, African countries need to address development deficits in the structural transformation of output and trade, infrastructure, human resources and science and technology; and capitalize on the opportunities and manage the risks in the emerging multipolar world and the shift in the resource balance to developing regions.

More specifically, to achieve global growth pole status Africa should sustain its 2000–2008 growth momentum (while the rest of the world maintains its rate of that period). If it does this, Africa will account for at least 5 per cent of world GDP by 2034.

Associated structural transformation targets, to be met by 2034 or earlier, include the following:

> African countries should reduce the share of agriculture in GDP to 15 per cent at most, increase the share of manufacturing to at least 25 per cent and restructure services from distributive trades towards more modern services.

> African countries should diversify their trade and render it more sophisticated, so that the shares of agricultural raw materials, fuel and ores and metals do not exceed 1 per cent, 6 per cent and 4 per

cent, respectively, of total exports, while the share of manufacturing exports should be at least 82 per cent. The shares of fuel and ores and metal in total imports should hover around 23 per cent and 7 per cent, while the composition of manufactured imports should change towards capital goods, industrial intermediates and components.

> Per capita electricity consumption and GDP per unit of energy use should be 1,129 kWh and 4 at least; the share of paved roads should be at least 44 per cent; telephone lines per 100 persons and Internet user per 100 persons should not be less than 16 and 6, respectively, in any African country.

> Secondary and tertiary enrolment should not be less than 16 per cent and 64 per cent, accompanied by quality assurance mechanisms.

> Adult and youth literacy rates should not be less than 77 per cent and 90 per cent, respectively, in any African country.

> Life expectancy should be 68 years at least and infant mortality rate should be 37 per 1,000 live births at most in any African country.

> All African countries should develop, nurture and support indigenous entrepreneurs capable of working with their foreign counterparts.

All these measures require collaboration among all stakeholders under the leadership of a developmental State. In that way, Africa can unleash its development capacity—as now discussed in detail.

Annex tables and figures

Annex table 3.1

Imperatives of changes in structure of output for Africa as a global growth pole

S/N	Country name	Agriculture (% of GDP)		Industry (% of GDP)		Services (% of GDP)		Manufacturing (% of GDP)	
		Value (2010)	%Change	Value (2010)	%Change	Value (2010)	%Change	Value (2010)	%Change
	SOUTHERN AFRICA								
	Upper Middle Income								
1	Botswana	2.9	16.5	45.3	-16.7	51.9	13.6	3.1	795.5
2	Mauritius	4.2	-21.3	28.6	31.8	67.2	-12.2	19.1	44.4
3	Namibia	7.5	-55.6	19.6	92.2	72.9	-19.1	7.7	257.2
4	South Africa	3.0	9.5	31.3	20.5	65.7	-10.2	15.2	81.6
	Lower Middle Income								
5	Angola	10.0	54.7	62.9	-39.9	27.1	72.3	5.8	313.3
6	Lesotho	7.9	95.7	34.2	10.5	57.9	-19.3	15.7	53.0
7	Zambia	9.2	68.9	37.2	1.4	53.6	-12.7	9.2	161.5
	Low Income								
8	Mozambique	31.9	-51.4	23.4	61.4	44.8	4.5	13.1	83.1
9	Malawi	30.5	-49.3	16.1	134.3	53.4	-12.3	10.0	138.3
10	Zimbabwe	17.4	-11.3	29.2	29.3	53.4	-12.3	14.9	60.6
	EAST AFRICA								
	Upper Middle Income								
11	Seychelles	1.9	70.9	19.1	97.3	78.9	-25.3	11.4	141.5
	Lower Middle Income								
12	Djibouti	3.9	301.2	16.9	123.6	79.3	-41.0	2.5	877.4
	Low Income								
13	Burundi	34.8	-55.6	20.0	88.7	45.1	3.6	8.8	171.2
14	Comoros	46.3	-66.6	12.1	211.8	41.6	12.5	4.3	458.0
15	Eritrea	14.5	6.5	22.4	68.2	63.0	-25.8	5.7	323.9
16	Ethiopia	47.7	-67.6	14.3	164.3	38.0	23.0	5.2	356.8
17	Kenya	19.4	-20.2	13.8	173.2	66.8	-30.0	7.7	212.9
18	Madagascar	29.1	-46.9	16.0	135.9	54.9	-14.8	14.1	69.4
19	Rwanda	33.9	-54.3	14.4	162.3	51.8	-9.6	6.4	276.6
20	Somalia	63.6	-75.7	10.1	273.1	27.5	70.0	4.5	426.8
21	Tanzania	28.1	-45.0	24.5	53.8	47.3	-1.1	9.8	143.6
22	Uganda	24.2	-36.2	25.5	48.3	50.3	-7.0	8.3	188.1
23	Congo, Dem. Rep.	42.9	-63.9	24.0	57.0	33.0	41.5	5.5	336.0
	CENTRAL AFRICA								
	High Income								
24	Equatorial Guinea	3.2	4.6	92.6	-59.3	4.2	1297.9	13.6	102.7
	Upper Middle Income								
25	Gabon	4.4	-23.6	53.5	-29.6	42.1	40.0	3.7	638.5
	Lower Middle Income								
26	Cameroon	19.5	-20.5	30.6	23.2	49.9	-6.2	16.5	45.1
27	Congo, Rep.	3.9	301.4	80.2	-52.9	15.9	193.6	3.8	523.1

S/N	Country name	Agriculture (% of GDP)		Industry (% of GDP)		Services (% of GDP)		Manufacturing (% of GDP)	
		Value (2010)	%Change	Value (2010)	%Change	Value (2010)	%Change	Value (2010)	%Change
28	Sao Tome and Principe	16.8	-8.0	20.5	83.9	62.7	-25.4	6.4	275.8
	Low Income								
29	Central African Republic	56.5	-72.6	14.8	154.9	28.7	62.9	7.6	214.8
30	Chad	13.6	13.5	48.8	-22.7	37.5	24.6	6.6	265.2
	WEST AFRICA								
	Lower Middle Income								
31	Côte d'Ivoire	22.9	-32.6	27.4	37.9	49.7	-5.8	19.2	24.5
32	Cape Verde	8.9	72.9	19.7	92.0	71.4	-34.5	6.6	263.5
33	Ghana	30.2	-48.8	18.6	102.5	51.1	-8.5	6.5	270.2
34	Nigeria	32.7	-52.7	40.7	-7.1	26.6	75.6	2.6	828.2
35	Senegal	16.7	-7.4	22.1	70.5	61.1	-23.5	12.8	87.6
	Low Income								
36	Benin	32.2	-52.0	13.4	181.4	54.4	-14.0	7.5	218.8
37	Burkina Faso	33.3	-53.5	22.4	68.8	44.4	5.5	13.6	75.8
38	Guinea	13.0	18.8	47.4	-20.3	39.6	18.2	4.8	403.2
39	Gambia	26.9	-42.6	15.7	140.0	57.3	-18.4	5.0	382.4
40	Guinea-Bissau	57.3	-73.0	13.1	187.3	29.6	58.2	10.6	125.8
41	Liberia	61.3	-74.8	16.8	124.7	21.9	113.6	12.7	88.6
42	Mali	36.5	-57.7	24.2	56.1	39.1	19.8	3.1	670.9
43	Niger	39.6	-61.0	17.1	120.5	43.2	8.2	6.3	277.2
44	Sierra Leone	49.0	-68.4	20.7	82.7	30.4	54.0	3.7	551.5
45	Togo	43.5	-64.4	23.9	58.0	32.6	43.5	10.1	136.9
	NORTH AFRICA								
	Upper Middle Income								
46	Algeria	11.7	-71.6	54.5	-30.9	33.7	74.8	6.1	353.3
47	Libya	1.9	78.6	78.2	-51.8	19.9	195.8	4.5	513.3
48	Tunisia	8.0	-58.4	32.3	16.8	59.7	-1.3	18.0	53.2
	Lower Middle Income								
49	Egypt	14.0	10.6	37.5	0.6	48.5	-3.5	15.8	51.6
50	Morocco	15.4	0.6	29.7	27.3	55.0	-14.9	15.3	56.5
51	Mauritania	20.2	-23.3	37.0	2.0	42.8	9.2	4.0	506.0
52	Sudan	23.6	-34.5	33.0	14.3	43.3	8.0	5.6	326.3

Source: *Computed based on data from World Bank (2011a).*

Note: *All values are for 2010 or latest available. South Sudan became an independent State on 9 July 2011. Separate data for the country is not yet available hence it is still combined with the Sudan. %Change is the percentage difference between the actual value for each country and the relevant benchmark.*

Annex table 3.2
Imperatives of structure of merchandise exports for Africa as a global growth pole

S/N	Country Name	Food exptors (% of merchandise exports)		Agric. raw materials exports (% of merchandise exports)		Fuel exports (% of merchandise exports)		Ores and metals exports (% of merchandise exports)		Manufactures exports (% of merchandise exports)	
		Value (2010)	%Change	Value (2010)	%Change	Value (2010)	%Change	Value (2010)	%Change	Value (2010)	%Change
	SOUTHERN AFRICA										
	Upper Middle Income										
1	Botswana	5.1	-79.2	0.2	320.5	0.4	1428.7	14.5	-88.3	79.5	14.2
2	Mauritius	37.2	-97.2	0.5	53.2	0.0	908560.2	0.4	379.4	60.2	51.0
3	Namibia	22.5	-95.3	0.4	86.7	0.5	1038.5	31.3	-94.5	44.7	103.3
4	South Africa	8.7	-87.9	1.9	-58.9	9.9	-45.1	32.7	-94.8	46.6	95.1
	Lower Middle Income										
5	Angola	0.3	1893.8	0.0	47857.5	94.8	-93.3	4.9	-6.3	0.0	4464917.4
6	Lesotho	13.5	-54.9	9.1	-90.1	0.4	1660.8	2.5	84.5	74.4	9.5
7	Zambia	5.9	3.3	1.0	-7.7	0.5	1135.8	86.0	-94.7	6.3	1195.8
	Low Income										
8	Mozambique	15.7	-61.3	4.4	-79.5	19.7	-67.9	54.4	-91.6	2.0	4026.5
9	Malawi	76.4	-92.0	3.3	-73.3	0.2	3300.0	11.1	-58.9	9.0	809.5
10	Zimbabwe	20.1	-69.7	7.0	-87.2	1.6	294.1	34.9	-87.0	36.4	123.7
	EAST AFRICA										
	Upper Middle Income										
11	Seychelles	58.5	-98.2	0.0	1790.6	0.0	227678.8	0.0	42764.9	2.4	3686.7
	Lower Middle Income										
12	Djibouti	0.4	1322.6	0.0	9274.0	6.5	-2.5	0.3	1327.3	90.7	-10.2
	Low Income										
13	Burundi	81.4	-92.5	4.9	-81.7	2.3	171.6	5.2	-12.9	5.9	1273.7
14	Comoros	13.8	-55.8	0.0	3527.0	0.0	134271.3	0.1	2940.2	6.3	1187.8
15	Eritrea	42.0	-85.5	26.0	-96.6	0.0	34655.1	1.8	159.2	30.3	169.3
16	Ethiopia	77.5	-92.1	11.9	-92.5	0.0	735453.9	0.8	492.2	8.7	841.6
17	Kenya	47.9	-87.3	10.9	-91.8	4.3	46.8	2.0	124.0	34.7	135.0
18	Madagascar	26.7	-77.1	3.2	-71.7	6.7	-5.1	9.5	-51.9	48.2	68.9
19	Rwanda	52.4	-88.4	3.1	-70.9	0.0	120390.5	36.9	-87.7	7.6	966.1
20	Somalia	93.7	-93.5	0.7	31.4	1.1	464.8	0.0	12481.0	1.3	5985.4
21	Tanzania	31.9	-80.9	7.4	-87.9	2.5	149.5	33.7	-86.5	24.1	238.6
22	Uganda	66.8	-90.9	7.2	-87.6	1.2	421.8	1.9	138.8	22.8	256.6
23	Congo, Dem. Rep.	32.5	-81.2	7.8	-88.6	1.3	379.7	51.8	-91.2	4.8	1580.8
	CENTRAL AFRICA										
	High Income										
24	Equatorial Guinea	57.9	-98.2	30.0	-97.3	1.7	219.4	7.5	-77.1	4.0	2185.9
	Upper Middle Income										
25	Gabon	0.8	39.9	8.9	-91.0	83.1	-93.4	3.0	-43.7	4.2	2069.1
	Lower Middle Income										
26	Cameroon	24.4	-75.0	14.8	-93.9	49.5	-87.3	3.0	53.6	7.5	981.0
27	Congo, Rep.	1.0	505.6	8.3	-89.2	87.6	-92.8	0.3	1299.1	2.7	2907.0

S/N	Country Name	Food exptors (% of merchandise exports)		Agric. raw materials exports (% of merchandise exports)		Fuel exports (% of merchandise exports)		Ores and metals exports (% of merchandise exports)		Manufactures exports (% of merchandise exports)	
		Value (2010)	%Change	Value (2010)	%Change	Value (2010)	%Change	Value (2010)	%Change	Value (2010)	%Change
28	Sao Tome and Principe	94.6	-93.6	0.7	33.6	0.0	-	0.0	30974.0	4.7	1646.8
	Low Income										
29	Central African Republic	3.6	71.2	31.6	-97.2	0.0	25738.2	62.0	-92.7	2.7	2941.1
30	Chad	16.2	-62.2	66.9	-98.7	7.9	-20.5	0.8	452.4	7.7	956.3
	WEST AFRICA										
	Lower Middle Income										
31	Côte d'Ivoire	49.5	-87.7	9.6	-90.7	24.1	-73.8	0.3	1326.5	16.2	403.8
32	Cape Verde	81.6	-92.5	0.0	1989.8	0.0	-	0.9	413.0	17.5	365.5
33	Ghana	60.7	-89.9	6.9	-87.1	0.3	1851.5	11.2	-59.6	20.7	294.0
34	Nigeria	3.3	82.7	1.6	-45.1	87.1	-92.8	1.1	320.5	6.7	1118.7
35	Senegal	28.6	-78.6	1.4	-37.4	26.1	-75.8	3.8	20.8	40.1	103.1
	Low Income										
36	Benin	40.6	-85.0	44.3	-98.0	0.4	1506.2	0.7	586.6	14.1	476.6
37	Burkina Faso	33.3	-81.7	55.9	-98.4	0.1	11975.6	1.6	176.4	9.1	797.8
38	Guinea	2.5	145.0	4.9	-81.8	1.5	317.4	59.2	-92.3	31.9	155.6
39	Gambia	53.0	-88.5	1.0	-13.3	0.0	106500.1	6.8	-33.6	39.1	108.3
40	Guinea-Bissau	98.7	-93.8	0.2	318.2	0.8	679.5	0.6	623.3	0.1	99459.3
41	Liberia	8.6	-28.7	25.6	-96.5	0.0	151787.2	64.8	-93.0	0.4	21433.6
42	Mali	29.8	-79.5	48.0	-98.1	0.1	4863.2	0.7	582.9	20.2	303.5
43	Niger	21.1	-71.1	2.8	-67.9	1.9	240.9	59.6	-92.4	14.1	479.5
44	Sierra Leone	91.6	-93.3	0.8	13.6	1.6	307.2	0.1	3854.9	7.5	992.4
45	Togo	15.0	-59.4	4.9	-81.8	0.1	4909.2	5.6	-18.9	74.2	9.8
	NORTH AFRICA										
	Upper Middle Income										
46	Algeria	0.6	88.6	0.0	4968.8	97.3	-94.4	0.3	486.0	1.8	4985.6
47	Libya	0.5	101.3	0.2	352.2	92.6	-94.1	0.0	7659.6	6.7	1263.3
48	Tunisia	7.7	-86.3	0.5	59.8	14.2	-61.5	1.6	9.1	76.0	19.5
	Lower Middle Income										
49	Egypt	17.2	-64.5	3.0	-70.3	29.8	-78.8	6.3	-27.3	43.4	87.7
50	Morocco	19.0	-67.9	1.7	-48.4	1.1	488.5	11.7	-61.0	66.3	22.8
51	Mauritania	57.8	-89.4	0.1	774.5	0.0	381452.2	30.4	-85.1	0.0	1731148.9
52	Sudan	5.6	9.6	1.4	-35.7	92.1	-93.1	0.3	1717.6	0.4	19197.9

Source: *Computed based on data from World Bank (2011a).*

Note: *All values are for 2010 or latest available. South Sudan became an independent State on 9 July 2011. Separate data for the country is not yet available hence it is still combined with the Sudan. %Change is the percentage difference between the actual value for each country and the relevant benchmark.*

Annex table 3.3

Imperatives of structure of merchandise imports for Africa as a global growth pole

S/N	Country Name	Food imports (% of merchandise imports)		Agric. raw materials imports (% of merchandise imports)		Fuel imports (% of merchandise imports)		Ores and metals imports (% of merchandise imports)		Manufactures imports (% of merchandise imports)	
		Value (2010)	% Change	Value (2010)	%Change	Value (2010)	% Change	Value (2010)	% Change	Value (2010)	% Change
	SOUTHERN AFRICA										
	Upper Middle Income										
1	Botswana	12.4	-64.1	0.8	134.9	14.7	73.6	2.0	245.8	68.5	-11.1
2	Mauritius	21.1	-79.0	2.2	-10.5	19.3	32.0	1.1	537.1	56.4	7.9
3	Namibia	13.9	-68.2	0.7	183.2	13.7	85.6	1.0	565.1	70.3	-13.4
4	South Africa	5.8	-24.0	0.9	115.9	19.7	28.9	1.5	340.4	65.4	-6.9
	Lower Middle Income										
5	Angola	32.5	-88.9	0.8	273.8	0.2	9316.3	1.4	411.0	65.1	-3.8
6	Lesotho	20.2	-82.1	1.9	56.9	10.5	120.3	0.8	736.5	53.3	17.5
7	Zambia	4.7	-23.2	0.6	424.7	11.6	99.2	21.0	-67.1	61.6	1.6
	Low Income										
8	Mozambique	11.6	-68.9	1.0	197.2	19.9	16.0	0.5	1257.9	49.6	26.3
9	Malawi	13.6	-73.4	1.1	167.4	10.0	131.9	1.0	580.7	74.1	-15.5
10	Zimbabwe	18.8	-80.8	2.6	15.5	11.2	106.1	13.8	-50.1	52.2	20.0
	EAST AFRICA										
	Upper Middle Income										
11	Seychelles	17.2	-74.1	2.1	-6.9	12.4	105.4	0.6	951.5	47.8	27.4
	Lower Middle Income										
12	Djibouti	29.3	-87.7	0.6	415.7	6.5	258.1	0.8	817.6	62.4	0.3
	Low Income										
13	Burundi	13.7	-73.6	1.4	109.2	2.1	993.0	0.7	943.7	81.6	-23.3
14	Comoros	19.5	-81.5	0.2	1161.5	0.7	3239.6	0.2	4338.7	53.5	17.0
15	Eritrea	45.6	-92.1	0.9	229.9	0.8	2646.5	0.9	651.3	51.7	21.1
16	Ethiopia	10.9	-66.7	0.5	487.6	15.9	45.9	1.2	468.0	71.5	-12.4
17	Kenya	12.0	-70.0	1.5	94.6	22.1	4.7	1.5	357.3	62.7	-0.2
18	Madagascar	13.6	-73.5	1.0	212.6	15.2	52.4	0.4	1576.3	69.5	-9.9
19	Rwanda	13.2	-72.6	1.6	83.0	8.1	186.5	1.2	462.3	75.6	-17.2
20	Somalia	22.4	-83.9	7.1	-57.3	12.4	85.9	0.4	1486.4	54.7	14.5
21	Tanzania	10.0	-63.7	0.9	252.7	27.6	-16.2	1.0	561.1	60.4	3.6
22	Uganda	12.4	-70.9	1.1	182.9	20.0	15.8	1.3	452.4	65.1	-3.8
23	Congo, Dem. Rep.	20.6	-82.4	1.8	68.2	9.9	132.9	1.2	461.5	65.6	-4.5
	CENTRAL AFRICA										
	High Income										
24	Equatorial Guinea	31.8	-86.0	0.2	973.4	2.7	826.1	1.0	571.4	64.2	-5.2
	Upper Middle Income										
25	Gabon	17.1	-74.1	0.4	350.0	7.3	246.9	1.0	579.0	73.8	-17.5
	Lower Middle Income										
26	Cameroon	17.7	-79.6	1.6	91.5	27.5	-15.7	0.8	719.8	52.4	19.5
27	Congo, Rep.	20.8	-82.6	0.9	249.8	19.6	18.3	0.8	795.1	58.0	8.0

S/N	Country Name	Food imports (% of merchandise imports)		Agric. raw materials imports (% of merchandise imports)		Fuel imports (% of merchandise imports)		Ores and metals imports (% of merchandise imports)		Manufactures imports (% of merchandise imports)	
		Value (2010)	% Change	Value (2010)	%Change	Value (2010)	% Change	Value (2010)	% Change	Value (2010)	% Change
28	Sao Tome and Principe	29.8	-87.9	0.8	289.2	16.1	43.7	1.1	537.3	52.0	20.5
	Low Income										
29	Central African Republic	39.3	-90.8	2.3	32.9	0.6	3581.3	1.7	310.9	55.9	11.9
30	Chad	24.3	-85.1	0.6	402.5	17.9	29.0	0.6	1008.3	56.1	11.7
	WEST AFRICA										
	Lower Middle Income										
31	Côte d'Ivoire	19.2	-81.2	0.9	251.7	23.7	-2.5	1.2	495.9	54.6	14.7
32	Cape Verde	27.7	-87.0	1.3	130.4	11.9	93.8	1.1	506.1	57.8	8.3
33	Ghana	15.3	-76.4	1.1	178.0	1.0	2273.6	1.2	496.0	81.1	-22.7
34	Nigeria	10.2	-64.7	0.8	287.9	1.4	1550.5	1.1	534.9	86.4	-27.6
35	Senegal	22.4	-83.9	1.5	98.8	29.9	-22.7	1.7	307.5	44.4	41.1
	Low Income										
36	Benin	30.7	-88.2	4.6	-34.3	21.6	6.9	1.0	599.0	41.8	49.8
37	Burkina Faso	15.1	-76.1	0.7	306.2	22.0	5.2	0.9	686.2	61.0	2.6
38	Guinea	13.2	-72.7	0.4	707.0	33.0	-29.8	0.2	3232.0	53.2	17.7
39	Gambia	35.2	-89.7	0.7	312.8	20.5	13.0	0.7	878.5	42.9	45.9
40	Guinea-Bissau	50.7	-92.9	0.6	397.7	16.6	38.9	0.1	7192.0	31.1	101.2
41	Liberia	25.0	-85.6	0.4	592.2	19.7	17.1	1.3	422.5	53.0	18.2
42	Mali	11.6	-68.9	0.5	567.9	26.0	-11.0	0.6	997.2	61.2	2.4
43	Niger	15.1	-76.1	2.1	44.2	12.5	84.9	0.9	659.3	69.4	-9.7
44	Sierra Leone	22.5	-84.0	7.6	-60.1	39.7	-41.7	0.8	744.4	29.3	113.6
45	Togo	15.7	-76.9	1.4	122.1	13.9	66.1	1.9	268.7	67.2	-6.8
	NORTH AFRICA										
	Upper Middle Income										
46	Algeria	16.3	-72.8	1.6	20.7	2.1	1093.9	1.5	346.5	78.4	-22.4
47	Libya	16.8	-73.5	0.6	247.2	0.7	3596.6	0.9	641.2	81.1	-24.9
48	Tunisia	9.3	-52.5	2.1	-9.2	12.6	101.8	3.6	90.2	72.3	-15.8
	Lower Middle Income										
49	Egypt	19.1	-81.1	3.2	-6.1	13.4	72.1	4.1	67.5	60.1	4.3
50	Morocco	11.4	-68.4	2.2	39.4	23.1	0.3	3.3	111.6	58.8	6.6
51	Mauritania	19.4	-81.4	0.5	505.5	26.4	-12.5	0.2	3270.1	52.9	18.4
52	Sudan	14.9	-75.8	1.1	179.1	4.0	473.9	0.9	662.6	77.8	-19.5

Source: Computed based on data from World Bank (2011a).

Note: All values are for 2010 or latest available. South Sudan became an independent State on 9 July 2011. Separate data for the country is not yet available hence it is still combined with the Sudan. %Change is the percentage difference between the actual value for each country and the relevant benchmark.

Annex table 3.4

Imperatives of energy use for Africa as a global growth pole

S/N	Country Name	Electric power consumption (kWh per capita)		GDP per unit of energy use (PPP $ per kg of oil equivalent)	
		Value (2010)	%Change	Value (2010)	%Change
	SOUTHERN AFRICA				
	Upper Middle Income				
1	Botswana	1503.3	419.1	12.6	-58.5
2	Mauritius		-	12.4	-57.8
3	Namibia	1576.2	395.1	8.2	-36.1
4	South Africa	4532.0	72.2	3.5	47.6
	Lower Middle Income				
5	Angola	202.2	458.5		-
6	Lesotho		-		-
7	Zambia	635.0	77.8	2.4	65.5
	Low Income				
8	Mozambique	453.4	149.0		-
9	Malawi		-		-
10	Zimbabwe	1026.2	10.0		-
	EAST AFRICA				
	Upper Middle Income				
11	Seychelles		-	8.9	-41.1
	Lower Middle Income				
12	Djibouti		-		-
	Low Income				
13	Burundi		-		-
14	Comoros		-		-
15	Eritrea	51.0	2113.7		-
16	Ethiopia	45.8	2367.3		-
17	Kenya	147.4	665.8		-
18	Madagascar		-		-
19	Rwanda		-		-
20	Somalia		-		-
21	Tanzania	85.7	1217.8	3.0	32.3
22	Uganda		-		-
23	Congo, Dem. Rep.	103.9	987.1	0.9	324.2
	CENTRAL AFRICA				
	High Income				
24	Equatorial Guinea		-		-
	Upper Middle Income				
25	Gabon	922.5	746.0		-
	Lower Middle Income				
26	Cameroon	271.2	316.2		-
27	Congo, Rep.	146.4	671.2		-
28	Sao Tome and Principe		-	5.9	-33.6

S/N	Country Name	Electric power consumption (kWh per capita)		GDP per unit of energy use (PPP $ per kg of oil equivalent)	
		Value (2010)	%Change	Value (2010)	%Change
	Low Income				
29	Central African Republic	-			-
30	Chad	-			-
	WEST AFRICA				
	Lower Middle Income				
31	Côte d'Ivoire	203.5	454.9		-
32	Cape Verde		-		-
33	Ghana	265.1	325.9		-
34	Nigeria	120.5	836.9	3.2	22.4
35	Senegal	196.0	476.0	7.8	-49.6
	Low Income				
36	Benin	91.3	1137.1		-
37	Burkina Faso		-		-
38	Guinea		-		-
39	Gambia		-		-
40	Guinea-Bissau		-		
41	Liberia		-		-
42	Mali		-		-
43	Niger				-
44	Sierra Leone		-		-
45	Togo	110.8	918.8	2.2	78.4
	NORTH AFRICA				
	Upper Middle Income				
46	Algeria	971.0	703.7		-
47	Libya	4170.1	87.1		-
48	Tunisia	1311.3	495.1	10.5	-50.2
	Lower Middle Income				
49	Egypt	1548.6	-27.1		-
50	Morocco	755.6	49.4		-
51	Mauritania		-		-
52	Sudan	114.3	888.0	5.9	-33.5

Source: Computed based on data from World Bank (2011a).

Note: All values are for 2010 or latest available. South Sudan became an independent State on 9 July 2011. Separate data for the country is not yet available hence it is still combined with the Sudan. %Change is the percentage difference between the actual value for each country and the relevant benchmark.

Annex table 3.5

Imperatives of roads and telecommunications for Africa as a global growth pole

S/N	Country Name	Roads, paved (% of total roads)		Telephone lines (per 100 persons)		Mob cellular subsc. (per 100 person)		Internet users (per 100 person)	
		Value (2010)	% Change	Value (2010)	% Change	Value (2010)	% Change	Value (2010)	% Change
	SOUTHERN AFRICA								
	Upper Middle Income								
1	Botswana	32.6	135.6	6.8	625.2	117.8	-32.4	6.0	1097.2
2	Mauritius	98.0	-21.6	30.3	64.1	93.0	-14.3	25.2	184.5
3	Namibia	12.8	500.2	6.3	686.3	67.2	18.5	6.5	1005.1
4	South Africa	17.3	344.0	8.5	487.6	100.8	-21.0	12.3	482.3
	Lower Middle Income								
5	Angola	10.4	322.1	1.6	890.1	46.7	-58.9	3.9	41.5
6	Lesotho	18.3	139.9	1.8	780.4	32.2	-40.3	3.9	43.0
7	Zambia	22.0	99.5	0.7	2157.1	38.3	-49.8	6.8	-19.1
	Low Income								
8	Mozambique	20.8	111.2	0.4	4078.7	30.9	-37.8	4.2	32.3
9	Malawi	45.0	-2.5	1.1	1364.2	20.4	-5.8	2.3	144.2
10	Zimbabwe	19.0	131.0	3.0	421.8	59.7	-67.8	11.5	-52.0
	EAST AFRICA								
	Upper Middle Income								
11	Seychelles	96.5	-20.4	25.5	94.9	135.9	-41.4	39.8	80.5
	Lower Middle Income								
12	Djibouti	45.0	-2.5	2.1	656.8	18.6	3.1	6.5	-15.1
	Low Income								
13	Burundi	10.4	320.5	0.4	3945.4	13.7	39.9	2.1	162.8
14	Comoros	76.5	-42.6	2.9	449.5	22.5	-14.6	5.1	8.2
15	Eritrea	21.8	101.4	1.0	1424.0	3.5	444.6	5.4	2.2
16	Ethiopia	13.7	221.0	1.1	1335.8	7.9	144.4	0.8	635.7
17	Kenya	14.1	210.9	1.1	1285.2	61.6	-68.8	25.9	-78.7
18	Madagascar	11.6	278.4	0.8	1792.6	39.8	-51.7	1.7	224.6
19	Rwanda	19.0	131.0	0.4	4113.9	33.4	-42.5	7.7	-28.3
20	Somalia	11.8	272.0	1.1	1368.0	6.9	176.5	1.2	375.4
21	Tanzania	7.4	494.8	0.4	3942.5	46.8	-59.0	11.0	-49.8
22	Uganda	23.0	90.8	1.0	1507.5	38.4	-50.0	12.5	-55.9
23	Congo, Dem. Rep.	1.8	2311.8	0.1	24615.2	17.2	11.6	0.7	666.4
	CENTRAL AFRICA								
	High Income								
24	Equatorial Guinea		-	1.9	2469.4	57.0	39.7	6.0	1097.2
	Upper Middle Income								
25	Gabon	10.2	652.4	2.0	2360.8	106.9	-25.5	7.2	893.5
	Lower Middle Income								
26	Cameroon	8.4	424.4	2.5	521.0	41.6	-53.8	4.0	37.9
27	Congo, Rep.	7.1	515.7	0.2	6372.4	94.0	-79.6	7.3	-24.4
28	Sao Tome and Principe	68.1	-35.5	4.6	239.8	62.0	-69.0	18.8	-70.6

S/N	Country Name	Roads, paved (% of total roads)		Telephone lines (per 100 persons)		Mob cellular subsc. (per 100 person)		Internet users (per 100 person)	
		Value (2010)	% Change	Value (2010)	% Change	Value (2010)	% Change	Value (2010)	% Change
	Low Income								
29	Central African Republic	2.7	1525.7	0.3	5669.9	23.2	-17.1	2.3	139.9
30	Chad	0.8	5386.9	0.5	3348.0	23.3	-17.5	1.7	224.6
	WEST AFRICA								
	Lower Middle Income								
31	Côte d'Ivoire	7.9	453.6	1.1	1291.2	75.5	-74.6	2.6	112.2
32	Cape Verde	69.0	-36.4	14.5	8.4	75.0	-74.4	30.0	-81.6
33	Ghana	14.9	194.0	1.1	1280.9	71.5	-73.1	8.6	-35.5
34	Nigeria	15.0	192.6	0.7	2273.1	55.1	-65.1	28.4	-80.6
35	Senegal	29.3	50.0	2.7	472.2	67.1	-71.4	16.0	-65.5
	Low Income								
36	Benin	9.5	362.1	1.5	943.5	79.9	-76.0	3.1	76.3
37	Burkina Faso	4.2	952.6	0.9	1699.7	34.7	-44.6	1.4	294.1
38	Guinea	9.8	348.4	0.2	8624.0	40.1	-52.1	1.0	474.8
39	Gambia	19.3	127.2	2.8	457.5	85.5	-77.5	9.2	-40.0
40	Guinea-Bissau	27.9	57.1	0.3	4667.6	39.2	-51.0	2.5	125.2
41	Liberia	6.2	608.0	0.1	10599.2	39.3	-51.2	0.1	7782.7
42	Mali	19.0	130.6	0.7	2013.3	47.7	-59.7	2.7	104.4
43	Niger	20.7	112.6	0.5	2819.4	24.5	-21.7	0.8	564.8
44	Sierra Leone	8.0	448.7	0.2	6493.5	34.1	-43.7	0.3	2022.3
45	Togo	21.0	109.0	3.5	343.7	40.7	-52.8	5.4	2.6
	NORTH AFRICA								
	Upper Middle Income								
46	Algeria	73.5	4.6	8.2	502.6	92.4	-13.8	12.5	474.6
47	Libya	57.2	34.3	19.3	156.9	171.5	-53.6	5.7	1155.8
48	Tunisia	75.2	2.2	12.2	306.2	105.4	-24.4	36.6	96.5
	Lower Middle Income								
49	Egypt	86.9	-49.5	11.9	32.7	87.1	-78.0	26.7	-79.4
50	Morocco	67.8	-35.2	11.7	34.1	100.1	-80.8	49.0	-88.7
51	Mauritania	26.8	63.5	2.1	660.5	79.3	-75.8	2.9	90.3
52	Sudan	36.3	20.9	0.9	1728.6	40.5	-52.6	10.2	-45.7

Source: Computed based on data from World Bank (2011a).

Note: All values are for 2010 or latest available. South Sudan became an independent State on 9 July 2011. Separate data for the country is not yet available hence it is still combined with the Sudan. %Change is the percentage difference between the actual value for each country and the relevant benchmark.

Annex table 3.6

Imperatives of human development for Africa as a global growth pole (education)

S/N	Country Name	School enrolment, tertiary (% gross)		School enrolment, secondary (% gross)		School enrolment, primary (% gross)		Lit. rate, adult total (% of people ages 15 and above)		Lit. rate, youth total (% of people ages 15-24)	
		Value (2010)	% Change	Value (2010)	% Change	Value (2010)	% Change	Value (2010)	% Change	Value (2010)	% Change
	SOUTHERN AFRICA										
	Upper Middle Income										
1	Botswana	7.4	1157.3	80.0	21.9	107.7	-5.7	84.1	-8.6	95.2	-5.5
2	Mauritius	24.9	276.0	89.4	9.1	99.4	2.2	87.9	-12.6	96.5	-6.8
3	Namibia	9.0	943.9	64.0	52.3	107.5	-5.5	88.5	-13.2	93.0	-3.2
4	South Africa	15.0	521.4	93.8	3.9	101.7	-0.1	88.7	-13.4	97.6	-7.8
	Lower Middle Income										
5	Angola	3.7	307.3	31.3	102.8	124.5	-10.6	70.0	9.8	73.1	23.1
6	Lesotho	3.5	329.5	46.4	36.9	103.2	7.7	89.7	-14.3	92.0	-2.1
7	Zambia	2.4	527.6	20.4	211.8	115.3	-3.5	70.9	8.4	74.6	20.7
	Low Income										
8	Mozambique	1.5	935.0	25.5	149.5	115.1	-3.3	55.1	39.5	70.9	27.0
9	Malawi	0.5	2862.7	32.1	97.7	135.5	-17.9	73.7	4.3	86.5	4.1
10	Zimbabwe	6.2	144.2	44.7	42.2	102.4	8.6	91.9	-16.4	98.9	-9.0
	EAST AFRICA										
	Upper Middle Income										
11	Seychelles	-		114.7	-14.9	116.8	-13.0	91.8	-16.3	99.1	-9.2
	Lower Middle Income										
12	Djibouti	3.4	338.3	30.2	110.3	54.5	104.0		-		-
	Low Income										
13	Burundi	3.2	365.4	24.8	156.2	156.3	-28.8	66.6	15.4	76.6	17.5
14	Comoros	7.9	90.8	46.3	37.0	104.3	6.7	74.2	3.6	85.3	5.5
15	Eritrea	2.0	658.0	31.9	98.8	44.6	149.4	66.6	15.4	88.7	1.5
16	Ethiopia	5.5	176.7	35.7	77.8	101.6	9.5	29.8	157.7	44.6	101.8
17	Kenya	4.0	275.3	60.2	5.5	113.3	-1.8	87.0	-11.7	92.7	-2.9
18	Madagascar	3.7	309.2	31.1	104.2	148.6	-25.1	64.5	19.2	64.9	38.6
19	Rwanda	4.8	213.8	32.2	97.4	142.6	-22.0	70.7	8.7	77.2	16.5
20	Somalia	2.6	487.7	7.8	715.2	32.5	242.7		-	77.4	16.2
21	Tanzania	1.5	934.8	27.4	131.7	102.3	8.7	72.9	5.4	87.4	3.0
22	Uganda	4.2	260.8	28.1	126.1	121.1	-8.2	73.2	5.0	67.7	33.0
23	Congo, Dem. Rep.	6.2	144.0	37.9	67.5	93.2	19.3	67.0	14.7	97.9	-8.1
	CENTRAL AFRICA										
	High Income										
24	Equatorial Guinea	3.3	2737.6	27.5	254.7	86.6	17.3	93.3	-17.7	97.6	-7.8
	Upper Middle Income										
25	Gabon	7.0	1227.0	53.1	83.7	132.4	-23.3	87.7	-12.4	83.1	8.3
	Lower Middle Income										
26	Cameroon	11.5	31.7	42.2	50.5	119.8	-7.1	70.7	8.7	80.5	11.8
27	Congo, Rep.	5.5	174.3	44.6	42.3	115.0	-3.3		-		-
28	Sao Tome and Principe	4.5	237.6	50.9	24.7	130.7	-14.9	88.8	-13.4	95.3	-5.6

S/N	Country Name	School enrolment, tertiary (% gross)		School enrolment, secondary (% gross)		School enrolment, primary (% gross)		Lit. rate, adult total (% of people ages 15 and above)		Lit. rate, youth total (% of people ages 15-24)	
		Value (2010)	% Change	Value (2010)	% Change	Value (2010)	% Change	Value (2010)	% Change	Value (2010)	% Change
	Low Income										
29	Central African Republic	2.6	488.0	12.6	403.5	93.4	19.1	55.2	39.1	64.7	39.2
30	Chad	2.2	596.9	25.7	147.3	90.0	23.6	33.6	128.6	46.3	94.6
	WEST AFRICA										
	Lower Middle Income										
31	Côte d'Ivoire	8.9	70.4	27.1	134.0	79.1	40.6	55.3	39.0	66.6	35.2
32	Cape Verde	17.8	-15.3	87.5	-27.4	109.6	1.5	84.8	-9.4	98.2	-8.3
33	Ghana	8.8	71.7	58.3	9.0	106.3	4.6	66.6	15.3	80.1	12.4
34	Nigeria	10.3	47.3	44.0	44.2	83.3	33.6	60.8	26.3	71.8	25.3
35	Senegal	7.9	90.8	37.4	69.7	86.8	28.1	49.7	54.6	65.0	38.4
	Low Income										
36	Benin	6.0	150.4	37.1	71.3	125.9	-11.6	41.7	84.5	54.3	65.6
37	Burkina Faso	3.3	353.7	20.7	206.5	75.6	47.1	28.7	167.5	39.3	129.2
38	Guinea	9.5	59.8	38.1	66.8	94.4	17.8	39.5	94.7	61.1	47.4
39	Gambia	4.1	267.0	54.1	17.4	82.6	34.6	46.5	65.3	65.5	37.5
40	Guinea-Bissau	2.7	455.2	36.0	76.3	123.1	-9.7	52.2	47.2	70.9	27.0
41	Liberia	16.1	-6.2	34.8	82.4	96.0	15.8	59.1	30.1	75.6	19.0
42	Mali	5.8	160.6	37.7	68.4	80.4	38.3	26.2	193.5	38.8	131.8
43	Niger	1.5	935.1	13.4	375.0	66.3	67.8	28.7	168.0	36.5	146.2
44	Sierra Leone	2.1	619.5	27.6	130.0	85.8	29.7	40.9	87.8	57.6	56.2
45	Togo	5.9	157.0	50.9	24.9	139.6	-20.4	56.9	35.1	76.5	17.7
	NORTH AFRICA										
	Upper Middle Income										
46	Algeria	30.8	203.9	94.9	2.7	110.2	-7.8	72.6	5.8	91.8	-1.9
47	Libyan Arab Jamahiriya	54.4	72.0	93.4	4.4	114.2	-11.1	88.9	-13.5	99.9	-9.9
48	Tunisia	34.4	171.8	90.5	7.8	108.8	-6.6	77.6	-0.9	96.8	-7.0
	Lower Middle Income										
49	Egypt, Arab Rep.	30.4	-50.4	84.7	-25.1	105.7	5.2	66.4	15.8	84.9	6.0
50	Morocco	13.2	14.3	56.1	13.2	111.4	-0.1	56.1	37.0	79.5	13.2
51	Mauritania	4.4	246.8	24.4	159.8	102.0	9.1	57.5	33.7	67.7	33.0
52	Sudan	6.1	148.2	39.0	62.9	72.7	53.0	70.2	9.4	85.9	4.7

Source: *Computed based on data from World Bank (2011a).*

Note: *All values are for 2010 or latest available. South Sudan became an independent State on 9 July 2011. Separate data for the country is not yet available hence it is still combined with the Sudan. %Change is the percentage difference between the actual value for each country and the relevant benchmark.*

Annex table 3.7

Imperatives of human development for Africa as a global growth pole (health)

S/N	Country Name	Life expectancy at birth, total (years)		Mortality rate, infant (per 1,000 live births)		Survival to age 65, male (% of cohort)	
		Value (2010)	% Change	Value (2010)	% Change	Value (2010)	% Change
	SOUTHERN AFRICA						
	Upper Middle Income						
1	Botswana	53.0	48.0	36.1	-87.5	41.7	93.5
2	Mauritius	72.9	7.6	13.0	-65.4	66.5	21.4
3	Namibia	61.6	27.3	29.3	-84.6	54.7	47.5
4	South Africa	51.6	52.0	40.7	-88.9	32.0	151.9
	Lower Middle Income						
5	Angola	50.3	34.9	97.9	-61.2	38.1	73.3
6	Lesotho	46.7	45.2	64.6	-41.3	25.4	159.6
7	Zambia	47.8	41.7	68.9	-44.9	33.9	94.7
	Low Income						
8	Mozambique	49.3	37.5	92.2	-58.8	36.3	81.7
9	Malawi	52.7	28.6	58.1	-34.7	44.9	47.0
10	Zimbabwe	48.5	39.9	50.9	-25.4	26.4	150.0
	EAST AFRICA						
	Upper Middle Income						
11	Seychelles	73.0	7.4	11.7	-61.5		-
	Lower Middle Income						
12	Djibouti	57.1	18.6	73.0	-48.0	48.2	36.9
	Low Income						
13	Burundi	49.4	37.1	87.8	-56.8	42.6	54.8
14	Comoros	60.2	12.5	62.8	-39.6	63.3	4.2
15	Eritrea	60.6	11.9	42.3	-10.3	47.1	40.0
16	Ethiopia	58.1	16.6	67.8	-44.0	49.6	32.9
17	Kenya	55.8	21.4	55.1	-31.1	47.5	38.8
18	Madagascar	66.2	2.4	43.1	-11.9	57.8	14.2
19	Rwanda	54.7	24.0	59.1	-35.8	41.0	60.9
20	Somalia	50.6	33.8	108.3	-65.0	42.3	55.8
21	Tanzania	56.6	19.8	50.0	-24.1	49.6	33.1
22	Uganda	53.1	27.7	63.0	-39.8	45.3	45.5
23	Congo, Dem. Rep.	47.8	41.8	111.7	-66.0	38.8	70.1
	CENTRAL AFRICA						
	High Income						
24	Equatorial Guinea	50.5	55.2	80.5	-94.4	42.9	88.0
	Upper Middle Income						
25	Gabon	61.8	26.8	54.4	-91.7	56.4	43.0
	Lower Middle Income						
26	Cameroon	50.6	34.0	84.4	-55.0	43.3	52.4
27	Congo, Rep.	56.6	19.8	60.8	-37.6	46.2	42.6
28	Sao Tome and Principe	64.1	5.7	53.1	-28.5	67.7	-2.6

S/N	Country Name	Life expectancy at birth, total (years)		Mortality rate, infant (per 1,000 live births)		Survival to age 65, male (% of cohort)	
		Value (2010)	% Change	Value (2010)	% Change	Value (2010)	% Change
	Low Income						
29	Central African Republic	46.9	44.5	106.0	-64.2	36.4	81.0
30	Chad	48.9	38.6	98.9	-61.6	42.2	56.5
	WEST AFRICA						
	Lower Middle Income						
31	Côte d'Ivoire	54.1	25.4	85.9	-55.8	54.1	21.9
32	Cape Verde	73.6	-7.9	29.2	30.0	72.1	-8.6
33	Ghana	63.4	6.9	50.0	-24.1	51.9	27.0
34	Nigeria	50.9	33.0	88.4	-57.1	39.9	65.2
35	Senegal	58.6	15.6	49.8	-23.8	48.2	36.8
	Low Income						
36	Benin	55.2	22.8	73.2	-48.2	62.6	5.3
37	Burkina Faso	54.5	24.4	92.6	-59.0	46.0	43.5
38	Guinea	53.2	27.5	81.2	-53.3	55.9	18.0
39	Gambia	57.8	17.2	56.9	-33.3	48.5	36.0
40	Guinea-Bissau	47.3	43.2	92.0	-58.8	39.4	67.4
41	Liberia	55.5	22.2	73.6	-48.4	56.9	15.9
42	Mali	50.5	34.1	99.2	-61.7	39.5	67.1
43	Niger	53.8	25.9	72.5	-47.7	44.7	47.5
44	Sierra Leone	47.0	44.3	113.7	-66.6	30.2	118.5
45	Togo	56.2	20.6	66.0	-42.5	61.9	6.6
	NORTH AFRICA						
	Upper Middle Income						
46	Algeria	72.6	8.0	30.5	-85.2	78.6	2.7
47	Libya	74.5	5.2	13.4	-66.4	75.7	6.6
48	Tunisia	74.5	5.3	13.8	-67.4	78.6	2.6
	Lower Middle Income						
49	Egypt	72.7	-6.8	18.6	104.0	72.4	-8.9
50	Morocco	71.6	-5.3	30.4	24.8	74.6	-11.6
51	Mauritania	57.9	17.0	75.3	-49.6	50.5	30.6
52	Sudan	60.8	11.5	66.4	-42.8	53.9	22.4

Source: Computed based on data from World Bank (2011a).

Note: All values are for 2010 or latest available. South Sudan became an independent State on 9 July 2011. Separate data for the country is not yet available hence it is still combined with the Sudan. %Change is the percentage difference between the actual value for each country and the relevant benchmark.

Annex figure 3.1

Imperatives of primary enrolment for Africa as a global growth pole

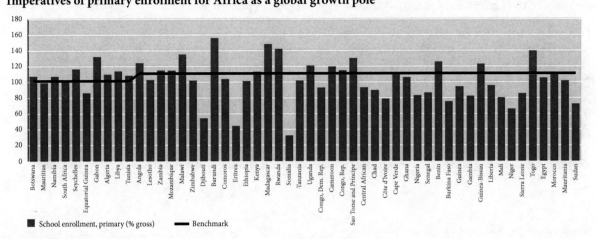

Source: *World Bank (2011a).*

Annex figure 3.2

Imperatives of secondary enrolment for Africa as a global growth pole

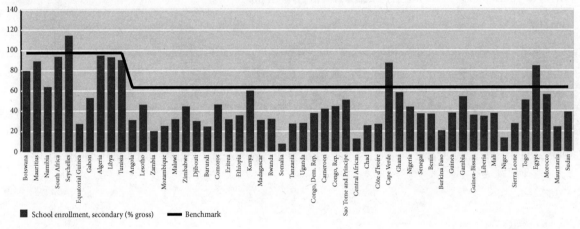

Source: *World Bank (2011a).*

Annex figure 3.3

Imperatives of tertiary enrolment for Africa as a global growth pole

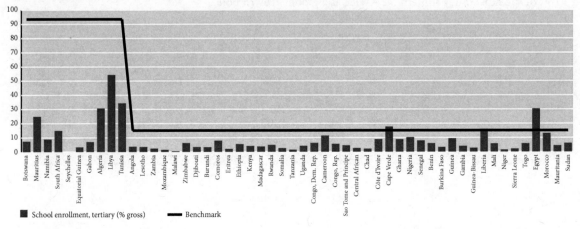

Source: *World Bank (2011a).*

Annex figure 3.4

Imperatives of the adult literacy rate for Africa as a global growth pole

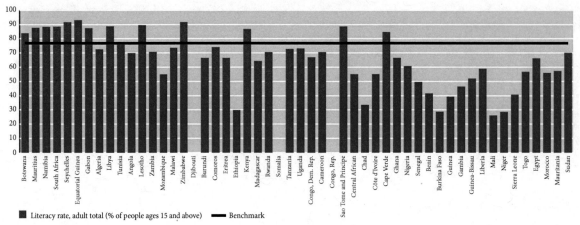

■ Literacy rate, adult total (% of people ages 15 and above) ▬ Benchmark

Source: World Bank (2011a).

Annex figure 3.5

Imperatives of youth literacy rate for Africa as a global growth pole

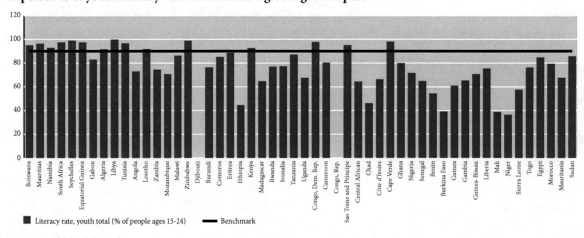

■ Literacy rate, youth total (% of people ages 15-24) ▬ Benchmark

Source: World Bank (2011a).

Annex figure 3.6

Imperatives of life expectancy at birth for Africa as a global growth pole

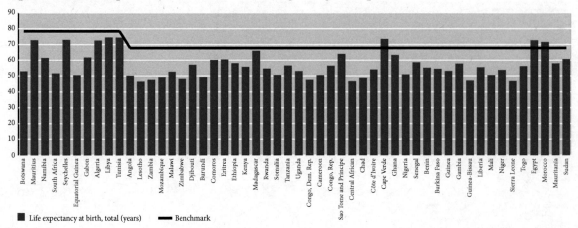

■ Life expectancy at birth, total (years) ▬ Benchmark

Source: World Bank (2011a).

Annex figure 3.7

Imperatives of infant mortality rate for Africa as a global growth pole

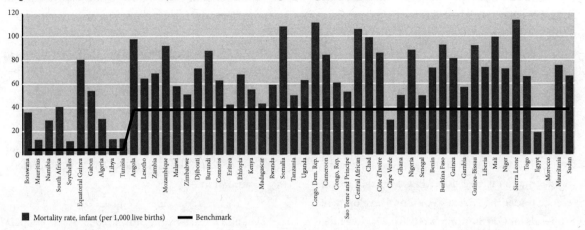

■ Mortality rate, infant (per 1,000 live births) ▬ Benchmark

Source: World Bank (2011a).

Annex figure 3.8

Imperatives of survival to age 65 for Africa as a global growth pole

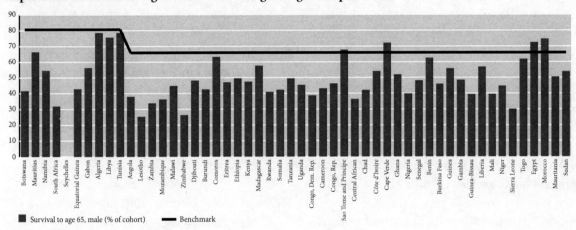

■ Survival to age 65, male (% of cohort) ▬ Benchmark

Source: World Bank (2011a).

References

Adam-Kane, J., and J. Jerome Lim. 2011. "Growth poles and multipolarity." Policy Research Working Paper 5712. World Bank, Washington, DC.

AfDB (African Development Bank), Committee of Ten, UNECA (United Nations Economic Commission for Africa), AUC (African Union Commission) and (Korea Institute for International Economic Policy). 2010. Achieving Strong Sustained and Shared Growth in Africa in the Post Crisis Global Economy (A presentation at the 2010 KAFEC Ministerial Conference under the Africa's Voice on Development: Proposals for G20 Summit, Seoul, Korea, November

Ajakaiye, O. 2007. "Recent economic development experiences of China, India, Malaysia and South Korea: some lessons from capacity building in Africa." Commissioned Paper for the 2nd Pan African Capacity Building Forum, Maputo, Mozambique, August 1–3.

Ajakaiye O., R.E.B. Lucas, and J.T. Karugia. 2006. "Africa's resurgence and international migration: an overview." *Journal of African Economies* 15 (S2): 1–20.

Bevan, D.C., A.J. Okidi, and F. Muhumuza. 2003. "Poverty Eradication Action Plan Revision 2002/3." Discussion Paper on Economic growth, Investment, and Export Promotion. Kampala: Ministry of Finance, Planning and Economic Development.

Chenery, H. 1986. "Growth and transformations." In *Industrialization and growth: a comparative study*, ed. H. Chenery, S. Robinson, and M. Syrquin. New York: Oxford University Press.

Cilliers, J., B. Hughes, and J. Moyer. 2011. "African futures, 2050: the next forty years." Institute for Security Studies Paper 175, Pretoria.

Finger M. P. 2012. "Evolving Wave of Competition in the International Market: Challenges for Africa through the Rise of China and India." In *Trade Infrastructure and Economic Development*, ed Ajakaiye Olu and T.A. Oyejide. London and New York: Routledge.

Juma, C. 2006. "Reinventing growth." In *Going for growth: science, technology and innovation in Africa*. London: London Smith Institute.

Kaplinsky, R., S. Robinson, and D. Willenbockel. 2007. *Asian drivers and sub-Saharan Africa: the challenge of development strategy*. New York: Rockefeller Foundation.

Kar, D., and D. Cartwright-Smith. 2008. *Illicit financial flows from developing countries, 2002–2006 executive report*. Washington, DC: Global Financial Integrity.

Kuznets, S. 1955. "Economic growth and income inequality." *American Economic Review* 45 (1): 1–28.

Leke, A., S. Lund, C. Roxburgh, and A. van Wamelen. 2011. *What's driving Africa's growth*. Washington, DC: McKinsey Global Institute.

Lewis, W.A. 1954. "Economic development with unlimited supplies of labour." *The Manchester School* 22 (2): 139–191.

McKinsey Global Institute. 2010. *Lions on the move: the progress and potential of African economies*. Washington, DC: McKinsey.

Moyo, M., R. Simson, A. Jacob, and F.-X. de Mevius. 2011. "Attaining middle income status: Tanzania." Working Paper 11/1019. International Growth Centre, London.

Ndikumana, L., and J.K. Boyce. 2008. "Is Africa a net creditor? new estimates of capital flight from severely indebted sub-Saharan African countries, 1970–1996." Political Economy Research Institute Working Paper. University of Massachusetts, Amherst, MA.

Ndulu, B.J., L. Chakraborti, L. Lijane, V. Ramachandran, and J. Wolgin. 2007. *Challenges of African growth: opportunities, constraints and strategic directions.* Washington, DC: World Bank.

Page, J. 2011. "Can Africa industrialise?" *Journal of African Economies* 21 (Supplement 20):ii86–ii124.

Ratha D, A Shimeles, W. Shaw, C. Ozden and S. Mohapatra. 2011. Leveraging Migration for Africa; Remittances, Skills and Investment, World Bank, Washington D.C.

Soludo, C., O. Ogbu, and H.-J. Chang. 2004. *The politics of trade and industrial policy in Africa.* Trenton, NJ: Africa World Press.

Stein, H. 1992. "De-industrialization, adjustment, the World Bank and the IMF in Africa." *World Development* 20 (1): 83–95.

Thandika, M., and C. Soludo. 1999. Our continent our future: African perspectives on structural adjustment. Dakar: CODESRIA.

UNCTAD and UNIDO (United Nations Conference on Trade and Development and United Nations Industrial Development Organization). 2011. *Economic Development in Africa Report 2011: Fostering Industrial Development in Africa in the New Global Environment,* United Nations: New York & Geneva.

UN-DESA (United Nations Department of Economic and Social Affairs). 2012. World Economic

Situation and Prospects. UN-DESA. New York.

UNECA. 1990. African Alternative Framework to Structural Adjustment Programmes for

Socio-economic recovery and Transformation (AAF-SAP). UNECA. Addis Ababa

_____. and AUC. 2011. *Economic report on Africa 2011: governing development in Africa—*

the role of the state in economic transformation. Addis Ababa.

World Bank. 2011a. *World Development Indicators 2011.* Washington, DC: World Bank.

_____. 2011b. *Global Development Horizons 2011—multipolarity: the new global economy.* Washington, DC: World Bank.

Notes

1   ISI in Africa generally involved the following elements: restriction of imports to intermediate inputs and capital goods required by domestic industries; extensive use of tariff and non-tariff barriers to trade; currency overvaluation to facilitate the import of goods needed by domestic industries; subsidized interest rates to make domestic investment attractive; direct government ownership or participation in industry; and provision of direct loans to firms as well as access to foreign exchange for imported inputs (Mkandawire and Soludo, 1999; UNCTAD and UNIDO, 2011).

2   In particular, the focus of ISI was more on setting up factories than building the entrepreneurial capabilities that would foster industrial dynamism and the development of competitive export sectors. In addition, the domestic economic policies adopted during the period implicitly taxed agriculture and exports, so reducing foreign exchange earnings.

3   This negates the initial premise of the ISI strategy to reduce foreign dependency through local production of industrialized products. The gap between import and export shares in GDP, which was gradually closing between 1960–1965 and 1966–1970, started widening, with imports rising steadily but exports rising more slowly.

4   The policy conditions included deregulating interest rates, liberalizing trade, privatizing SOEs (parastatals), withdrawing government subsidies and devaluing the currency. One of the key objectives of SAPs was to reduce the role of the state in the development process and give market forces more room in allocating resources. The assumption was that markets are more efficient than the state in this and that the appropriate role of the state should be to provide an enabling environment for the private sector to flourish in.

5   The most detailed analysis of the major flaws of SAPs was contained in the UNECA (1990) African Alternative Framework to Structural Adjustment Programmes (AAF-SAP).

6   Discussed in detail in chapter 4, these include reducing transaction costs for private enterprises, supporting innovation and improving skills and institutional capacity (Ndulu et al., 2007).

7   Also analysed in chapter 4, responses include increasing agricultural productivity to support industrialization.

8   Including integrating its small, national markets to create a larger, pan-African market—chapter 4.

9   Under the title "Africa's Voice on Development: Proposals for G-20 Summit"

10   See, for instance, World Bank (2011), McKinsey Global Institute (2010) and Institute for Security Studies (2011).

11   In his address to the AU Executive Council in Malabo, Equatorial Guinea, June 2011.

12   The others are Brazil, Indonesia and Russia. The six are referred to as the BRIICKs (World Bank, 2011). The benchmarking approach to specifying the imperatives is similar to the idea first proposed and applied to Uganda by Bevan et al. (2003) and subsequently applied to Tanzania by Moyo et al. (2011) and recently applied by Page (2011) in a multi-country context.

13   Computation of the growth polarity index proposed by Adam-Kane and Lim (2011) is $P_t = \dfrac{y_{i,t-1}}{Y} \cdot \dfrac{\Delta y_i}{v_{i,t-1}} \equiv s_{i,t-1}^y \cdot g_{i,t-1}^y$ where y_{it} is the GDP of country i at time t, $Y_t = \sum_j^N y_j$ is global GDP which simply aggregates GDP for all $N \in C$ countries, and $\Delta y_i = y_i - y_{i,t-1}$ is the change in GDP of economy i,. s_t^y and g_t^y are the output share and growth rate of country i at time t, which means that a growth pole is simply the size-adjusted growth rate of the economy.

14   This is consistent with the proposition that in order to sustain their growth momentum and serve as global growth poles, emerging economies should undertake structural changes that will generate self-sustaining, internally driven growth through a combination of sustained productivity advances and robust domestic demand (World Bank, 2011).

15   This requires all components of GDP to grow but the growth rate of the other sectors will be higher than that of agriculture such that their shares in total GDP will be higher than that of agriculture over time.

16   This is without prejudice to Africa maintaining its comparative advantage in producing these commodities. Indeed, as industrialization proceeds, its demand for these commodities will be so large that imports may be necessary to complement domestic production

17   The SOEs in resource-rich African countries are not really involved in exploring, extracting and exporting minerals, unlike those in Brazil, Malaysia and Jamaica, where indigenous enterprises are some of the industry's global players.

18   The discussion in this section is inspired by the scoping studies, in-depth country case studies and policy briefs that emanated from the AERC Collaborative Research on China–Africa Economic Relations led by Ajakaiye, Kaplinsky, Mlambo, Mwega, Morris and Oyejide between 2006 and 2010, as well as by the various presentations on this project at seminars and workshops by project leaders and case study authors.

19   Ndikumana and Boyce (2008), for example, estimate that illicit capital flight from sub-Saharan Africa in 1970–2004 was nearly 82 per cent of 2004's GDP; Ndikumana and Boyce (2008) and Kar and Cartwright-Smith (2008) identified that the top 14 countries in illicit capital flight are resource-rich countries to some degree. Examples include the leasing of large parcels of land by investors from the Middle East, in particular for producing agricultural commodities that are exported in their crude forms to processors back home. This business practice essentially makes such FDI an enclave, like those in extractive industries.

Unleashing Africa's Development Capacity

AFRICAN ECONOMIES HAVE grown impressively over the past decade, but the sources of growth have been mainly agriculture and natural resources (see chapters 2 and 3). Taking advantage of global conditions, Africa must now unleash its potential and grow even faster. To do this, it must diversify its economic foundations, industrialize further, address key development challenges in governance and institutions, human capital, technology, infrastructure and agriculture, and promote regional integration and new development partnerships.

Underlying many of Africa's socio-economic issues is bad governance, and without a stable, predictable and rule-based political order, Africa's productive potential cannot be unlocked. Its development potential cannot be set free unless the intellectual capital of the continent is maintained and developed. In a knowledge-based world, investment in science and innovation is the foundation of a competitive and resilient national economy. African economies are among the least competitive in the world because of the huge underinvestment in critical infrastructure, such as roads, electricity, water and ports. Without modern infrastructure, Africa's development potential cannot be harnessed to its fullest.

The continent's marginal position in the global economy is not "destiny" or "fate". It can be reversed with the right type of political leadership committed to mobilizing all sectors of society in support of a common national development vision. The institutional framework required for this task demands a capable and pragmatic bureaucracy, which can develop clear development objectives and targets as well as a common understanding among all stakeholders, through formal and informal ties with the private sector and civil society.

In turn, building national consensus that supports a common development vision requires a social contract in which the State, private sector and civil society are mutually accountable for realizing the development vision. As one aspect of good governance, the social contract must be cemented in societal structures through well-targeted policy interventions to ensure the legitimacy of the overall growth process.

Taking advantage of global conditions, Africa must now unleash its potential and grow even faster.

4.1 Promoting good governance

MANY OF THE socio-economic challenges confronting Africa are associated with bad governance and lack of a broad-based and inclusive national development vision (UNECA, 2009). Unresolved issues of political leadership, legitimacy and widespread "elite capture" are preventing Africa from developing. Since the 1990s, with the spontaneous growth of people's democratic movements across the continent, African leaders have also acknowledged the results of poor governance. The New Partnership for Africa's Development (NEPAD, 2002) identified the entrenchment of good governance principles and practices as preconditions for Africa's development. More significantly, the APRM provides a framework through

which African leaders can hold each other accountable for their commitment to uphold norms of good political, economic and corporate governance in their countries.

There is growing consensus on the key elements of governance reforms in Africa (UNECA, 2005 and 2009). These include: strengthening the institutions of the State in order to foster predictability and accountability, and promoting a free and fair electoral process; fighting corruption; enhancing the capacity of public service delivery systems; and instituting programmes of social protection for those who are too poor or too sick to work. This section reviews some of these elements in a political then economic light.

Encouraging good political governance

Even with the progress in promoting democracy in Africa since the early 1990s, the picture is rather mixed, one of progress and reversals, what Karl Polanyi called "the double movement" (Polanyi, 1957). The fact that undemocratic rulers extend their hold on power through the ballot box with increasing regularity serves as a sobering reminder of how tentative and fragile the experiment with

liberal democracy has been. When the basic conditions for democracy (table 4.1) are either non-existent or are too weak, the excesses of the executive branch of government cannot be checked. Yet, despite recent democratic reversals and the resurgence of a seemingly "predatory" so-called democratic State, the thirst of Africans for democracy remains strong (Lynch and Crawford, 2011).

Table 4.1

Top 10 performers on measures in the Ibrahim Index, 2011

Rule of Law	Score	Accountability	Score	Personal Safety	Score	Participation	Score	Rights	Score
Continental Average	48	Continental Average	43	Continental Average	44	Continental Average	42	Continental Average	43
Botswana	97	Botswana	86	Mauritius	80	Cape Verde	83	Cape Verde	86
Mauritius	94	Mauritius	82	Cape Verde	77	Mauritius	80	Mauritius	81
Cape Verde	88	Cape Verde	82	Seychelles	70	Liberia	78	Ghana	75
South Africa	85	Namibia	76	Sao Tome & Principe	69	Benin	78	Namibia	69
Ghana	85	South Africa	72	Botswana	65	South Africa	75	Benin	68
Namibia	81	Seychelles	68	Comoros	65	Seychelles	75	South Africa	67
Seychelles	74	Lesotho	65	Namibia	63	Botswana	75	Mali	67
Lesotho	66	Ghana	61	Djibouti	61	Sao Tome & Principe	73	Sao Tome & Principe	65
Uganda	65	Rwanda	59	Benin	59	Ghana	72	Lesotho	62
Malawi	64	Swaziland	59	Burkina Faso	59	Comoros	68	Zambia	61

Source: Mo Ibrahim Foundation (2011)

Moreover, the democratization experience in Africa has focused more on abstract rights and less on achieving concrete economic rights. Rapid economic growth has not translated into improved welfare for the majority of Africans, and the trend is towards wealth concentrating in the hands of small elites.

For democracy to succeed, there must be significant social reform and a reduction in socio-economic inequalities. Political freedom and participation cannot be divorced from other kinds of freedom. There is an organic link between political freedom and freedom from hunger, ignorance and disease (Sen, 1999). In the absence of real changes in people's lives, zero-sum mentalities will prevail instead of moderation, thus undermining the chances for democratic consolidation and deepening.

Africa governments must therefore tread carefully to ensure that efforts to reform the economy along free-market lines do not undermine the equally important responsibility of a government to protect and promote the economic and social rights of its citizens. To overcome its democratic deficit, government must address important issues critical for restoring the faith of citizens in the integrity of public institutions, and ensure that the rules governing social and economic interactions are predictable and stable.

Strengthening the institutions of accountability

The task of strengthening democratic governance must, at the very least, include the following enabling mechanisms: the rule of law and constitutional legitimacy; a system of representation, with well-functioning political parties and interest associations; freedom of expression and association; an electoral system that guarantees regular free and fair elections; and a system of checks and balances based on the separation of government powers. Ensuring compliance requires strong institutions of accountability.

Strengthening these institutions, such as the office of the auditor-general, internal revenue service, anti-corruption bureau, electoral commission and relevant parliamentary budget committees, will greatly assist in improving transparency and accountability in government performance. Such strengthening will require enhanced investment in data gathering and analysis, as well as cost-effective computerization and information sharing among government

> *Despite recent reversals, Africans' thirst for democracy remains strong.*

agencies. Doing more with less is not just a matter of efficiency gain. It is also about instilling a culture of responsibility, accountability and service orientation in government institutions.

Strengthening the capacity of non-State actors

Democratic participation becomes meaningful only when individual citizens, through their respective popular organizations, take an active part in shaping public policy, and hold their governments and elected representatives accountable. Meaningful participation also requires grassroots civic education to create more active, self-confident and politically aware citizens. However, many civil society organizations and social movements in Africa suffer from a poverty of ideas, poor leadership and lack of basic resources, hindering them from becoming an effective force in protecting and promoting the democratic system of government, locally and nationally. This institutional weakness makes it hard for civil society to regularly check excesses of State power.

The challenge for African governments in the coming years is how to build strong, vibrant and autonomous organs of civil society across the political spectrum through which citizens can influence public policy, and assert and fight for their social and economic rights. Only by expanding visions and raising consciousness can people participate effectively in the political process and hold public officials accountable. A weak civil society and a

> *For democracy to succeed there must be significant social reform and a reduction in socio-economic inequalities.*

weak state are not good for the practice of democracy. Both have to be strengthened and sustained.

Constructing an inclusive and viable social contract

The crucial challenge for African governments is how to expedite democratization while revitalizing the economy. This dual task demands an effective and competent State capable of mobilizing the population in support of a common national vision to bring about the material emancipation of the poor majority. Economic growth has little meaning unless it is accompanied by complementary policies to reduce inequality, to ensure access of the poor to education and basic social services and to strengthen infrastructure. Growth should lift the ability of the poor to engage in productive employment and some African countries are achieving this, as shown in table 4.2. Since investment in the social sector has a direct impact on the productive efficiency of the economy, social policy should become an integral part of democratization and development (see chapter 2 for a more detailed discussion on social development issues).

Table 4.2

Africa's top 10 performers on human development indicators in the Ibrahim Index, 2011

Human Development	Score	Welfare	Score	Education	Score	Health	Score
Continental Average	56	Continental Average	52	Continental Average	51	Continental Average	66
Tunisia	88	Mauritius	89	Seychelles	96	Seychelles	99
Mauritius	87	Tunisia	83	Tunisia	87	Libya	98
Seychelles	86	Cape Verde	81	Mauritius	84	Cape Verde	95
Cape Verde	83	South Africa	80	Libya	83	Tunisia	95
Libya	82	Botswana	77	South Africa	82	Botswana	91
Botswana	82	Ghana	69	Algeria	81	Namibia	88
Algeria	77	Algeria	68	Egypt	79	Mauritius	87
South Africa	77	Djibouti	68	Botswana	78	Sao Tome & Principe	87
Egypt	76	Egypt	68	Cape Verde	74	Morocco	84
Namibia	72	Rwanda	66	Ghana	66	Swaziland	84

Source: Mo Ibrahim Foundation (2011)

For democracy to survive, let alone flourish, it should embody social and economic characteristics that are relevant to the aspirations of the majority and that protect the rights of minorities. This implies a completely different kind of politics in which the social contract between the State, private sector and civil society is renegotiated along equitable, inclusive and emancipatory lines (Ake, 1996). Formalized social contracts are an essential ingredient of a political society. One cannot understand or even begin to theorize governance and accountability without a sense of the nature of the social contract in any given political system (Adesina, 2007). Without the social contract, citizens cannot seek to exert accountability as members of that political community.

> *Social policy should become an integral part of democracy and development.*

African States should therefore strive to build a form of democracy that emphasizes concrete political, social and economic rights as opposed to abstract political rights. There must, as said earlier, be an organic link between political freedom and freedom from hunger, ignorance and disease. The main bases for a more inclusive growth process are access to productive assets, such as land, and expansion of productive employment. Important policies for achieving this goal include agrarian reform and rural development policies, greater access to high-quality education and health services, and stronger critical infrastructure, thus enabling citizens to have equal opportunities for upward mobility.

Expanding national policy space

Part of the challenge for restoring and renewing democracy in Africa is that African policy institutions and the process of policymaking have been captured to a point where rulers exercise power, but the determinants of policy appear to be external to the continent. This process took the form of structural adjustment in the 1980s and has since been extended to core areas of social and economic policy, such as the PRSPs and the MDGs—and even democratization (UNCTAD, 2007).

Many of these donor-driven initiatives have added to erosion of domestic policy space through debt structures, unfair trade practices and endless loan conditions that characterize donor–recipient relationships (Utting, 2006). How to rebuild policy space and reconfigure the politics surrounding policymaking and how to exercise institutional innovations for pursuing autonomous national development are critical issues that African countries must address pragmatically. An effective State with considerable policy space is a prerequisite for consolidating democracy and a well-functioning market (UNECA and AUC, 2011).

Improving economic governance

Alongside the politics runs the economics. Countries with strong institutions and an independent and effective bureaucracy generally have solid economic growth by securing property rights, checking corruption, promoting and protecting individual rights and freedoms, and restraining the government's discretionary power (Evans, 1995; UNCTAD, 2009a). Conversely, the absence of transparent and predictable institutional frameworks allows discretionary interpretations that could give rise to rent seeking and corrupt practices. In countries where strong and effective government institutions are missing, public confidence in the integrity of the policy and regulatory frameworks is diminished and the operation of the market is distorted (Miller and Holms, 2011).

Since promoting democracy is a political process, it cannot exclude the central issue of State power. Although the State in Africa has frequently been the object of popular resistance, it is unrealistic to assume that any society can be put on a democratic footing without an effective and functioning State system (Mkandawire, 2001).

Effective governance of economic development therefore requires a capable State that does two things: maintain macroeconomic stability as the foundation for successful productive development policy; and implement structural and social policies to unleash productive capacity for immediate poverty reduction and for building foundations for long-term growth. Indeed, part of the democratic movement in Africa is precisely how to build such a State, that responds to the concerns of the majority of the population and empowers all to strive to realize their full potential (Edigheji, 2010; Mkandawire, 2001).

Certainly, the policy and institutional environment for doing business in Africa has improved considerably over the past decade. In 2012, for example, 36 out of 46 economies in sub-Saharan Africa improved their business regulations. However, much more remains to be done. The following section outlines some of the elements required to build the foundations for broad-based, sustainable structural economic transformation.

> *It is wrong to assume that any society can be put on a democratic footing without an effective and functioning State system.*

A comprehensive development planning framework and industrialization

African countries need comprehensive development frameworks underpinned by effective development plans and policies, including industrial and other sectoral policies (UNECA and AUC, 2011a). The experience of emerging economies presents three important lessons. The first is that there are discernible common characteristics in the patterns of structural change and economic development processes in general, and industrialization and diversification in particular. The second is that countries that have achieved high growth in recent history are not the ones that implemented the prescriptions of the Washington Consensus such as deregulation, privatization, maintaining a balanced budget, and reducing the role of the State in the economy. This is illustrated by Republic of Korea, Taiwan (Province of China) and China, whose growth policies exhibit significant departures from that approach.

The third and overarching lesson is that the State plays a central role in guiding and promoting successful structural transformation. Indeed, the historical evidence shows that all countries that have successfully transformed from agrarian economies to modern advanced economies had governments that played a proactive role in assisting individual firms in the shift.

For the development frameworks adopted by African countries to be effective, States must tackle the weaknesses outlined in box 4.1. In addition to rebuilding and strengthening State capacity, a development framework should focus on promoting high, sustainable and shared economic growth through diversification and transformation. The framework must steer economic and social policies to work in a complementary manner.

Box 4.1: Weaknesses in Africa's structural transformation

Structural transformation involves continuous technological innovation, industrial upgrading and diversification, and improvements in the various types of infrastructure and institutional arrangements that constitute the context for business development and wealth creation.

However, Africa's experience with a range of development approaches (see chapter 3) has not led to genuine transformation, suggesting the need to rethink the role of the State, both in the continent's economic transformation and in country-level planning and policy frameworks. It is essential that African States assume their developmental responsibilities and guide sustainable social and economic development.[1]

Economic transformation in Africa has remained weak for several interacting reasons. First, development strategies have been ineffective in reallocating factors of production from less to more productive sectors as a means of diversifying the economies from primary commodities to industry and services with high value added. This has prevented many countries from fostering the kind of growth that creates decent jobs and reduces poverty. Second, natural-resource abundance is often associated with distorted incentives to diversify; a problem compounded by the continent's challenging environment and geography. Together, these issues lower labour productivity, access to large markets, economies of scale and production efficiency, and raise production costs.

Third, Africa lags behind the rest of the world in the quality of its economic and political institutions as well as its business environment. This weakness in quality feeds through to ineffective resource allocation and lack of incentive systems for innovative long-term investment and private sector development. It also partly accounts for the continent's inadequate provision of public goods and social expenditure. Many African countries suffer from large deficits in the State's ability to enhance the human capacity of its citizens. Therefore, the degree of public participation and ownership of development programmes is often low.

Note: 1. See UNECA and AUC (2011) for a detailed discussion of the role of the State in economic transformation in Africa.

The impact of these economic policies will create winners and losers among various economic agents, both as producers and consumers. Indeed, all segments of society may be called on to make short-term socio-economic sacrifices for long-term benefits. Hence, the framework must contain incentives and sanctions, so that economic agents who meet targets are rewarded and those who fail are penalized. This system accords the State a large role in designing and implementing appropriate conflict-management arrangements.

Since free-market forces will not drive economic transformation on their own—issues of market failure abound in this area—the State must play a central role in allocating resources and in efficiently coordinating crucial economic activities. This is particularly relevant to infrastructure, agriculture and industry.

Industrial production creates job opportunities at high skill levels, and facilitates dense linkages among service and agricultural sectors, rural and urban economies, and consumer, intermediate and capital-goods industries. In addition, the prices of manufactured exports are less volatile and less susceptible to long-term deterioration than those of primary goods, making industrialization particularly strategic in highly commodity-dependent developing countries. The move to industry is therefore a critical tool in creating jobs, reducing poverty and developing outlying regions. Finally, it can spur technological advances and innovation as well as productivity gains. In short, it can play the leading development role more suitably than any other sector.

> *Poor delivery of services by State-owned utility companies is a major obstacle to entrepreneurship.*

Virtually all today's successful nations supported and protected their industries through specific policies and institutions. They also relied on government policies to promote growth by accelerating structural transformation. China is an example, as its phenomenal manufacturing power rests in large part on public assistance to new industries (Lin et al. 2003). The Chilean Government has also played a crucial role in developing every significant new export (Pietrobelli and Rabellotti, 2006). The United States also owes much of its innovative industrial power to government support (Lazonick, 2011).

Africa, with its rich endowment of natural and mineral resources, is the least industrialized continent. Post-independence industrial strategies were abruptly discontinued in most countries when SAPs were promulgated (see chapter 3). The slow pace of industrialization of the continent may be attributed to numerous factors, among them inappropriate industrial investment policies, and constraints associated with infrastructure, market size and technology. Still, despite the early challenges faced, African governments continue to rate industrialization among their highest policy priorities, as evidenced by Africa-wide initiatives (box 4.2).

Box 4.2: Industrializing Africa

The Lagos Plan of Action of 1980 considered industrialization as the means of attaining self-reliance and self-sustained development. This was strongly reflected in proposals for Industrial Development Decades for Africa. However, despite isolated successes, the effects of these proposals were deemed disappointing by most African countries, as they were hampered by an absence of mechanisms for implementation, coordination and monitoring.

Subsequently, the African Productive Capacity Initiative was adopted by AU and NEPAD in 2004 as the overarching framework for sustainable industrial development in Africa. Further, during the AU Summit in 2008, the Heads of State and Government adopted the Plan of Action for the Accelerated Industrial Development of Africa.

The issue of national industrial policies has been making its way back onto the 'radar screens' of many African governments, with the adoption of new industrial policies in recent years. Some of these policies combine both active industrial instruments and broader macroeconomic measures. In addressing Africa's industrial development challenges in the twenty-first century, consensus is being built on the need to create competitive industries (Africa Union, 2007b). From a technical perspective, it is implicitly recognized that competitiveness can be drawn not only from existing (static) comparative advantages, such as Africa's immense natural resources base, but also from created (dynamic) comparative advantages.

Improving public service delivery and reducing costs

The cumulative effects of unreliable power supply, bad roads and poor communications on competitiveness, overall economic growth and job creation are immense. In many African countries, poor and ineffective delivery of services by State-owned utility companies is a major obstacle to entrepreneurship and the right of citizens to enjoy healthy living. Access to reliable electricity and clean water are two of the most pressing challenges that consumers and private operators face on a daily basis (figure 4.1). Frequent power outages impose a substantial loss on sales and working hours. In Nigeria, for example, almost 40 per cent of electricity is privately provided by generators, and businesses report that outages occur almost every day of the year. The country's main electricity company, the State-owned Nigerian Electric Power Authority, is riddled with inefficiency yet is allowed to continue running at a loss.

Figure 4.1

Power outages and lost sales

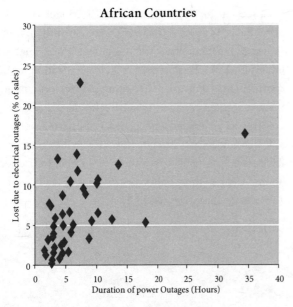
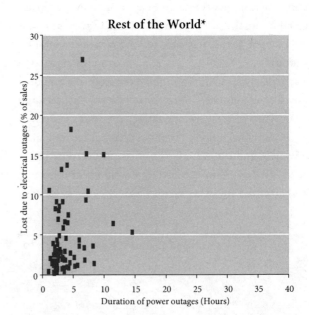

Source: World Bank Enterprise Surveys 2005-2011.

*Notes: the information per country corresponds to the last available year within the period 2005-2011; * African countries not included.*

Nigeria is not alone. The problem of poor service delivery is widespread across the continent. What has been missing in many African countries is decisive political leadership to dismantle inefficient utility companies. The need is often acknowledged, but rarely acted on.

Nevertheless, the situation today is far from hopeless. It also varies widely, as a glance at the indicators shows (figure 4.1). Improving service delivery by State utility companies requires deliberate State action to force them to operate on market principles, and to hold their managers and regulatory agencies accountable. Greater efficiency can be brought into these company operations—provision of electricity and water in particular—by fostering competition through deregulation and privatization, public–private partnerships (PPPs) and various forms of joint ventures, management contracts and other market-driven approaches. Whatever approach is chosen must be based on empirical evidence rather than political bias, and the power of regulators should be strengthened to ensure that utility companies do not cut corners to save money.

Figure 4.2
Costs of doing business

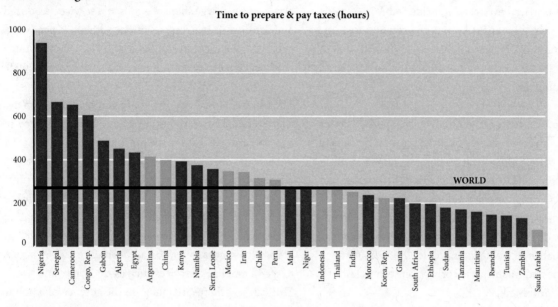

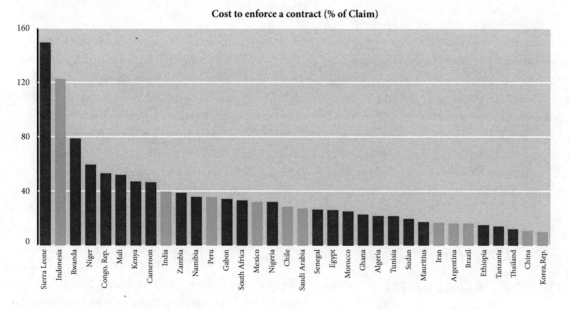

Source: *World Bank Doing Business and Enterprise Surveys 2005-2011.*

Note: *the information per country corresponds to the last available year within the period 2005-2011.*

Creating an enabling business environment

African private sector operators face greater regulatory and administrative burdens, and less protection of property and investor rights, than businesses in any other region (World Bank, 2011b; Okey, 2011). Nevertheless, the situation is ameliorating. Both Doing Business

> *The war against corruption should be stepped up.*

2012 (World Bank, 2011b) and the Africa Competitiveness Report 2011-2012 (WEF, 2011) point out that several African countries have recently made impressive gains in economic governance. Among the top 30 most improved economies between 2001 and 2008, a third is in sub-Saharan Africa. In the top 10 are five sub-Saharan African countries.

These improvements are generally attributed to better regulations and ease of doing business, improved access to credit and better enforcement of contracts. However, much remains to be done to upgrade conditions to international standards. Corruption remains too common, with 27 of 47 African countries classified as having "rampant corruption". In another 17 countries, corruption is regarded as a "serious challenge" by business people. Only in Botswana, Cape Verde and Mauritius is corruption seen as less of a burden (World Bank, 2011b).

In order to unleash the productive potential of Africa's private sector, decisive government actions are needed to cut unnecessary and costly red tape in such areas as accessing electricity or telephone connections, securing building permits and land titles, or an operator's licence to start a business. The war against corruption should be stepped up—and will last a long time. Waging war requires persistence, a balanced approach that combines incentives as well as regulation, and an effective State with the capacity to implement and monitor outcomes

> *Bridging the informal-formal divide should be central to creating a conducive business environment in Africa.*

and ensure that the benefits far outweigh the costs. In addition, the fight must be broad-based and targeted at all sectors of society—not just political rivals or opponents.

Then there is the issue of informality. The nature and characteristics of the private sector in Africa, with high and dominant informality, demand a particular approach to getting the most out of it. Informality is pervasive, and accounts for a large share of goods and services produced and consumed. It is responsible for perhaps 78 per cent of urban employment in sub-Saharan Africa, and as much as 93 per cent of new jobs (Xaba, Horn and Motola, 2002).

The International Labour Organization (ILO) estimates that 80 per cent of the non-agricultural workforce in sub-Saharan Africa is in the informal economy, as are 92 per cent of non-agricultural job opportunities for women (ILO, 2009). As a share of gross national income, informality ranges from under 30 per cent in South Africa to nearly 60 per cent in Nigeria, Tanzania and Zimbabwe (Verick, 2006). Yet, informal operators face many challenges, from harassment by authorities to lack of access to credit and basic services such as electricity and water. This can largely be attributed to the absence of a policy framework.

Bridging the informal–formal divide should be central in plans to create a conducive and inclusive African business environment, one that supports various categories of informal operators, especially youth and women, helping them to move up the technological and entrepreneurship ladder through programmes of education and training, skills and technological transfer, and subcontracting possibilities with formal firms and with government procurement (ILO, 2009; Hallward-Driemeier, 2011). In this way, informal enterprises could grow to become more productive formal enterprises, generating jobs and growth, and usefully boosting tax receipts.

Creating an enabling environment for enterprises to leap-frog onto a green growth path
Efforts to improve the business environment have to go beyond increasing efficiency and profits. They also need to promote innovation and the intensive use of science and technology by domestic firms through market mechanisms rather than administrative fiat. National

governments should consider creating an enabling business environment to help enterprises to take up new environment friendly technologies in production so as to enable them to make the transition to a green economic future without having to incur huge costs. Through tax incentives and subsidies, and working with the private sector, governments should promote environmentally sustainable models of production among domestic firms.

4.2 Investing in human capital and technology

TAPPING DEEPER INTO Africa's productive potential cannot happen unless the intellectual capital of the continent is at least maintained, and then developed.[1] Education, both basic and tertiary, provides the basis for building national capabilities to improve productivity and competitiveness. Africa has greatly improved access to primary education but still faces a daunting challenge in improving the quality of secondary and tertiary education.

One troubling aspect of the current system is the disconnect between what is taught in the formal system and the demands of public and private employers for graduates with skills in business administration, entrepreneurship, finance, and science and technology (Gyimah-Brempong and Ondiege, 2011). Too many graduates leave secondary school or universities with only a general education qualification while jobs for individuals with technical and management skills remain vacant. Bridging this gap requires a plethora of actions in priority areas.

Prioritizing science and technology, and business development education

In the newly industrialized countries of East Asia, technological advance has been a key driving force, accounting for the major part of productivity growth. The situation in Africa is quite different despite huge government investment in education. While about half or more of students enrolled in tertiary educational institutions in fast-growing economies such as Republic of Korea, Taiwan (Province of China) and China are enrolled in science, engineering, technology or business disciplines, the equivalent figure for Africa is about one fifth. The majority are enrolled in other disciplines, including about one third in the social sciences and slightly less in education (Gyimah-Brempong and Ondiege, 2011). The result is that, while graduates of African tertiary educational institutions go unemployed, African counties continue to face shortages of skilled labour.

The key to sustained growth, competitiveness and economic transformation is a progressive upgrade of national technological capacity, and quality and relevance should be the hallmark of higher education reform in Africa. Greater emphasis must be given to improving scientific and technological skills, business management and other fields that will set the key to unlocking Africa's productive potential (Gyimah-Brempong and Ondiege, 2011). This can largely be achieved through a radical restructuring of the existing tertiary education system via curricular reform, appropriate funding mechanisms and incentives for innovation and high performance.

Quality and relevance should be the hallmark of higher education reform in Africa.

Investing in programmes to retrain and retool unemployed graduates

The mismatch between the skills needed in the labour market and the academic-focused training of graduates is a huge waste of human capital. In the short and medium term, human resource development policy should move to retrain and retool unemployed school graduates from secondary and tertiary educational institutions in order to meet the growing demand for other skills on the labour market. Such skills include ICT, services, and transport and logistics. Governments should also work with the private sector to link potential employees and employers.

Developing national strategies to attract skilled members of diasporas

African governments recognize the contributions of their people living in the diaspora to the economic development of their home countries, both as investors and transmitters of remittances, knowledge and skills (Brinkerhoff, 2006; Kapur, 2001). Some 15 African countries have set up diaspora-related institutions or ministries. In addition, the AUC has created the African Citizens Directorate to deal with overarching issues in the relationship between diasporas and home governments.

Initial interest by African governments in engaging members of their diasporas in developing the homeland may have been motivated by financial or economic considerations, but diasporan communities also transfer non-financial resources—or "social remittances"—such as skills and modern values from the West to Africa. Eventually, these resources may have more profound impact on the attitude of societies to freedom, gender equality, tolerance of differences, human rights, governance and political practices. Skilled diasporans, particularly those in teaching and research at leading Western universities, can play a critical role in transforming African universities through their research, teaching and mentoring of young scholars and future graduate students (box 4.3).

Box 4.3: Tapping into diaspora knowledge: The Migration for Development in Ethiopia programme

The International Organization for Migration (IOM), with the Diaspora Coordinating Office of the Ethiopian Ministry of Capacity Building, administer the Migration for Development in Ethiopia (MidEth) programme, an IOM country-specific programme of its larger initiative—Migration for Development in Africa.

Set up to address skills gaps in Ethiopia, the programme offers several components, including a transfer of knowledge and technology scheme. The objective of such transfer is for skilled diaspora members to return to Ethiopia temporarily, preferably six months or more, to provide support to ministries and public institutions.

The programme is coordinated by Ethiopian embassies, which recruit members of the diaspora, and by he Ministry of Capacity Building, which assesses the needs for skilled workers in Ethiopia. IOM in Ethiopia coordinates logistics. A focus of the programme is universities in Ethiopia seeking skilled professionals, and lists of positions are available on embassy websites. The Ministry of Capacity Building partly funds the programme by paying for the flights and housing costs of temporary returnees. The United Nations Development Programme (UNDP) funds other aspects of the programme, including IOM coordination activities and paying the diasporan member a top-up of a maximum of $300 a month.

A successful programme is that with the Ethiopian North American Health Professionals Association (ENAHPA). Established in 1999, ENAHPA is a network of diasporan and non-diasporan volunteers dedicated to improving health in Ethiopia. Each year, via MidEth, ENAHPA sends health professionals to Ethiopia to train, lecture and run workshops with medical professionals. ENAHPA organizes the health professionals, IOM funds their flights and the Government of Ethiopia approves their mission.

Source: Kuschminder and Siegel (2010).

Transforming the university system to become a catalyst for change

No country in the world has managed to join the knowledge-based global economy by investing only in primary education. As Africa prepares to become the next global growth pole, national governments must emphasize post-graduate and university education, with a particular focus on science and technology, business studies, and a strong research culture in African universities. University reform should involve the way knowledge is produced, the nature and content of knowledge, the place of research and knowledge production and how to pay for it, and the kinds of partnerships that universities in Africa should seek to be equal players in the global arena while remaining relevant nationally and locally (Zeleza and Olukoshi, 2004; Aina, 2010). These important issues have major implications for the future of Africa's universities.

Investing in regional centres of excellence

African governments need to support centres of excellence in science and technology. The more proficient countries in this field, such as Egypt, Kenya, Nigeria and South Africa, can become regional incubators to cover smaller countries. National and regional centres of excellence, along the lines of the Indian Institute of Science and Technology and the University of Botswana Business Clinic, should be established.

Such centres aim to promote high-quality research to be shared by geographically dispersed institutions. The African Economic Research Consortium (AERC) has collaborative MA and PhD degrees in economics, as one example. The approach can be replicated for agriculture, business management, engineering and ICT training programmes.

4.3 Investing in physical infrastructure

NO COUNTRY HAS sustained rapid growth without keeping up fairly steep rates of public infrastructure investment. Infrastructure affects growth in two main ways—directly through physical capital accumulation and indirectly through improvements in productivity. At the microeconomic level, investment in infrastructure enhances private activity by lowering the cost of production and opening new markets, and presenting new production and trade opportunities. At the same time, infrastructure investment in power generation, water, sanitation and housing improves the social well-being of citizens.

The inadequate and poor quality of infrastructure in Africa is a major obstacle to unleashing Africa's development potential. Empirical research indicates that Africa's infrastructure deficit is lowering the continent's per capita economic growth by 2 percentage points a year and reducing the productivity of firms by as much as 40 per cent (Foster and Briceño-Garmendia, 2010; Ramachandran, Gelb and Shah, 2009).

The continent faces huge infrastructure challenges, in particular:

> Access to electricity for 30 per cent of the population compared with 70–90 per cent for Asia, Latin America and the Middle East.

> A telecommunications penetration rate of about 6 per cent compared with an average of 40 per cent for other regions of the world. Africa has the lowest Internet penetration—3 per cent.

Inadequate and poor infrastructure is a major obstacle to unleashing Africa's development potential.

> A road access rate of 34 per cent compared with 55 per cent on average for other regions, and some of the highest transport costs in the world.

> Access to water and sanitation (65 per cent urban and 38 per cent rural) compared with water access rates of 80–90 per cent for other regions.

Largely due to this underinvestment (table 4.3), African countries are among the least competitive in the world. Alone, increasing per capita growth in electricity output from 2 per cent to 6 per cent would lead to a one-half percentage point increase in economic growth. Infrastructure in Africa is in dire need of rehabilitation, upgrading and expansion to make up for many years of poor maintenance and even neglect.

Table 4.3

Density of infrastructure

Normalized units	Sub-Saharan low-income countries	Other low-income countries
Paved-road density	31	134
Total road density	137	211
Main-line density	10	78
Mobile density	55	76
Internet density	2	3
Generation capacity	37	326
Electricity coverage	16	41
Improved water	60	72
Improved sanitation	34	51

Source: *Adapted from Foster and Briceño-Garmendia, 2010:3*

Recent initiatives and the financing gap

African leaders have shown renewed commitment to addressing the continent's infrastructure gap through strong partnerships with global and regional institutions. Various planning frameworks developed by NEPAD since its inception[2] were brought together under one umbrella, the Programme for Infrastructure Development in Africa, in July 2010. This covers all four key sectors of transport, energy, trans-boundary water and ICT (AfDB et al., 2011). It will be carried out in two stages—study and implementation—and is therefore work in progress.

Sub-Saharan Africa's infrastructure requires an estimated $93 billion a year, two thirds for capital spending (table

4.4). Actual spending is put at $45 billion a year, and after accounting for potential efficiency gains that could amount to $17 billion, Africa's infrastructure gap remains substantial at close to $31 billion a year, or 12 per cent of its GDP (Foster and Briceño-Garmendia, 2010). About half the total investment needs are for power, followed by transport and water.

As scope for raising additional tax or user fees to fill the financing gap is highly constrained, simultaneous actions on two fronts are required: mobilizing resources and getting more out of current investments.

Table 4.4
Sub-Saharan Africa: infrastructure needs, 2006–2015, ($billion a year)

	Capital expenditure	Operations and maintenance	Total spending
ICT	7.0	2.0	9.0
Irrigation	2.7	0.6	3.3
Power	26.7	14.1	40.8
Transport	8.8	9.4	18.2
Water and sanitation	14.9	7.0	21.9
Total	60.4	33.0	93.3

Source: Foster and Briceño-Garmendia, 2010, p. 58.

Mobilizing resources

Efforts to encourage more domestic and external development finance should have high political priority at international and national levels. There is considerable scope for further innovation in mobilizing new sources of development finance if the political will exists. This section looks at the options open to Africa. Chapter 5 discusses matters in more detail.

Developing domestic financial and capital markets

Much effort is going towards attracting investments for infrastructure from external private and official finance for infrastructure development, but harnessing domestic resources has not been sufficiently explored (Inderst, 2009; UNCTAD, 2007). Approaches would include pension funds, sovereign wealth funds (in the case of mineral-rich African countries) and insurance funds. Several countries in Africa, such as Ghana, Kenya, Nigeria and Senegal, have started to tap into pension and insurance funds for infrastructure financing.

Through structural reforms, African governments can also develop long-term local capital markets, which include government and non-government bond markets and equity markets. New instruments, such as diaspora bonds and commodity-linked bonds, are already being used (Ratha and Ketkar, 2007; Kuschminder and Siegel, 2010). A domestic bond market is fundamental to the pricing of credit risk associated with long-term financing. Local stock markets could be strengthened to absorb large public offerings of shares in order to increase availability of long-term financing. Measures could be taken to enhance the role of banks as intermediaries for infrastructure projects by creating instruments and markets to shape risk, maturity and duration.

Encouraging FDI from emerging economies

The increasing importance of emerging and developing countries such as Brazil, China, India and Turkey in global trade, finance and investment has opened up opportunities for closer economic relations between Africa and these players. The contributions of China and India to Africa's infrastructure have been quite visible and very hard to ignore (Foster et al., 2008). These emerging powers have relatively large financial resources as well as appropriate skills and technology that African countries need to address their development needs. China has been the biggest investor in African infrastructure (box 4.4).

Resource-rich African countries should leverage the commodity boom to negotiate "resource-for-infrastructure" deals.

Box 4.4: China and Africa's infrastructure development

Chinese infrastructure financing commitments in Africa surged in 2001–2009 to $14 billion. In 2008 alone, among the top 225 international contractors, Chinese contractors had 42.4 per cent of the African market.

Most Chinese financing commitments are in electricity, ICT and transport. By value, power projects account for approximately half the Chinese-financed projects. Around one third of these financing commitments went to 10 of the 16 landlocked African countries, and about two thirds went to low-income economies. Rehabilitation of projects previously financed by China account for 18 per cent of Chinese-financed projects, most of them in rural areas.

The entry of Chinese construction companies and infrastructure developers into the equity/PPP project market is still in initial stages, but the firms recognize this as a growing market. According to one survey, competitive bidding represents slightly less than 90 per cent of contracts won in Africa by Chinese contractors. They are localizing more, by creating jobs for Africans and investing in training for local employees.

Source: Chen (2010).

African countries should therefore make all efforts to attract FDI from these countries into physical infrastructure development. Not only do the Chinese have the financial resources but also the proven expertise and know-how. Resource-rich African countries should leverage the commodities boom to negotiate "resource-for-infrastructure" deals from a better informed platform.

Accelerating institutional and governance reform

Essential for mobilizing the necessary domestic and external private finance for infrastructure development is designing and establishing the relevant policies, laws and regulations that provide predictable and accountable rules, mechanisms, and procedures on tendering and bidding, and that enforce contracts between the public and private sectors (Shendy, Kaplan and Mousley, 2011). This also entails improving regulatory performance and applying more explicit competition rules and procedures.

Getting more out of current infrastructure investment through efficiency gains

Achieving greater efficiency in service delivery and ensuring value for money are essential in their own right, as well as complementary to mobilizing finance. By accelerating reform in the infrastructure sector, Governments can reap huge savings through efficiency gains. The World Bank estimates that some $17 billion can be saved through greater efficiency in infrastructure (Foster and Briceño-Garmendia, 2010). Some key approaches are outlined in the following section.

Promoting PPPs through a transparent engagement framework

Infrastructure investment in Africa has remained low for so long for several reasons. First, infrastructure investments have the characteristics of a public good (i.e.,

they are non-exclusive in consumption), which gives the private sector very little incentive to invest. Second, the lack of long-term stable finance, high sector-specific risks, political instability and poor governance limit private participation. Third, the public sector has too few resources to provide infrastructure financing.

In recent years, the idea of PPPs for infrastructure has gained acceptance in African policymaking circles. Given the fiscal crisis of African countries and the shortage of long-term locally denominated debt, several African countries are encouraging PPPs, including joint ventures, build-operate-transfer schemes and similar arrangements, which could help to upgrade and expand the infrastructure base (Shendy, Kaplan and Mousley, 2011; Foster and

Briceño-Garmendia, 2010). For PPPs to succeed, however, governments have to develop clear and transparent institutional frameworks that cover many sides of PPP transactions, from project development to contract compliance. PPPs also need strong bodies to monitor implementation, evaluate results and ensure overall compliance in meeting performance targets (UNECA, 2011b).

Dismantling monopolies and encouraging competition

Operational inefficiencies and corruption are widespread problems in publicly run utilities. Such inefficiencies in power cost Africa $2.7 billion a year, or around 0.8 per cent of GDP (Foster and Briceño-Garmendia, 2010).[3] It is estimated that the continent's average power distribution losses are 23.3 per cent, more than twice the norm

> *Transforming agriculture is a precondition for unleashing the continent's development potential.*

of 10 per cent for developing countries. Although this affects all countries to some degree, these inefficiencies reduce the pace of electrification, drain the public purse and undermine the performance of utilities. The problem is not just limited to poor network coverage, but comes through in the exceptionally high price of infrastructure services in Africa (table 4.5).

Table 4.5

High-cost of African infrastructure

Sector	Africa	Other developing regions
Power tariffs ($ per kilowatt-hour)	0.02–0.46	0.05–0.1
Water tariffs ($ per cubic metre)	0.86–6.56	0.03–0.6
Road freight tariffs($ per ton-kilometre)	0.04–0.14	0.01–0.04
Mobile telephony ($ per basket per month)	2.6–21.0	9.9
International telephony ($, 3 minutes to US)	0.44–12.5	2.0
Internet dial-up ($ per month)	6.7–148.0	11

Source: Foster and Briceño-Garmendia, 2010, p. 50.

Note: Ranges reflect prices in different countries and consumption levels.

Governments can secure greater efficiency and lower costs in electricity and water by fostering competition through deregulating and privatizing. The best example in Africa in recent years is telecommunications. Deregulating the sector, which allowed competition among private providers, was responsible for the rapid expansion of mobile telephony in many parts of the continent. Similar efforts should be made to foster competition in energy, transport, banking and finance. Privatization has to be complemented with enabling regulation to ensure that private monopolies do not arise.

The problem of corruption and inefficiency in operating and managing State utilities in Africa is part of the broader unfinished economic governance agenda. Africa's State utilities embody only about 40 per cent of good governance practices for such enterprises (Vagliasindi and Nellis, 2009), despite the substantial sums spent on, for example, management training, internal accounting and auditing, as well as regulatory agencies. Some efforts have led to successful outcomes—the Botswana Power Corporation and the Kenya Power and Lighting Company, for instance—but results generally have disappointed (Nellis, 2005). The best laid plans for institutional reform can be stymied unless Governments make a commitment to hold ministries, regulatory agencies, contractors and the management of utilities accountable.

4.4 Unleashing Africa's agricultural potential

AGRICULTURE REMAINS THE mainstay of Africa's economies. It employs 90 per cent of the rural workforce, 60 per cent of the total (urban plus rural) labour force, accounts for as much as 40 per cent of export earnings and provides over 50 per cent of household needs and income (UNECA, 2007a). Yet, the sector received the least attention from national governments until 2003 when African leaders adopted the Comprehensive African Agriculture Development Programme (CAADP). Failure to transform agriculture has kept millions of rural Africans trapped in a cycle of underproduction, underemployment, low incomes and chronic poverty (UNECA and AUC, 2009).

The sector's poor performance is largely due to the lack of critical rural and interregional infrastructure, limited access by farmers to credit, the low skills base of small farmers, absence of security of land tenure and pervasive taxation of smallholding farmers by national governments (World Bank, 2007). Value chains and innovative small-farming systems are embryonic, while irrigation and fertilizers are underdeveloped. Thus, food production per capita has fallen as agricultural output has stagnated, and the demographic transition remains delayed (UNECA and AUC, 2009b).

The persistent and widespread anti-rural bias in Africa is in sharp contrast to the successfully industrialized economies of East Asia, such as Korea and Taiwan (China), where agrarian reform and the green revolution were major channels of wealth creation and income distribution in the early phase of development. A critical force in transforming agriculture in countries such as China and Korea was an activist and development-oriented State that invested heavily in transport and communications infrastructure, agricultural research and extension, irrigation systems and storage facilities—all essential factors for raising productivity and increasing income for the poor.

East Asia's agrarian transformation served as the basis for economies to industrialize, paving the way for a more diversified base to emerge. Increased incomes for farmers created buoyant demand in rural areas for farm inputs, for processing and marketing services as well as for consumer goods and services. This was followed by the switch to export-led industrialization strategies, which sparked rapid growth in industry and in urban centres. This in turn resulted in major spillover benefits for rural areas, generating remittances from workers who had migrated to urban areas and bringing non-farm opportunities to rural areas. Furthermore, urban-based industries have sought to locate some of their labour-intensive activities (such as food processing and metal fabrication) to lower-wage rural areas. The final push came from market liberalization in the late 1990s, which unleashed the full force of the market and brought international competition and FDI into these economies, including rural areas.

The successful experience of Asia and Latin America in transforming agriculture is known to many African policymakers, who increasingly recognize, along with their development partners, that transforming agriculture is a precondition for unleashing the continent's development potential (UNECA and AUC, 2009b; UNECA, 2007b). The priority tasks ¬¬of Africa's agricultural revolution are complicated and multifaceted, and involve technological, macroeconomic, institutional and ecological dimensions—purposes for which AU formulated CAADP (box 4.5).

Box 4.5: Transforming African agriculture: new opportunities

The prospects for agricultural transformation, which would propel industrialization and social development, have never been better in Africa (UNECA and AUC, 2009b). The emergence of the continental and regional policymaking machinery alongside national policies in recent years has been a major turning point. CAADP is now the basic reference point for African governments to improve agricultural productivity and reduce hunger on the continent (AUC, 2003 and 2006).

Development partners, private foundations and the international private sector are showing increasing interest in raising Africa's productivity in agriculture, so as to ensure food security and to use agricultural transformation as the foundation for industrializing Africa. Some of the most notable examples are the Africa Food Security Initiative launched by the G-8 at the L'Aquila Summit in 2009, with the commitment of $22 billion over two years; US President Barack Obama's Feed the Future Program; the Alliance for a Green Revolution in Africa, a private initiative headed by former UN Secretary-General Kofi Annan; and the New Vision for Agriculture, an initiative of the World Economic Forum, whose aim is to expand partnerships, catalysing investment and integrating best practices in the way private actors from outside Africa should support agriculture on the continent.

Progress in implementing the CAADP framework

CAADP as a framework has continental reach but envisages that a thorough assessment of country-level agricultural and food security programmes, policy frameworks and institutional arrangements has to precede any credible investment planning. CAADP also uses key analytics, such as critical review of constraints and policy gaps, economic modelling, growth-option analysis, and external review of investment plans. The latter is supported by the Regional Strategic Analysis and Knowledge Support System, an Africa-wide network of regional nodes supporting the implementation of CAADP.

The roadmap for CAADP focuses on expanding areas under cultivation, managing land and water sustainably, improving market access and infrastructure, increasing food supplies, improving responses to food emergencies, and improving dissemination and adoption of agricultural research and technology. In the Maputo Declaration on Agriculture and Food Security in Africa, adopted by the AU Conference of Ministers of Agriculture in July 2003, African countries were urged to allocate 10 per cent of their national budgets to agriculture within five years. Only four countries have done so, however: Ethiopia (13 per cent), Ghana (10 per cent), Malawi (14 per cent) and Mali (17 per cent). Many countries hardly reach 4 per cent of GDP and have to depend on ODA for funding agriculture and other sectors (Benin et al., 2010).

Implementation of the CAADP framework is in its early phases—some 40 countries are at different stages, from formally recognizing CAADP as having value addition to efforts to formulate CAADP-aligned programmes and projects. As of September 2011, 27 countries had completed the CAADP roundtable process and signed their compacts. Of these, around 20 had developed CAADP-based Agriculture and Food Security Investment Plans and were subjected to AUC and NPCA-led independent technical reviews. Fourteen countries have organized CAADP business meetings that showcase the outcome of the independent technical review that aims to garner domestic support and mobilize international assistance. These moves are taken as a demonstration of a strong joint commitment by government, private sector, civil society, farmers and development partners. ECOWAS has also signed a regional compact (Benin et al., 2010).

As CAADP implementation moves forward, experimenting, piloting and capturing best practices for wider application should be the manner of operation. Policy reforms should begin with modest and pragmatic interventions that bring small farmers, the State and markets together, and progressively unlock agriculture's potential. Experimentation and piloting can help to reduce risks and improve the success rate of reforms through scaling up pilot projects that worked and eliminating unsuccessful policy options that could potentially produce disastrous spillover effects (Hoffman and Wu, 2009).

Among the many priority issues identified by CAADP for transforming African agriculture, four stand out:

Increasing land under cultivation

It is estimated that 60 per cent of cultivable land in Africa is not under production, which gives considerable room for increasing agricultural production, both for staple foods as well as exports (McKinsey Global Institute, 2010;). A comprehensive review of archaic tenure systems is needed, as are different types of property ownership and use. Reforms on land tenure can be initiated either top down, or bottom up from small, local experiments. Such approaches can bring huge tracts of unused land into production. Particularly important in Africa is the need to rehabilitate large tracts of degraded land using soil and water conservation measures, and through sustainable use of modern technology and inputs (UNECA and AUC, 2009).

New modalities of land ownership and use would provide an opportunity to attract FDI in agriculture through joint ventures of lease arrangements, though they must not be permitted if they displace communities already using the land for production (AUC, AfDB and UNECA, 2010).

Raising yields of staple foods

High rates of population growth, urbanization and high global food prices are putting pressure on governments to increase the yields of staple foods. This remains a particular challenge for Africa where investment in infrastructure, technology and agricultural research is weak, and use of yield-enhancing practices (such as fertilizers and pesticides, mechanical tools and irrigation) is very low relative to other developing regions.

Improving the productivity of small farmers should be a key policy target over the next two decades. This demands high and sustained levels of investment in key public goods for the rural sector, such as roads and irrigation infrastructure, as well as support for innovative farming technologies and learning systems for small farmers. Experience from countries that have undergone a successful green revolution shows that access to science and technology for small farmers, via research institutes and demonstration centres, is crucial for fully realizing their potential. Such an approach, along with agricultural extension centres and access to credit and seeds, should be expanded (OECD-DAC/IPRCC, 2010).

Linking farmers to markets

Most African farmers produce for subsistence, yet with help they have considerable scope to farm more profitably by producing high-value products. Beyond capacity building and improved access to inputs, farmers need to be linked to markets through regional value chains (UNECA and AUC, 2009). This requires development of small- and medium-sized rural industries—the vital links to global and regional markets.[1] More FDI is also needed in agriculture, with well-defined forward and backward linkages, spawning new manufacturing and service sectors (UNECA and AUC, 2009).

Expanding opportunities for non-farm rural employment

Beside increasing productivity in agriculture and linking farmers to global value chains, it is vital to generate non-farm jobs by diversifying the rural economy—arguably an even greater challenge than the technical rehabilitation of agriculture. Despite the preponderance of smallholder agriculture, the rural population is becoming less agrarian. This process, which started in the final days of colonialism, has been accelerating as a result of environmental degradation, population growth and land subdivision, which make it hard for large numbers of small farmers to rely only on subsistence agriculture.

Expanding non-farm rural jobs should be an integral part of an agriculture-led rural industrialization strategy. Rural productivity increases can be achieved through public works programmes such as secondary roads, reforestation and soil conservation, clean water supplies, rural electrification, and construction or rehabilitation of rural schools and health centres. Such non-farm employment activities, while providing additional incomes for the rural poor, would also strengthen the internal working of the rural economy by stimulating production and consumption of local goods and services.

Note: 1. Such as agro-processing and packaging industries; providers of agricultural inputs and cold storage; marketing agents; clearing agents and freight handlers at ports; and quality assurance and certification agents.

For the first time in many decades, African policymakers are looking to smallholder farming as an option for sparking a successful rural transformation. This hope feeds on the successful rural transformation in China, where smallholder-focused land and price reforms triggered a massive increase in agricultural production. Rural manufacturing and allied activities now account for the largest share of income and employment in rural China. In Africa's own contexts, the following options require the most serious attention.

Improving access to land through tenure reform

Although Africa has some 60 per cent of the world's arable land, access to land—particularly by women—remains a huge problem, and insecure tenure prevents farmers from investing their labour and meagre resources in technology to improve the land's productivity. The need for land reform is recognized, but rarely acted on (Chambers, 1991; Pausewang et al., 1990). This problem still persists although countries such as Ethiopia are experimenting with new land-use practices to reduce uncertainty among farmers. Ethiopia's community-driven land certification has been an effective way to improve land-use practices to reduce encroachment and improve soil conservation (Deininger et al., 2007).

There is no single universal model of land reform that countries should follow. Land ownership patterns in each country are historically and culturally determined and each country must pursue a land reform policy that takes into account the local ecological, social and cultural contexts. Neither the old system of communal land ownership nor the modern form of private ownership can adequately address the problem of land scarcity, which has been accentuated by rapid population growth, decades of land degradation and new threats from climate change.

There is no universal model of land reform that countries should follow.

State control of land, as in Ethiopia at present, hampers investment and productivity since smallholders feel insecure and fear expropriation by the State at a stroke of a pen (Cheru, 2002). Equally, the shift towards private ownership concentrates land in the hands of a few and often excludes poor farmers and women. Thus, any strategy to address land scarcity must strike a balance between the interests of landless peasants and those of private land owners who want to engage in commercial production for profit.

Investing in research and technology

Crucial means to transform African agriculture are research and technological innovation. Increasing yields, adding value to products, raising the efficiency of resource use—from water to land—will not happen without determined efforts to devote resources in these areas. Yet as seen, spending on agriculture usually falls far short of the 10 per cent of national budgets agreed at the 2003 Maputo Summit.

The amount spent on research and technology is also very low, even though its economic rate of return is very high (Ehui and Tsigas, 2006). Many analysts consider public spending as a share of GDP adequate at 2 per cent or more—the figure for the continent stands at 0.7 per cent, lower than the global average of about 1 per cent. Southern Africa shows 2.3 per cent, and South Africa 3.0 per cent (UNECA and AUC, 2009).

Huge investments in innovations are needed to enhance food production and accelerate economic transformation (partly because of agriculture's strong multiplier effect). African governments should therefore spend more on agricultural research and technology if they are going to improve the sector's productivity.

Reaching rural areas with financial services

The demand for financial services in rural Africa is huge, but providers are too few or are absent. In countries where microfinance institutions exist, their coverage is low owing to insufficient capital or high collateral requirements

African governments should spend more on agricultural research and technology if they are going to improve the sector's productivity.

discourage potential borrowers. Moreover, microfinance institutions are focused more on lending to, rather than mobilizing savings from, the rural population. The underdeveloped status of rural banks is now a major impediment to generating savings and to providing essential financial services in rural areas.

A key task for governments is therefore to broaden financial intermediation in rural areas by liberalizing the financial and banking sector and to encourage competition among different providers, including credit unions, savings and loan associations and domestic commercial banks. This would encourage competition and the spread of banking services (box 4.6).

Box 4.6: Financial inclusion in Tanzania: The National Microfinance Bank

The National Microfinance Bank (NMB) in Tanzania makes financial inclusion—extending banking services to previously "unbankable" communities—a priority. According to a survey conducted in 2009 by FinScop, a pan-African market research company, the proportion of the country's adult population that was using banks and other formal institutions was just 12.4 per cent. The large segment of the unbanked population thus represented a huge opportunity for NMB, and it has been making good progress. Over the past five years, customer numbers have more than doubled from 600,000 to 1.4 million in 2011.

This rapid expansion has been possible for two reasons: the expansion of its branch network from 100 to 140, giving NMB an on-ground presence in 80 per cent of the country's administrative districts; and the bank's enthusiasm for new technology, which has enabled it to reach out to remote rural clients who do not have easy access to a bank branch. NMB is the first bank in Tanzania to offer mobile banking, enabling customers to check balances, transfer funds and buy top-ups for their electricity accounts via their mobile phones. With the launch of its PeasaFasta cardless ATM service in April 2011, NMB customers are now able to send money to people who do not have a bank account. Unbanked Tanzanians can withdraw funds sent to them via any of the NMB 400 cash machines nationwide, using a code sent to their mobile phone, rather than the traditional card.

For unbanked customers, it is a matter of convenience and security—a vast improvement on keeping money under the mattress. In addition, interest on savings provides an incentive to start saving in the first place. Once previously unbanked customers have acquired a record with their bank, they can access other services, such as insurance against crop failure and, over time, micro-loans.

Source: Twentyman (2011).

Building a climate-resilient economy

Efforts to release the potential of African agriculture will be incomplete without attention to the ill effects of climate change. Unchecked, climate change will alter rainfall patterns, decrease the areas suitable for agriculture, the length of growing seasons and crop yield potential, and potentially force millions to migrate to urban areas (Low, 2006). The continent has opportunities to profit from its vast carbon sinks, leap-frog dirty technologies and embark on a path of low-carbon growth and clean development. Along with innovations in research and technology, as well as sustainable management of land and water resources, Africa will be able to make the transition to a green economy growth model in transforming agriculture (UNECA and AUC, 2009). This will require African governments to take decisions on mainstreaming climate change adaptation and mitigation policies, and to institute policies and incentives in assisting farmers to adopt clean technology and production practices.

Taking bold steps to empower women farmers

In sub-Saharan Africa, women produce up to 80 per cent of all basic food products and constitute a sizeable part of the agricultural labour force. Yet they have less access than men to agricultural assets, inputs and services, credit, education and training, and rural jobs. The gender gap imposes real costs on society through lost agricultural output, food security and economic growth (World Bank, 2011a).

> *Promoting gender equality is not only good for women—it is also good for agricultural development.*

Policies need to be directed to empowering women farmers, particularly through better access to the above elements, in order to raise their incomes (World Bank, 2011a). Promoting gender equality is not only good for women—it is also good for agricultural development.

Industrializing through agriculture

Productivity growth in agriculture on its own is unable to solve the problem of chronic food insecurity, underemployment and poverty in rural Africa. Agriculture has to be sufficiently harnessed to serve as the foundation for wider industrialization. This requires a wide range of experiments to channel local productive endowments, capture best practices and scale them up nationally and regionally (Fan, Nestorova and Olofiniyi, 2010).

Agriculture-led rural industrialization can enhance the dynamism of rural economies—generating non-farm employment in industrial clusters in value addition, packaging, processing, shipping and ensuring vital inputs and services to make agriculture itself more productive. It can produce local and regional spillovers by increasing access to dynamic markets and by strengthening links between farmers, industry and services (World Bank, 2007).

African countries can learn from the experience of new development partners (AfDB et al., 2011). Each new partner has a comparative advantage—China in infrastructure development and rural-based special economic zones, India in the green revolution and skills-intensive learning, and Brazil in agriculture and agro-processing.

In particular, the lesson from China and East Asia generally is that rural transformation requires pragmatic and hands-on leadership from the top, supported by a goal-oriented and competent bureaucracy committed to building the country's unique strengths rather than concentrating on removing general "negatives" (box 4.7). This implies the need for selectivity, innovation in new institutional arrangements at central and local levels, experimentation and pilot testing, and a public–private alliance to identify and act on concrete constraints (Bruce and Li, 2009). State and local governments have to be given the power to attain concrete goals, grounded in the local context. New organizations may have to be created. Pragmatism also implies flexibility in moving limited human and financial resources to where they are needed most.

Box 4.7: Lessons from China's agriculture-led industrialization

Agricultural liberalization and gradual international integration were fundamental to Deng Xiaoping's "going out" policy of China's economic transformation. A grass-roots originated experimental reform of land ownership, along with price reform for agricultural products and inputs, sparked an agricultural revolution. New special economic zones played a key role for testing economic reforms, attracting FDI, catalysing industrial clusters, learning new technologies and incubating new management practices.

The Chinese enabling environment for enterprise development involved: job creation through rural and micro-enterprises; labour and wage policies; training and capacity building through joint ventures and aid programmes; local autonomy and decision-making; competition between regions and cities; bureaucracy and regulatory reform; access to financing; and creation of appropriate technology and infrastructure. This in turn contributed to a massive flow of people from rural areas into more productive employment in manufacturing and services in the towns, and out of poverty (Fan, Nestorova and Olofiniyi, 2010).

Chinese political leadership was supported in these reforms by research institutions such as the China Development Research Group, the Chinese Academy of Social Sciences, and the Development Research Centre of the State Council. The gradualism of the reform process and its reliance on evidence from local experiments helped to secure political support and reinforced its credibility.

Source: *Extracted from notes of the China-DAC Study Group Bamako Meeting, April 2010.*

Harnessing South–South cooperation

As well as the lessons of industrializing through agriculture, South–South cooperation offers opportunities for transferring policy experiences, technologies and finance to boost agricultural productivity (UNCTAD, 2009d). These new development partners can bring a commercial approach to cooperation, in which agro-industry enterprises play an important role, creating management and technical know-how with inputs such as "high-tech seeds". Strong cooperation with new development partners could therefore contribute to an African green revolution if the relationship is managed strategically (Cheru and Modi, 2012).

Among the new development partners, China's engagement has been the most extensive. Agriculture is a top priority, involving over 40 countries and over 200 projects, with a strong focus on land management, breeding technologies, food security, and machinery and processing. In recent years, China has intensified its technology cooperation, organizing training courses in practical technologies and carrying out experimental agricultural technology projects. It has sent more than 10,000 agro-technicians to

Africa to train local farmers and provide technical support (Cheru and Obi, 2010).The Action Plan 2007–2009 of the Third Forum for China-Africa Cooperation (FOCAC, 2006) included setting up 14 centres for agricultural research in Africa.

India—through the Africa-India Forum Summit launched in April 2008—has sought to reinforce cooperation, especially by transferring agricultural technologies that meet the needs of Africa's smallholders. Indian companies,

South-South cooperation offers opportunities for transferring policy experiences, technologies and finance to boost agricultural productivity.

> *A fresh and pragmatic approach is needed to reinvigorate regional integration in Africa.*

such as Karturi Global and Karluskor, have become major investors in agriculture. India is also active in interregional initiatives for Africa, involving India, Brazil and South Africa (IBSA), which established the IBSA Facility Fund for the Alleviation of Poverty and Hunger in Africa in 2003. South Africa, itself a leader on the continent in agricultural technology, is a key player in technology transfer to other African countries (Arkhangelskaya, 2010).

Within IBSA, the establishment of Embrapa in 2008 in Ghana points to a new phase in Brazil's deeper engagement in African agriculture. Embrapa is a Brazilian agricultural research and training institution and is a driving force in agricultural development. Several African countries have signed technical cooperation agreements and begun implementing joint projects with Embrapa and[4] the Forum for Agricultural Research in Africa (FARA) also has regular dialogue and joint research with this institution.

In addition, the Brazil–Africa Dialogue on Food Security, Fight Against Hunger and Rural Development, which gathered more than 40 African Ministers of Agriculture in Brasilia in 2010, highlights cooperation on sharing expertise in policies and best practices aimed at family farming, such as public-purchase schemes linked to domestic food aid and school feeding programmes, concessional loans for importing Brazilian farming machinery, and investment and technology transfer in producing bio-fuels on African soil (Government of Brazil, 2010). Such initiatives can help to release Africa's agricultural potential, by increasing smallholder productivity as well as expanding large-scale commercial farming for export.

Countries such as China, India and Brazil are championing new technologies and production systems in an attempt to move away from the old resource-intensive method of production to one in which agricultural productivity is boosted by using and managing natural resources (both land and water) more efficiently. Tapping into their vast knowledge and expertise should be a major priority for African States, while developing appropriate land policies to ensure that foreign investments in African agriculture do not compromise the land rights of local populations (AfDB et al., 2011).

Forging non-State strategic partnerships

In addition to establishing stronger relationships with governments, African governments need to maximize inputs from bilateral and multilateral donors, philanthropic foundations, universities, agricultural research consortia and agri-businesses.

In recent years, several philanthropic bodies have invested in green revolution experiments to boost the productivity of small farmers. The Alliance for a Green Revolution in Africa, with financial support from the Bill & Melinda Gates Foundation and the Alliance for a Green Revolution in Africa, a private initiative headed by former UN Secretary-General Kofi Annan, among others, are leading the way in smallholder farming by applying yield-enhancing technology and inputs, and offering training. Measures such as linking farmers to research and technology so that

they can raise their outputs, enabling them to get their products to the market quickly along better roads, and providing them with real-time information on market conditions and commodity prices will help to raise the incomes of small farmers.

In summary, if Africa's small farmers are to improve productivity and develop profitable niches in agricultural value chains, the State must be active in two main ways: investing in agricultural research and extension, technological innovation, and transport and communication; and ensuring that credit is available and essential inputs are provided This would play a pivotal role in spawning rural industrialization through raising farmers' incomes.

4.5 Intra-African economic integration

CONTINENTAL INTEGRATION HAS enormous potential for promoting growth and unleashing the development potential of African countries by easing the binding constraints to growth (such as poor transport networks) and by lowering direct and indirect costs of doing business (Ramachandran, Gelb and Shah, 2009). Integrating Africa's fragmented markets can therefore help to attract the required investment—from Africa and the rest of the world—and to build competitive and more diversified economies. This requires better links between countries—from paved roads to banking cooperation—to spur economic growth mutually, which in turn should strengthen integration of African countries into the global economy.

Africa has more regional organizations than any other continent, and most African countries are members of more than one. Yet, they have failed to set free the continent's development potential and ensure sustainable growth and liberalization, mainly because of institutional and economic impediments to intra-African trade. The policy and regulatory environment, the transparency and predictability of trade and business administration, and the business climate for promoting intra-African trade remain weak and complicated. Other institutional challenges include bureaucratic and physical hindrances, such as road charges, transit fees and administrative delays at borders and ports. The economic obstacles include the high dependence of most countries on exports of primary commodities, strict rules of origin emanating from trade liberalization schemes and poor infrastructure (UNECA, 2011).

Africa's RECs—the key pillars for carrying out the economic integration agenda—face numerous challenges, including inadequate financial and human resources, weak institutional infrastructure, multi-membership of countries, duplication of mandates, poor policy coordination and harmonization, and lack of political will among member States to push through the packages of agreed-on protocols (UNECA, 2010). Although some RECS such as the Economic and Monetary Community of Central Africa) (CEMAC) and COMESA have made some progress in specific sectors, the performance of many others has been quite disappointing. Consequently, the level of intra-African trade remains low compared with trade within other global regions, both developed and developing.

Changing tack: a modest proposal for intra-African integration

A fresh and pragmatic approach is needed to reinvigorate regional integration in Africa, promote entrepreneurship, increase the international competitiveness of African firms and remove supply-side constraints. An ambitious market integration approach along the lines of the EU is many years away. Given the diversity, institutional weaknesses and huge infrastructure gap of African economies, more flexible institutional arrangements to promote regional integration may have more potential because of their responsiveness to immediate national priorities and interests.

The most recent AU initiative in this area—the Minimum Integration Programme (MIP) — is an important first step. It attempts to identify priority sectors and sub-sectors that would produce immediate benefits to cooperating countries within RECs. The MIP is divided into three 4-year phases until 2020, aligned with the AU Strategic Plan. The first phase (2009–2012) has a long list of initiatives.

The cost of implementing the MIP is not specified, although collaboration with the RECs is likely to cost over $100 million. This implies that, if Africa is to properly own and accelerate its integration agenda, sustainable financing must be sought for the MIP as well as for the implementation plan for the priority sectors identified by the Action Plan for Boosting Intra-African Trade (Africa

The African consumer market holds great potential for trade and investment.

Union, 2011a). This plan aims to strengthen productive capacity, trade policy, trade finance and trade-related regional infrastructure, agriculture and integration of factor markets (Africa Union, 2011a). The MIP has the potential to improve coordination and harmonization between the AUC and the RECs as well as among the RECs, to implement the 1990 Abuja Treaty for establishing an African Economic Community in a timely manner and to strengthen the leadership and coordination role of the AUC (Africa Union, 2011a).

Eliminating supply-side constraints and weak productive capacities

The most important binding constraint to raising productive capacity in Africa is poor infrastructure. Unreliable power supply and poor roads in particular, along with red tape, stifle private sector productivity—an acute problem for trade among African countries.

The Action Plan for Boosting Intra-African Trade is a pragmatic and focused approach to tackling the interlocking problems of infrastructure, along with radical measures to improve the business environment (AUC, 2011a). More specifically, governments have to make significant public investment in both "hard" and "soft" infrastructure (box 4.8), invest in human capital formation, provide credit and maintain a growth-oriented macroeconomic environment—all within a sustainable fiscal environment.

Such measures to remove supply-side constraints must be joined by efforts to reduce demand-side constraints through, for example, forming trade promotion councils, subregional credit and insurance systems and subregional banks to finance production and trade, as well as by developing a common framework for financing regional infrastructure.

Box 4.8: Hard and soft infrastructure

Crucial as improvements in hard infrastructure are for economic growth, they represent only a part of the solution to the constraints limiting intra-Africa trade. Many others issues—together termed "soft" infrastructure—impose heavy costs on intra-Africa trade.

These include the policy and regulatory environment, transparency and predictability of trade and business administration, and the quality of the business environment more generally. Other institutional challenges include administrative delays, overly zealous inspection of goods at borders, poor coordination of inspection between different actors, short opening times at the points of entry, corruption at border crossing points, and cumbersome and time-consuming customs procedures (box table 1).

Box table 1: Export and import procedures, time and cost for selected global regions, 2012

Region	Number of documents for exporting	Time for export (days)	Number of documents for importing	Time for import (days)
OECD average	4.4 (4.5)	10.5 (11)	4.8 (5.1)	10.7 (11.5)
East Asia & Pacific	6.5 (6.8)	21.9 (24.3)	7 (7.6)	23 (25.9)
Latin America Caribbean	6.4 (6.4)	17.8 (21.7)	6.9 (7.2)	19.6 (26.6)
Middle East & North Africa	6.3 (7.3)	19.7 (24.9)	7.6 (8.8)	23.6 (31.1)
Eastern Europe & Central Asia	6.9 (7.6)	27 (32.6)	7.8 (8.7)	28.8 (35.3)
Sub-Saharan Africa	7.7 (8.2)	32.5 (36.7)	8.8 (9.3)	37.1 (45.3)

Source: World Bank (2011b).

Note: Data in parentheses are for 2011.

Capturing growing trade and services opportunities

African countries have made real progress in liberalizing since the early 1980s to open themselves up to the world economy, but the scope and pace of such moves for intra-African trade and investment have been disappointing. Tariff and non-tariff barriers, complicated customs procedures and documentation, poor infrastructure, and poor trade information and finance are some of the obstacles to intra-African trade and investment (UNECA, 2010).

The African consumer market holds great potential for trade and investment. Although Africa has low per capita incomes, the situation is changing fast. Over the past decade, several African countries have recorded per capita income higher than that of the BRIC countries (AfDB et al., 2011). Recent projections indicate that consumer spending in Africa will rise from $860 million in 2008 to $1.4 trillion in 2020. The share of African households with discretionary income is projected to rise from 35 per cent in 2000 to 52 per cent in 2020, to 128 million (McKinsey Global Institute, 2010).

African governments should note this untapped consumer market right on their doorstep and begin to put enabling policies in place and the institutional framework to increase intra-African trade and investment, and to open up new market opportunities for domestic producers and retailers (Africa Union, 2011a). Increased consumer demand could help spawn small- and medium-sized firms specializing in consumer goods.

Services must not be forgotten. The current approach focuses on trade in goods and has only recently started to focus on the untapped opportunities for trade in services, which have the potential to become substantial sources of export earnings for many African economies. Prime examples are tourism, trade logistics services such as transport and harbours, and construction.

In the next decade, the national and African markets in consumer goods and services will represent ever-rising shares of Africa's trade and investment opportunities. As countries urbanize and a middle class forms, demand for basic consumer goods and services will grow quickly—spurring economic development—yet capacity is not growing to be ready to meet this demand (Boston Consulting Group, 2010). Continental trade in services is only slowly liberalizing (Africa Union, 2011a), hampering the ability of private service providers to exploit Africa-wide opportunities. Governments therefore need to liberalize such trade faster, as progress nationally is a precondition for progress throughout Africa.

Achieving intra-African integration

Regional economic integration—when designed and carried out with a broader development strategy to promote economic diversification, structural transformation and technological development—could enhance the productive capacities of African economies, realize economies of scale, improve competitiveness and serve as a launching pad to make Africa a global growth pole (see chapter 3).

Some major obstacles—and ways to remove them so as to unleash Africa's productive potential are discussed below. Policymakers should not look at any of them in isolation, but should strike the right balance between developing the hard and soft infrastructure necessary for the private sector to thrive in a business-friendly, enabling environment.

Closing the infrastructure gap

Infrastructure in Africa needs work on many fronts—mobilizing additional resources for investment, getting more out of current spending, tackling inefficiency, expanding private sector participation and promoting good governance.

Transport costs are arguably the most important impediment to intra-African trade (Ndulu, 2006). One estimate has put transport costs in Africa to be 136 per cent higher than those on other continents (Foster and Briceño-Garmendia, 2011). For landlocked African countries, freight costs are roughly 10–25 per cent of the total value of their imports, against a global average of 5 per cent (UNCTAD, 2007). The potential gains that should accrue to African countries from worldwide tariff reductions are offset by high transport costs that impose higher effective protection than tariffs (Foster and Briceño-Garmendia, 2010).

Better physical infrastructure is therefore crucial in raising intra-African trade, particularly for landlocked countries, thus exploiting unused productive capital to the fullest (Foster and Briceño-Garmendia, 2010). One study estimates that improving the main intra-African road network alone could generate trade expansion of around $250 billion over a period of 15 years for an investment of $32 billion, including maintenance (Buys et al., 2006). The same study estimated that landlocked African countries could increase their trade five-fold—Chad 507 per cent, Uganda 741 per cent and Sudan 1,027 per cent, for the same investment. Other studies estimate a five-fold trade increase from halving transport costs in a typical landlocked country (Limao and Venables, 2001).

Building a strong regional financial market

Expanded investment in infrastructure has to be complemented with a well-functioning banking and financial sector for private operators to have reliable access to credit and payment arrangements. Recent surveys of African firms indicate that access to credit is a major obstacle to investment in the region. Moreover, without a continental guaranteed payments system, African firms are increasingly dependent on international letters of credit and other forms of guaranteed payments, which entail onerous transaction costs. Many resources that should be used in productive economic activity are tied up as payment guarantees (Ramachandran, Gelb and Shah, 2009).

Liberalizing the financial sector is the first step towards developing an Africa-wide network of banking services. Such a network will foster trade, mobilize savings and facilitate payments (UNCTAD, 2009c). Two of the most successful examples are in West Africa (box 4.9).

Box 4.9: Spreading banking services in West Africa

Aided by a more open and liberal environment, Ecobank (Togo) and Nigerian banks have expanded their operations across West Africa, step by step, through mergers and acquisitions. These banks have also ventured outside West Africa and have established a presence in Burundi, Cameroon, Democratic Republic of the Congo, Rwanda, South Africa, Uganda and Zambia (UNCTAD, 2009c).

In 2008, nine of the 20 largest banks in Africa were Nigerian. Banks from that country accounted for over 25 per cent of African bank capital, and seven Nigerian banks had capital of well more than $1 billion (*Africa Business*, 2008).

The expansion of banks across Africa would boost investment and trade, for several reasons. First, it would inject capital in the economy, offer employment to locals and introduce new products as well as managerial and technical skills. Second, it would help to increase economic activity through lending and mobilizing savings. Third, increasing competition among banks would reduce the cost of their services (UNCTAD, 2009b).

Reinforcing political will for wider gain

Despite developing broad regional agreements to expedite the process of liberalization and institutional reforms in order to promote intra-Africa trade, little progress has been made in enforcing the agreements. The political commitment must be found to go beyond narrow national interests and create conditions for larger economies of scale that would benefit all the member States in RECs and, ultimately, the African continent. Individual economies are too small on their own to take advantage of the opportunities available on the global market. Moreover, the lack of compensatory mechanisms to assist the poorest member countries in a regional community further discourage their effective participation in enforcing regional agreements as these would entail immediate costs.

Reducing the information gap

Africa's ability to participate in the global economy and negotiate with trade partners from a strong and well-informed base depends on the access that negotiators for African countries have to trade information, knowledge of trading systems and their skills in trade and contract negotiations. Although the rapid spread of the Internet and mobile telephony has started to break down such "information apartheid", national governments need to do much more in easing access to vital economic information. One approach would be to harness the knowledge and research capacity of African universities, research institutes and think-tanks.

In addition, private sector agents need up-to-date information on what other REC member States can offer to substitute for the products imported from developed countries. They also need access to the latest information on the rules and regulations, products in development, tariffs, and opportunities for co-financing in partner countries. Establishing a subregional trade information platform along the lines of the COMESA Trade Information Network would improve direct communication among private sector agents within RECs.

Strengthening entrepreneurship

The need to strengthen State capacity is well acknowledged by national governments and donor partners, equally important is the need to strengthen the capacity of the indigenous private sector in Africa.

Africa's entrepreneurial capacity in many sectors is constrained by the absence of a broad-based, competing business network, which further limits the ability of domestic

> *Better physical infrastructure is crucial in raising intra-Africa trade, particularly for landlocked countries.*

investors to grow and thrive. Many African countries lack the institutional capacity to provide the necessary support services to producers and exporters, highlighting again the great competitive disadvantages the continent labours under compared with other developing regions (Ramachandran, Gelb and Shah, 2009; WEF, 2011). The State's underdevelopment has contributed to that in the private sector. Simply drafting a national competition policy does not automatically render the private sector competitive.

A big part of the reform agenda to liberate Africa's productive potential must therefore focus on strengthening the capacity of the domestic private sector to compete effectively in global markets. Special efforts are needed that would bring together universities, research centres and bodies representing the private sector to develop continuing education and training programmes that offer customized skills development for entrepreneurs. Such steps can help entrepreneurs to adopt the latest technologies and management systems, and to link up with regional and global firms. One of the lessons from East Asia is that entrepreneurial capacities are built during industrialization—they were not prepared before as a precondition for growth (Ohno and Shimamura, 2007).

4.6 Harnessing new partnerships

THE INCREASING ROLE of new global economic powers such as China, India and Brazil in world trade, finance and investment has opened opportunities for economic cooperation with Africa. Not only do they have large financial resources—they also have the skills and technology that African countries need. Infrastructure is one area where Africa's new development partners, particularly China, are making sterling contributions.

These new development partners with increasing global clout present opportunities and challenges for Africa—as well as questions: How best can Africa benefit from their rise? What are the risks to economic diversification and transformation? How can these risks be contained? What can be done to ensure that Africa–South cooperation does not replicate the current unequal pattern of economic relations with the rest of the world?

These are important questions that African policymakers must carefully examine before jumping into partnership arrangements (Cheru and Obi, 2010). The ultimate impact of South–South cooperation on African development will depend on the extent to which African countries can maximize the benefits, while minimizing potential risks, through well thought-out national and regional strategic measures. The benefits of South–South cooperation are most likely to accrue to those countries that have taken adequate steps to exploit the complementarities between trade, investment and ODA to promote structural change. Those countries may well have focused on the following three priority areas.

Attracting Southern FDI to develop productive potential

FDI is an important source of private capital for developing countries. It has the potential to increase national income and promote economic growth and diversification. It can do this through creating jobs, enhancing skills development, facilitating transfer of technology and access to foreign markets, enhancing competitiveness of local firms by creating capacity for value addition, and encouraging new manufacturing and service sectors (Ajayi, 2006; UNCTAD, 2005). FDI also contributes by removing constraints to productivity and growth. Both Malaysia and Mauritius, for example, have used FDI successfully in this way, attracting FDI into sectors producing goods and services with a high value-added element.

Africa has never been the most popular destination for FDI (figure 4.3), even though profitability from FDI is higher in Africa than elsewhere. Some reasons advanced for this conundrum include political instability, the information deficit, poor infrastructure and a general perception of Africa as a riskier investment environment than other developing regions

Figure 4.3
FDI inflows by region, 1990–2010 (%)

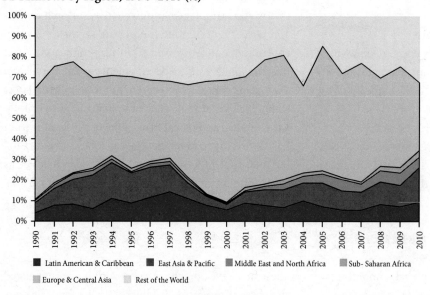

Source: Calculations based on data from the World Bank (2011)

The last reason is exaggerated. The crisis period of the 1980s and 1990s has passed, the political landscape in Africa is changing and the process of economic policymaking has improved greatly. One of the most important regional frameworks for this is NEPAD, which has not only identified FDI as a crucial source of financing for the continent's development, but has also clearly outlined steps to be taken, including governance reforms inspired and monitored by the APRM (UNECA, 2006).

Creating an enabling policy environment to attract FDI will not on its own produce the desired results—structural change and industrialization. These will very much depend on three factors.

First, the host country must have a strategic vision of how FDI fits into its overall development. African countries must ensure that FDI is channelled into priority sectors—agriculture, natural resource extraction, infrastructure and manufacturing—which are critical to unlocking the continent's productive potential. Second, FDI promotion should not be at the expense of the domestic private sector. FDI should be a means for developing the domestic

> *African countries must ensure that FDI is channelled into priority sectors that are critical for unlocking the continent's productive potential.*

technological base by encouraging joint ventures, and so create linkages between FDI and domestic enterprises. Third, as the quality of the host country's human capital and infrastructure stock strongly influences the type and quantity of FDI flows, African countries need to make concerted efforts to improve this stock—a leitmotif running through this document.

Prioritizing FDI in infrastructure

The new Southern powers—China in particular—with huge financial resources and proven experience in major infrastructure development can become important sources of infrastructure finance and expertise to address Africa's infrastructure gap. Resource-rich African countries in particular should leverage the commodities boom to negotiate the supply of infrastructure with China,

India and Brazil. Resource-for-infrastructure deals must, however, be based on deep analysis of the costs and benefits for the host country, underlining the need for African governments to build their research and analytical base as well as their negotiation skills, in order to extract the most benefits from FDI (AfDB et al., 2011).

Building strong governance frameworks for natural resources

Mineral-rich African countries face difficult challenges in managing FDI in natural resources, particularly mining and energy. Large-scale corruption remains a serious problem, where a significant portion of economic rents from resources do not make it to the central treasury or the local community. Many resource-rich African countries do not have transparent plans for how wealth from the extractive sector is to be used, whether for poverty reduction or for investment to diversify the economy (Transparency International, 2008; Standing, 2007).

The pervasive corruption in Africa's extractive industries has brought growing international pressure to stamp out corruption and allow revenues to go to development and poverty reduction. The three most recognized anti-corruption initiatives—the Kimberley Process (for diamonds), the Extractive Industries Transparency Initiative (EITI), and the Publish What You Pay Initiative—aim to increase revenue accountability through full corporate and government disclosure (table 4.6). Although these are voluntary measures, several African countries—sponsored by the APRM—have signed up to one or more initiatives (UNECA, 2009a).

Table 4.6

International initiatives against corruption in the extractive industries, African signatories

	Kimberley Process	Publish What You Pay	EITI
Objectives	Launched in 2000, the Kimberley Process promotes transparency and accountability in the diamond trade, specifically stopping the illicit trade used by rebel movements. The certification scheme requires member States to certify that diamonds mined within their borders are conflict free	An initiative launched in 2006 by Global Witness, the Catholic Agency for Overseas Development, the Open Society Institute and Oxfam, the aim is to improve transparency and accountability for revenue generated from natural resource rents	Launched in 2002, EITI is an independent, internationally agreed voluntary standard for creating transparency in the payments made by companies and revenues received by governments related to exploitation of extractive resources, such as oil, gas and minerals
Member countries	Of the 48 members, 17 are African: Angola, Botswana, Central African Republic, Democratic Republic of the Congo, Côte d'Ivoire, Namibia, Sierra Leone, South Africa, Tanzania, Togo and Zimbabwe	Chad, Republic of Congo, Democratic Republic of the Congo, Côte d'Ivoire, Gabon, Guinea, Liberia, Mali, Niger, Nigeria, Sierra Leone and Zambia	Cameroon, Chad, Republic of Congo, Democratic Republic of the Congo, Equatorial Guinea, Gabon, Ghana, Guinea, Liberia, Madagascar, Mali, Mauritania, Niger, Nigeria, Sao Tome and Principe and Sierra Leone

Source: Compiled from UNECA (2009).

The responsibility for putting the necessary governance framework for natural resources into place rests with African governments. Their laws must ensure that concessions are awarded on merit in a transparent way, and that activities undertaken do not undermine environmental sustainability, or lead to instability and conflict (African Union, 2007). In the case of non-renewable resources, such as minerals, the framework should ensure that up- and downstream development activities ensure sustainability and protect the interests of local communities.

Moreover, governments must also ensure that the stream of revenues produced by such investment is properly accounted for in national budgets (Global Witness, 2007). If revenues are channelled into investment in infrastructure, education and social programmes, they are likely to play a major part in inducing structural change and laying the foundations for high and robust growth.

The key challenge for governments is how to put a transparent system in place for managing and using resource wealth, with the full participation of community groups and other stakeholders (Revenue Watch Institute & Publish What You Pay, 2006; Transparency International, 2008). This is primarily an issue of governance. If resource-rich countries are governed properly, and if they invest the windfall from resource rents into sovereign wealth funds, they could become important sources of development finance for their resource-poor neighbours.

4.7 Conclusions and policy recommendations

SUSTAINING THE CURRENT growth momentum in Africa and unleashing the continent's productive capacity requires innovative and bold actions on the following fronts.

Improving political and economic governance

Entrenching good governance principles and practices is a precondition for Africa's development. African governments should therefore continue their efforts to deepen democratic governance by improving people's participation in the political process, promoting free and fair elections, and strengthening accountability and transparency in decision-making. Combating corruption and inefficiency should be accorded top priority by governments. It is particularly crucial that they create a policy environment supportive of entrepreneurship and private sector development by reducing the cost of doing business.

Repurposing education for development

The educational system in Africa should assign greater emphasis to science and technology and to entrepreneurship training, which will help to unlock Africa's productive potential. African universities must be placed centre stage to become catalysts for technological change.

Reversing underinvestment in infrastructure

Investment in critical infrastructure is a necessary condition for unlocking productive capacity. Given the financing gap though, African governments should take extra measures to galvanize the domestic banking and insurance sector, the stock market and pension funds in order to mobilize the necessary resources for infrastructure development. Such measures should be complemented by efforts to attract FDI from emerging economies, such as China and India. Governments should also take measures to get more out of existing infrastructure investments through efficiency gains.

Boosting productivity in agriculture

No country has moved up the technological ladder without first developing agriculture. It is therefore imperative that African governments invest more in agricultural research and farm technology to increase productivity and enable farmers to move into producing more remunerative, high-valued products. These steps must be backed by policies to expand non-agricultural employment through public works programmes and rural industrialization in food processing and packaging.

Accelerating regional integration and intra-African trade

Regional integration is an important first step towards global integration, and requires better links between countries—from paved roads to banking cooperation—to spur mutual economic growth. African governments should therefore give a push to developing trade-related regional infrastructure by encouraging private sector participation (domestic and foreign) in infrastructure—while not omitting to strengthen the skills of their negotiators. They should also upgrade regional banking services to facilitate payment mechanisms. Finally, governments must redouble their efforts to simplify procedures and harmonize policies in a wide range of areas such as customs, border control and cargo inspection.

Harnessing new development partnerships

African governments should ensure that the emerging powers' trade, investment and financial flows support Africa's structural transformation, capital accumulation and technological progress. They should particularly encourage investments in infrastructure and agri-businesses. Moreover, the governments of resource-rich African countries should develop strong governance frameworks for extractive industries to stamp out corruption and avoid the problem of the "resource curse"—a theme of the next chapter.

References

Adesina, J.O. 2007. *Social policy in sub-Saharan African context: in search of inclusive development*. Basingstoke, UK: Palgrave Macmillan.

Africa Business. 2008. "Africa-wide pool of winners scoops the 2nd African Banker." Africa Business, November.

AfDB (African Development Bank). 2002. *African Development Report 2002: rural development for poverty reduction in Africa*. Tunis.

AfDB and UNECA (United Nations Economic Commission for Africa). 2006. "Infrastructure development and regional integration: problems, opportunities and challenges." Joint note. Sirte, Libya.

AfDB, OECD (Organisation for Economic Co-operation and Development), UNDP

(United Nations Development Programme), and UNECA. 2011. *African Economic Outlook 2011*. Paris: OECD Publishing.

AUC (African Union Commission). 2003. *Maputo Declaration on food security*. Addis Ababa.

_____. 2006. "Declaration of the Abuja Food Security Summit." Abuja, Nigeria, 4–5 December.

_____. 2007. "From the ground up: natural resource governance for reconstruction and sustainable development." PCRD/Workshop/1(II), Lusaka, Zambia 17–19 July.

_____. 2011a. "Boosting intra-Africa trade." Issue paper prepared for the 7th AU Trade Ministers Conference and the 18th Ordinary Session of the AU Assembly of Heads of State and Government, January/February 2012.

_____. 2011b. "Progress with CAADP

AUC, AfDB, and UNECA. 2010. "Framework and guidelines on land policy in Africa." AUC-UNECA-AfDB Consortium, Addis Ababa.

Aina, T.A. 2010. "Beyond reforms: the politics of higher education transformation in Africa." *The African Studies Review* 53 (1): 21–40.

Ajayi, S.I. 2006. "FDI and economic development in Africa." Paper presented at the AfDB/AERC International Conference on Accelerating Africa's Development, Tunis, 22–24 November.

Ake, C. 1996. *Democracy and development in Africa*. Washington, DC: Brookings Institution Press.

Arkhangelskaya, A. 2010. "India, Brazil and South Africa Dialogue Forum: a bridge between three continents—challenges, achievements and policy options." NAI Policy Notes Issue 8. Nordic Africa Institute, Uppsala, Sweden.

Benin, S., A. Kennedy, M. Lambert, and L. McBride. 2010. "Monitoring African agricultural development processes and performance: a comparative analysis." ReSAKSS Annual Trends Outlook Report. International Food Policy Research Institute, Washington, DC.

Boston Consulting Group. 2010. *The African challengers: global competitors emerge from the overlooked continent*. Boston: Boston Consulting Group.

Brinkerhoff, J. 2006. "Diasporas, skills transfer, and remittances: evolving perceptions and potential." In *Converting migration drains into gains: harnessing the resources of overseas professionals*, ed. C. Wescott and J. Brinkerhoff, 127–153. Manila: Asian Development Bank: Manila.

Bruce, J.W., and Z. Li. 2009. "Crossing the river while feeling the rocks: incremental land reform and its impact on rural welfare in China." Discussion Paper

926. International Food Policy Research Institute, Washington, DC.

Buys, P., U. Deichmann, and D. Wheeler. 2006. "Road network upgrading and overland trade expansion in sub-Saharan Africa." Policy Research Working Paper 4097. World Bank, Washington, DC.

Chambers, R. 1991. "The state and rural development: ideologies and an agenda for the 1990s." IDS Discussion Paper 269. University of Sussex, Sussex, UK.

Chen, V. 2010. "Chinese participation in infrastructure development in Africa." Note submitted to the OECD-DAC China Study Group, Beijing, 19–20 September.

Cheru, F., and C. Obi. 2010. *The rise of China and India in Africa: challenges, opportunities and critical interventions.* London: ZED Books.

Cheru, F., and R. Modi, eds. 2012a. *Agricultural development and food security in Africa: the impact of Chinese, Indian and Brazilian investments.* London: ZED/Palgrave.

Cheru, F., and R. Modi, eds. 2012b. *Promoting food security through South–South cooperation: the role of India, China and Brazil.* London: ZED Press.

China-DAC Study Group. 2010. "Economic transformation and poverty reduction: how it happened in China: helping it happen in Africa." Main findings and summaries, Beijing, 8 June.

Deininger, K., Ayalew, D.A., Holden, S., Zevenberger, J., 2007. Rural Land Certification in Ethiopia: process, initial impact and implications for other African countries, Washington, DC: World Bank

Edigheji, O., ed. 2010. *Constructing a democratic developmental state in South Africa: potentials and challenges.* Cape Town, South Africa: HSRC Press.

Ehui, S., and E. Tsigas. 2006. "Identifying agricultural research and development investment opportunities in Sub-Saharan Africa: a global, economy-wide analysis." Paper presented at the International Agricultural Economics Conference, Queensland, Australia, 12–18 August.

Evans, P. 1995. *Embedded autonomy: states and industrial transformation.* Princeton, NJ: Princeton University Press.

Fan, S., B. Nestorova, and T. Olofiniyi. 2010. "China's agricultural and rural development: implications for Africa." Paper presented at the China-DAC Study Group on Agriculture, Food Security and Rural Development, Bamako, Mali, 27–28 April.

FOCAC (Forum for China-Africa Cooperation). 2006. *Beijing Action Plan 2007–2009.* November 2006, www.foac.org/eng/ltda/dscbzjhy/DOC32009/t280369.htm.

Foster, V., and C. Briceño-Garmendia. 2010. *Africa's infrastructure: a time for transformation* Washington, DC: World Bank.

Foster, V., W. Butterfield, C. Chen, and N. Pushak. 2008. "Building bridges: China's growing role as infrastructure financier for sub-Saharan Africa." World Bank- PPIAF, Washington, DC.

Global Witness. 2007. "Make it work: why Kimberley Process Must do more to stop conflict diamonds." www.globalwitness.org.

Government of the Federal Republic of Brazil. 2010. "Brazil and African Countries Cooperation: Opportunities for enhancing smallholder farming productivity through small scale irrigation and rainwater harvesting", Outcome Document of the Brazil-Africa Ministerial Meeting, Brasilia: May 10-12, 2010.

Gyimah-Brempong, K., and P. Ondiege. 2011. "Reforming higher education: access, equity, and financing in Botswana, Ethiopia, Kenya, South Africa and Tunisia." In *The Africa Competitiveness Report 2011,* 39–66. Geneva: World Economic Forum.

Hallward-Driemeier, M. 2011. "Strengthening Women's Entrepreneurship." In *The Africa Competitiveness Report 2011*, 67–88. Geneva: World Economic Forum.

Hoffman, B., and J. Wu. 2009. "Explaining China's development and reforms." Working Paper 50, Commission on Growth and Development, Washington, DC.

IBSA (India-Brazil-South Africa). 2006. "Memorandum of understanding on trilateral cooperation in agriculture and allied fields between the governments of the Republic of India, the Federal Republic of Brazil, and the Republic of South Africa under the India-Brazil-South Africa (IBSA) Dialogue Forum Initiative." Official document signed June 2006.

ILO (International Labour Organization). 2009. *The informal economy in Africa: promoting the transition to formality*. Geneva.

Inderst, G. 2009. "Pension fund investment in infrastructure." OECD Working Papers on Insurance and Private Pensions 32., OECD Publishing, Paris.

Kapur, D. 2001. "Diasporas and technology transfer." *Journal of Human Development* 2 (2): 265–286.

Kuschminder, K., and M. Siegel. 2010. "Diaspora engagement and policy in Ethiopia." Unpublished paper.

Li, X. 2010. "To develop agriculture-led growth and poverty reduction in Tanzania." International Poverty Reduction Center in China and World Bank, July 2010.

Lazonick, W. (2011), Nine Government Investments That Made Us an Industrial

Economic Leader. http://www.newdeal20.org/2011/09/08/nine-government-investments-that-made-us-an-industrial-economic-leader-57814/

Limao, N., and A.J. Venables. 2001. "Infrastructure, geographical disadvantage and transport costs." *World Bank Economic Review* 15 (3): 451–479.

Low, P. S., ed. 2006. *Climate change and Africa*. New York: Cambridge University Press.

Lynch, G., and G. Crawford. 2011. "Democratization in Africa 1990–2010: an assessment." *Democratization* 18 (2): 275–310.

McKinsey Global Institute. 2010. *Lions on the move: the progress and potential of African economies*. Washington, DC.

Miller, T., and K. Holms. 2011. *Index of Economic Freedom: promoting economic opportunity and prosperity*. Washington, DC: The Heritage Foundation.

Mkandawire, T. 2001. "Thinking about developmental states in Africa." *Cambridge Journal of Economics* 25 (3): 289–314.

Mo Ibrahim Foundation. 2011. *2011 Ibrahim Index of African Governance Report*. London.

Ndulu, B. 2006. "Infrastructure, regional integration and growth in sub-Saharan Africa: dealing with the disadvantages of geography and sovereign fragmentation." *Journal of African Economics* (AERC Supplement 2): 212–244.

Nellis, J. 2005. "The evolution of enterprise reform in Africa: from state-owned enterprises to private participation in infrastructure—and back?" Research Paper 117. Fondazione Eni Enrico Mattei, Milan, Italy.

NEPAD (New Partnership for Africa's Development). 2002. *Declara*

OECD-DAC/IPRCC (Organisation for Economic Co-operation and Development–Development Assistance Committee and International Poverty Reduction Center in China). 2010. "Agricultural transformation, growth and poverty reduction." China-DAC Study Group background paper prepared for the international conference on "Agriculture, Food Security and Rural Development," Bamako, Mali, 27–28 April.

Ohno, I., and M. Shimamura. 2007. *Managing the development process and aid: East Asian experience in building central economic agencies.* Tokyo: GRIPS Development Forum.

Okey, M.K.N. 2011. "Institutional reforms, private sector, and economic growth in Africa." Working Paper 2011/140, UNU-WIDER, Helsinki.

Pausewang, S., E. Chole, F. Cheru, and S. Brune, eds. 1990. *Ethiopia: options for rural development.* London: ZED Press

Pietrobelli, C. and Rabellotti, R. (2006), Upgrading in Clusters and Value Chains in Latin

America. The Role of Policies. Inter-American Development Bank, Washington, D.C.

Polanyi, K. (1957), The Great Transformation: The Political and Economic Origins of Our Time, London: Beacon Press

Ramachandran, V., A. Gelb, and M.K. Shah. 2009. *Africa's private sector: what's wrong with the business environment and what to do about it.* Washington, DC: Center for Global Development.

Ratha, D., and S. Ketkar. 2007. "Development finance via diaspora bonds: track records and potentials." Policy Research Working Paper 4311. World Bank, Washington, DC.

Ravallion, M. 2009. "Are there lessons from China's success against poverty?" *World Development* 37 (2): 303–313.

Revenue Watch Institute & Publish What You Pay. 2006. *Eye on EITI: civil society perspectives and recommendations on the Extractive Industries Transparency Initiative.* New York: Revenue Watch Institute.

Sen, A. 1999. *Development as freedom.* New York: Oxford University Press.

Shendy, R., Z. Kaplan, and P. Mousley. 2011. *Toward better infrastructure: conditions, constraints, and opportunities in financing public-private partnerships in selected African countries.* World Bank: Washington, DC.

Standing, A. 2007. "Corruption and extractive industries in Africa: can combating corruption cure resource curse?" Institute for Security Studies Paper 153, Pretoria.

Transparency International. 2008. *Promoting revenue transparency: report on revenue transparency and oil and gas companies.* Berlin: Transparency International.

Twentyman, J. 2011. "Financial inclusion proves both worthy and profitable." *Financial Times*, 20 September.

UNCTAD (United Nations Conference on Trade and Development). 2005 *Economic Development in Africa 2005: rethinking the role of foreign direct investment.* Geneva: United Nations.

_____. 2007. *Economic Development in Africa Report 2007: reclaiming policy space—domestic resource mobilization and developmental states.* Geneva: United Nations.

_____. 2009a. *The Least Developed Countries Report 2009: the state and development governance.* New York and Geneva: United Nations.

_____. 2009b. *Enhancing the role of domestic financial resources in Africa's development: a policy handbook.* Geneva: United Nations.

_____. 2009c. *Economic Development in Africa Report 2009: strengthening regional integration for Africa's development.* Geneva: United Nations.

_____. 2009d. "The role of south–south and triangular cooperation for sustainable agriculture development and food security in developing countries." Note by the UNCTAD secretariat, TD/B/C.II/MEM.2/5, Geneva, 14–16 December.

UNECA (United Nations Economic Report on Africa). 2005. *Africa Governance Report I: striving for good governance in Africa*. Addis Ababa.

_____. 2006. *Economic Report on Africa 2006: capital flows and development financing in Africa*. Addis Ababa.

_____. 2007a. *Economic Report on Africa 2007: accelerating Africa's development through diversification*. Addis Ababa.

_____. 2007b. "Fostering agricultural transformation for food security, economic growth and poverty reduction." Twenty-sixth Meeting of the Committee of Experts, Addis Ababa, 29 March–1 April.

_____. 2009. *Africa Governance Report II, 2009*. Oxford, UK: Oxford University Press.

_____. 2010. *Assessing Regional Integration in Africa IV: enhancing intra-Africa trade*. Addis Ababa.

_____. 2011. *Africa Youth Report 2011: addressing the youth education and employment nexus in the new global economy*. Addis Ababa.

UNECA and AUC. 2009. *Economic Report on Africa 2009: developing African agriculture through regional value chain*. Addis Ababa.

_____. 2011. *Economic Report on Africa 2011: governing development in Africa—the role of the state in economic transformation*. Addis Ababa.

Utting, Peter (ed.) 2006, Reclaiming Development Agenda: Knowledge, power and international policy-making, UNRISD/Palgrave Macmillan: Basingstoke

Vagliasindi, M., and J. Nellis. 2009. "Evaluating Africa's experience with institutional reform for the infrastructure sectors." Working Paper 23. World Bank, Africa Infrastructure Sector Diagnostic, Washington, DC.

Verick, S. 2006. "The impact of globalization on the informal sector in Africa." www.iza.org/conference_files/worldb2006/verick_s872.pdf.

Wade, R. 2004. *Governing the market: economic theory and the role of governments in East Asian Development*. Princeton, NJ: Princeton University Press.

World Bank. 2007. *World Development Report 2008: agriculture for development*. Washington, DC.

_____. 2010.

_____. 2011a. *World Development Report 2012: gender equality and development*. Washington, DC.

_____. 2011b. *Doing Business 2012: doing business in a transparent world*. Washington, DC.

WEF (World Economic Forum). 2011. *Africa Competitiveness Report 2011*. Geneva.

Xaba, J., P. Horn, and S. Motola. 2002. "The informal sector in Sub-Saharan Africa: working paper on the informal economy." International Labour Organization, Geneva.

Zeleza, P.T., and A. Olukoshi, eds. 2004. *African universities in the twenty-first century*, Volumes 1 and 2. Dakar: CODESRIA.

Notes

1   See chapter 2 on other aspects of investment in people including health and other MDG and social development targets.

2   The NEPAD Short-Term Action Plan, the NEPAD Medium-to-Long Term Strategic Framework and the AU Infrastructure Master Plan.

3   This includes costs associated with under-collection of revenues and uncounted distribution losses.

4   Including Benin, Democratic Republic of the Congo, Ethiopia, Ghana, Guinea and Kenya.

5   As well as the value added of the associated technology transfer (Wade, 2004).

Mobilizing Resources for Structural Transformation

5

DESPITE THE UPTURN in Africa's economic fortunes in the new millennium, the failure of African economies—resource-rich and resource-poor alike—to diversify commodity-dependent structures has prevented them escaping from persistent fragility. Their growth prospects, and hence, capacity for resource mobilization, remain vulnerable to external shocks.[1]

The commodity boom has not yet succeeded in generating strong positive, economy-wide spill-over effects to other sectors within resource-rich countries or to resource-poor countries on a visible, continent-wide scale. Resource-poor and income-poor countries are heavily constrained by their meagre capacity to mobilize domestic resources as well as attract external resources—apart from official aid flows sustaining a minimum level of investment that prevents the development process from stalling altogether.

Governments face a range of challenges stemming from foreign investment activity. A fair share of the natural resource rents does not go to host countries but rather to the multinational enterprises (MNEs)—as do the benefits of productivity improvements stemming from FDI, instead of to the fragmented producers and farmers. Equally, domestic firms too often miss out on skill and technology transfer and productivity spillovers from FDI. Portfolio capital in resource-rich economies is very volatile, rendering it unsuitable as stable, development finance. Finally, high levels of informality, a shallow tax base and the unbalanced tax mix (often grounded in a heavy reliance on resource or trade taxes, including excessive tax preferences to MNEs), limit a country's domestic resource base.

For the resource-rich countries specifically, the challenge—as long as the commodity boom continues—is not so much how to mobilize external resources, but how to manage the flood of investment. Their windfall should be deployed purposely to help diversify and transform economic structures, including distributing resource rents for ensuring an inclusive growth pattern. Highly competent macroeconomic management over the commodity price cycle is required to avoid Dutch disease and to use resource rents for structural transformation.

The policy challenge shared by all African countries is therefore how to deploy resources for advancing the socio-economic development agenda, mainly because Africa's growth over the last three decades has not translated into meaningful job creation and poverty reduction.

The commodity boom has not yet succeeded in generating strong, positive, economy-wide spillover effects to other sectors.

One strand in meeting this challenge is to take a strategic position with all types of external actors and investors—traditional aid donors, new development partners from emerging economies, MNEs and private stock market investors, even workers abroad sending remittances. It is important to concentrate efforts on deepening financial markets and strengthening institutional capacity so that mobilized funds are effectively intermediated and used for productive investments and socio-economic development. This may entail new financial instruments, as well as substantial changes in public resource management to address at core the structural weaknesses in domestic public resource mobilization.

Policymakers should address these pressing challenges by taking advantage of new opportunities for bringing about structural transformation through improved mechanisms for mobilization, use, and distribution of resources, in order to create a foundation for inclusive growth.

5.1 The need for resources

AFRICA'S RESURGENCE (see chapters 2 and 3) is raising hopes that Africa will finally emerge from its status as a fragile continent, despite its discouraging growth trends. Not only is Africa blessed with rich natural resources, but its demographic trend—a youthful workforce—is favourable. The continent embraces a heterogeneous group of countries in natural resources, per capita income and other socio-political and economic characteristics. This diversity is reflected in the varying capacities across countries for raising financial resources for economic development, including the domestic resource gap—the distance between domestic savings and investment, much of which is met by external funding.

New financial instruments and substantial changes in public resource management are needed to address structural weaknesses in domestic public resource mobilization.

Savings and investment ratios have varied considerably over time (figure 5.1). In sub-Saharan Africa, the gross domestic savings ratio declined sharply from over 25 per cent in 1980 to 13 per cent in 1992 and stayed just above 15–16 per cent until 2009. The gross capital formation ratio followed a similar sharp downward trend from 25 per cent in 1980 to 16 per cent in 1992–1993 and stayed in the 16–18 per cent range for a decade before gradually increasing to 20–21 per cent in 2008–2009. In these early decades, foreign funds, mainly ODA, used to fill the domestic resource gap of about 3 per cent of GDP. The rise in investment after 2002–2003 reflects reviving economic growth, although external flows filled a domestic resource gap that widened from 3 per cent in 2003 to 6 per cent in 2008, as domestic savings did not increase enough.

Both savings and investment climbed markedly in sub-Saharan Africa by 2–3 percentage points in 2010, after experiencing a small reduction in 2009, marking a faster recovery from the global crisis among African economies (and other developing regions) than among developed countries. It is too early though to assume that this trend will continue in 2012 or beyond (see chapter 1).

Figure 5.1

Gross domestic savings and gross capital formation in Africa, 1980–2010 (% of GDP)

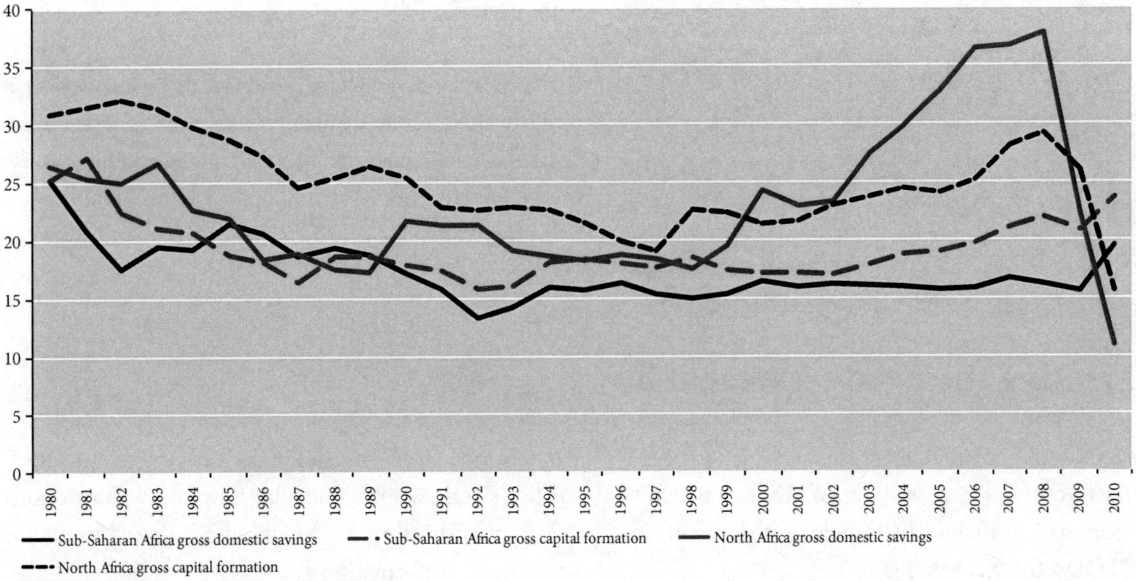

Source: World Bank and UNECA dataset, 2011.

Mainly because of differences in resource endowments and incomes, wide differences in aggregate savings and investment ratios stand out among country groups and subregions, particularly in low-income countries and in West Africa where savings ratios are around 2–6 per cent and investment ratios 5–9 per cent. These should be compared with the ECA estimate that for Africa to grow at 7 per cent a year—necessary to achieve the MDGs—the continent needs to maintain an investment rate of 33 per cent (UNECA, 1999).

In North Africa, too, these ratios experienced a steady decline through the 1980s to the late 1990s (see figure 5.1). The reduction in investment was particularly sharp, falling from 32 per cent of GDP in 1980 to 19 per cent in 1997. These two decades were indeed "lost" to economic development in Africa as a whole. Domestic savings in North Africa recovered quickly from the late 1990s, climbing to 38 per cent in 2008. This made North Africa a significant net creditor to the rest of the world, as domestic investment rose to only 30 per cent. Both savings and investment declined in 2010, however, reflecting the political upheavals (see chapter 1).

The recent impressive recovery in capacity to mobilize resources and invest is not seen in all African countries.

A dichotomy of resource-poor and resource-rich countries, dictated by their natural resource endowments, is a characteristic of the continent. Resource- and income-poor countries have been left out, and are still heavily constrained by their meagre capacity to mobilize domestic resources or attract external resources. ODA fills their wide domestic resource gaps, sustaining the minimum investment required to prevent development from stalling.

Certainly, the acceleration in investment and growth over the past decade has been more characteristic of oil- and mineral-rich countries, and is closely associated with the price hike of their commodities on world markets since 2002, buoyed by strong demand from emerging economies. As long as the boom continues, the task facing these countries is not so much how to mobilize resources as how to deploy newly mobilized resources for the structural transformation and diversification of their economies.[3]

Some countries not necessarily regarded as rich in mineral resources, such as Ethiopia, Kenya and Tanzania, have seen rising investment rates, though their domestic savings rates lag behind. Manufacturing and services have begun to attract private capital flows, which indi-

> *Africa has a wealth of opportunities rarely available in its post-independence years, but the challenges of turning optimism into reality are daunting.*

cates that African optimism is spreading to resource-poor countries and to activities not directly connected with minerals.

Africa is now at a critical juncture. It has a wealth of opportunities rarely available in its post-independence years. The challenges facing policymakers on how to use these opportunities—turning optimism into reality—are daunting.

5.2 Meeting the need—external flows

ACCORDING TO AfDB et al., (2011), total external financial flows to Africa increased from $27 billion in 2000 to $126 billion in 2010, and FDI flows for the first time surpassed ODA that decade (figure 5.2).[4]

We now look at the changes in each component of external flows (ODA, FDI, portfolio flows, as well as remittances), largely through the prism of Africa's needs for structural transformation and diversification.

Figure 5.2

FDI and ODA flows to Africa 2000–2011 ($billion)

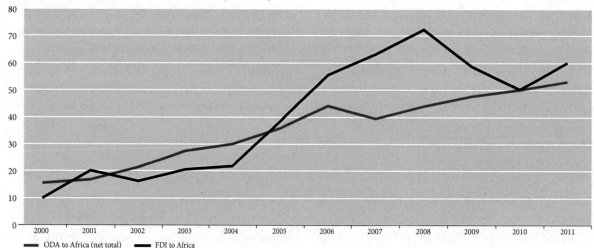

—— ODA to Africa (net total)   —— FDI to Africa

Source: AfDB et al. (2011).

ODA: the shifting ground of aid policy in Africa

Net ODA flows disbursed to all developing countries in 2009 was just more than $127 billion, an increase from around $50 billion in 2000. Africa received net aid flows of more than $45 billion, or 35 per cent (figure 5.3). Sub-Saharan countries received $42.3 billion—the largest share (33 per cent) of total ODA flows—and North African countries received $2.9 billion.[5]

Aid flows to sub-Saharan Africa increased sharply from $12.5 billion in 2000 to $42.3 billion in 2009—over a three-fold increase, though well short of the pledge of "doubling aid to Africa" made at the G-8 Gleneagles conference in the United Kingdom in 2005. Aid to North Africa fluctuated between $2 billion–$3 billion for almost three decades except for 1990–1994 when bilateral dis-

Figure 5.3

Total aid flows to developing regions ($ million)

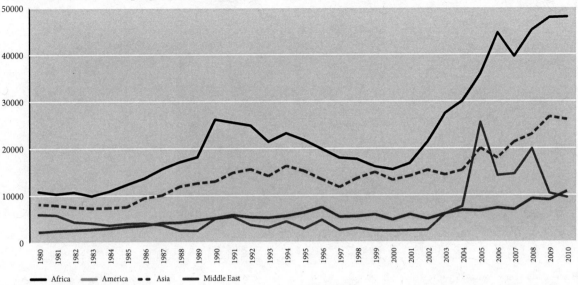

Source: OECD Statistics, 2011.

bursements to Egypt and other countries in North Africa doubled.

Both multilateral institutions and bilateral donors increased official aid to Africa in the past decade, but the sharp spike in aid to Africa in 2005–2006 came mainly from debt cancellation under the Multilateral Debt Reduction Initiative for the HIPCs (figure 5.4).

> *The sharp spike in aid to Africa in 2005-2006 came mainly from debt cancellation under the Multilateral Debt Reduction Initiative for HIPCs.*

Figure 5.4

Aid flows to Africa by type of donor ($ million)

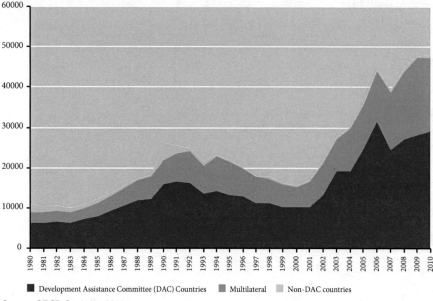

Source: OECD Statistics, 2011.

The grant–loan mix

Gross aid flows to sub-Saharan Africa and to North Africa have been dominated by grants in the last three decades (figure 5.5). In 2009, sub-Saharan Africa received $10.9 billion in loans and $36.1 billion in grants, almost 1:3; a larger share of 37 per cent in loans was disbursed to North Africa. This grant–loan mix, heavily in favour of grants, may partly be explained by recipient govern-ments' preference to avoid accumulating debt-service obligations. In sub-Saharan Africa it may also reflect a conscious decision by donors to eschew a repetition of the protracted debt crisis that stalled progress in socio-economic development in heavily indebted countries for 25 years before its resolution through the Multilateral Debt Reduction Initiative adopted in 2005.

Figure 5.5

Gross aid flows to Africa: loans versus grants ($ million)

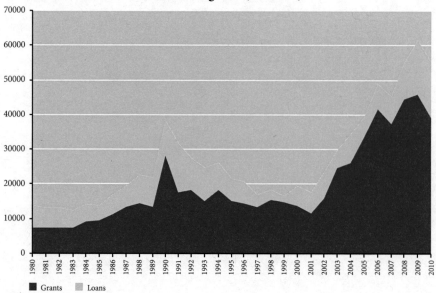

Source: OECD Statistics, 2011.

This section argues that the policy discourse on aid modality between loans and grants is somewhat over-simplistic, if not misguided. In fact, an example of the inappropriateness of such an approach is evident in the practice of the mechanical application of the "traffic light system" for deciding the grant–loan mix in the Debt Sustainability Framework used by the World Bank and IMF in the International Development Association (IDA) aid allocation. The use of properly structured, incentive-compatible loan contracts is technically preferable to outright grants in financing productive investment, with a greater growth dividend recuperated within a reasonable time of debt contracts (Nissanke, 2010b).

We should also consider that, if grants are the only instruments used for aid provision, the size of the overall aid envelope could be limited by the budget constraints that bilateral donor governments and multilateral development agencies face annually. Increasing aid through loans entails lower real costs for donors than providing the same nominal amount of aid as grants (Gunther, 2009). Indeed, the use of concessional loans allows augmentation of the overall aid resource envelope, as governments and agencies can use more funds mobilized through efficient inter-temporal management of their own resources.

An appropriate configuration of the grant–loan mix should thus be decided on, depending on what aid is used for. Many economic infrastructure projects that can alleviate various absorption capacity constraints and other critical supply bottlenecks could, in principle, bring about high growth dividends, faster. Indeed, they can generate high social returns if projects are managed efficiently to create a steady cash flow over a period corresponding to a negotiated debt payment schedule. Hence, for financing these types of projects, concessional loans can be a superior instrument to grants. The real issue for avoiding a protracted debt crisis in future is how to make terms and maturity structures of concessional loan contracts appropriate and generous enough to ensure a steady flow of debt service payment through an efficiently structured, contingent-financing facility that addresses low-income countries' high vulnerability to exogenous shocks.[6]

> *Investment in social infrastructure, such as health and education, would take longer to generate growth dividends.*

Investment in social infrastructure, such as health and education, would take longer to generate growth dividends. Returns to investment in human capital accrue more to individuals, hence widely dispersed, requiring an efficient and progressive tax system to recuperate. The latter takes time for governments to create and administer. Thus, grants can well be a more appropriate instrument of aid for this kind of investment or technical assistance and cooperation. Great care is required in deciding which aid instruments and modalities are appropriate, case by case.

ODA weaknesses in Africa

One might also challenge the basis of some of the key positions taken previously by the donor community in deciding how best ODA should be provided for low-income countries in Africa to overcome developmental bottlenecks. Experience with aid-funded economic infrastructure projects in the 1960s and 1970s was indeed astonishingly dismal in Africa, as many projects were conceived and carried out in an incorrect political-economy context.

For a start, ODA should have never been used for funding many of these politically motivated projects. Also, economic infrastructure projects require strong institutional and political commitment, equipped with dedicated professional management teams and adequate resources for operation and maintenance. Many valuable lessons have been drawn, but these mistakes cannot be used to justify reducing ODA support to economic infrastructure projects altogether. Further, ODA can play a pivotal role in both economic and social infrastructure development in low-income countries, through financial and technical assistance. The need for social infrastructure should not be used as a rationale for drastically curtailing ODA to economic infrastructure development, as happened in Africa in the 1980s and 1990s. Three reasons are put forward.

The first was the failure of many donor- and government-funded infrastructure projects, often dubbed "white elephants". Some of these projects were manifestly "wrong" from inception, as they were motivated almost exclusively by political considerations rather than carefully justified in economic terms. The others failed because of inadequate provision for recurrent and maintenance costs, unrealistic pricing, or prevalence of regulatory forbearance or gross mismanagement. The second reason was the relentless drive of the World Bank and IMF for public divesture, privatization and deregulation across infrastructure sectors in the 1990s. The third was the powerful advocacy for shifting public spending towards social sectors such as health and education, partly due to the deliberations of the Copenhagen Social Summit in 1995.[7]

In fact, it was the rise of a development paradigm emphasizing the virtues of liberalization, deregulation and privatization during the 1980s that had a profound impact on donor aid policy for infrastructure development. The World Development Report 1994 "Infrastructure for Development" is testimony to the dominant position taken by the donor community at the time. Its main recommendations were to "manage infrastructure like a business", "introduce competition" and "give users and other stakeholders a strong voice and real responsibility" (World Bank, 1994: 2). These policy measures had persuasive power in light of some real problems typically found in infrastructure development and management in Africa, such as inefficient operations, inadequate maintenance, fiscal drain, unresponsiveness to user demands and neglect of the poor and the environment.

Thus, reflecting both the shift in the dominant paradigm in the 1980s and these concerns on the ground, the World Bank then advocated greater private sector involvement and full cost recovery in utility provision, resulting in a major decline in donor-financed infrastructure projects in general. The prevailing view was that, once these sectors were deregulated and privatized, private investors would take over and turn around the coverage and quality of infrastructure services.

Yet, this optimism proved unfounded everywhere, particularly in Africa, which had attracted cumulatively just $28.1 billion of private flows for infrastructure investment in 1990–2002, compared with $199.4 billion in East Asia and $397.4 billion in Latin America and the Caribbean. Further, most of the private infrastructure investment in Africa took place in telecommunications (66 per cent) and electricity (18 per cent). Very little went to transport and water. Only a handful of countries in Africa, including South Africa, attracted private capital for running this infrastructure and these utilities in response to privatization initiatives (AfDB, 2006).

These conditions—especially the low private investment in Africa and in transport and water—partly reflect the well-known fact that there is a big wedge between private and social returns in providing utility services in poor areas. The initial sunk costs of infrastructure investment in poor, inaccessible areas are very high, yet cost recovery through pricing and user charges is impossible without commitments of substantial public financial resources, if the target is to improve the poor's access to infrastructure services. Appropriate pricing of services has often been one of the most difficult issues to address in infrastructure reforms.

The public economics literature has long acknowledged that market failure prevails in the presence of externalities. On account of high positive externalities and spillover effects, the provision of infrastructure development and services should be appropriately seen in the domain of public goods provision. Given that social returns are higher than private returns to infrastructure investment and that high risks are involved in large projects with long gestation periods, the public sector should shoulder a large share of financing infrastructure development and service provision in the early stages of economic development.

Yet, during the 1990s, the public sector throughout developing countries heavily cut its contribution to infrastructure development because of factors such as the unfounded optimism that private finance would be made available, the fiscal austerity required in protracted debt crises, and decentralization (that led to mismatches between resources and needs). Particularly in Africa, the sharp fall in domestic public financing (section 5.4) was exacerbated by an equally steep reduction in ODA for economic infrastructure in the 1990s. East Asia and the Pacific was an exception to this global trend, however (box 5.1).

Box 5.1: East Asian ODA for infrastructure: bucking global trends

In East Asia and the Pacific, about four fifths of aid in the last two or three decades has come from bilateral donors, with Japan the main source.[1]

Japan's ODA to the region is concentrated in economic infrastructure development, and the share of infrastructure financing in total aid followed an upward trend from the early 1970s. ODA for economic infrastructure and water-related infrastructure accounted for two thirds of infrastructure financing in the 1980s and 1990s. Public goods provision in economic infrastructure has thus been consistently higher in East Asia than in other developing areas. The contrast is sharpest between East Asia and Africa.

The East Asian experience unequivocally points to the central role of infrastructure provision in economic development. Financing infrastructure investment as public goods and strengthening State capacity to deliver infrastructure services sustainably are prerequisites for spurring and sustaining private initiatives and investment.

1. See Nissanke (2007) for further discussion.

In Africa, an inevitable correction to the damaging cull of infrastructure financing began by the mid-2000s, once donors identified infrastructure deficiencies as a critical gap in economic development. Given the continent's geographical disadvantages as one of the most binding growth constraints, the need for massive infrastructure investment was officially recognized as crucial for accelerating economic and productivity growth as well as for reducing poverty. This unfortunate delay reflected the unhealthy situation that has evolved since the early 1980s, whereby much of Africa's development agenda is set by donors, in particular IFIs.[8]

This belated official recognition—see, for example, the Commission for Africa Report (2005)—has entailed a

heavy cost in forgone economic growth and poverty reduction. Given the enormous infrastructure deficit, in its call for an immediate doubling of ODA to Africa to $50 billion a year, the Commission believed that about half of ODA should be spent on building infrastructure. The most recent estimate suggests that the cost of addressing Africa's needs in physical infrastructure is about $93 billion a year, some 15 per cent of Africa's GDP. About two thirds of this is needed for greenfield and rehabilitation investments, and the other third for maintaining current infrastructure.[9] Will a new development paradigm—South–South cooperation—be any better than the approach of the traditional donors?

Working with new development partners

China and other emerging economies such as Brazil, India, Korea, Turkey, Malaysia and capital-rich countries in the Middle East have increased aid and investment in Africa, offering a new kind of development partnership based on South–South cooperation.[10] Indeed, trade between Africa and its new development partners has increased at a phenomenal pace over the past decade, lead-

ing to a marked reduction in the share of the traditional partners from Europe and North America in the continent's trade and foreign investment.[11] In 2009, China's share in Africa's total trade with emerging partners was about 38 per cent, India's 14 per cent, and Brazil, Korea and Turkey each accounted for about 7 per cent (AfDB et al., 2011).

The emergence of China and other economies as new economic partners for Africa has attracted widespread attention and debate, receiving mixed reactions in policy circles around the world. Though the actual amount of aid provided by non-traditional partners to Africa is still small relative to the volumes from the traditional donors (that is, the members of the OECD-DAC), it has been increasing quickly.

The form of engagement among new partners varies (see chapter 4). For example, while Brazil focuses more on agriculture and agro-processing, a large proportion of India's aid, which has expanded alongside FDI and trade, is provided as technical assistance. India is active in learning, skills-intensive areas and services. At the first India–Africa Forum Summit in 2008,[12] India came up with new major initiatives including the Pan-African e-Network Project, the Techno-Economic Approach for the Africa-India Movement as well as Special Commonwealth African Assistance Programmes.

Saudi Arabia is reported to have provided Africa with $5.5 billion in gross ODA in 2008, using the Saudi Fund for Development to finance investment projects through concessional loans for transport and energy infrastructure. It allocated 28 per cent of its loans to countries in sub-Saharan Africa. Arab and Islamic funding institutions in aggregate are reported to have invested $2.4 billion in 2008 and $1.7 billion in 2009, in African infrastructure.[13] As a new member of the OECD-DAC, the Republic of Korea is now aligning its aid policy with those of other DAC members.

Yet, it is the form of China's engagement in Africa as well as its sudden surge in activities and the timing of its "re-turn" to Africa that has attracted perhaps the most commentary worldwide.[14]

The China card

China's aid is available without any policy conditionality attached, on the basis of a "coalition" engagement (a collaborative State–business approach through aid, trade and investment as a package). Though details of different components in the package are difficult to tease out, China's economic activities in Africa in aggregate have been expanding faster since 2001. In 2001–2008, bilateral trade is reported to have increased 10-fold, while total Chinese investment in Africa is estimated to have reached $26 billion by the end of 2008, according to a Chinese source.[15] China's pledge to double aid within three years (2007–2009), made at the summit meeting of the third Forum for China–Africa Cooperation in Beijing in 2006 was fulfilled, despite the global crisis. China has also agreed debt relief or cancellation with 31 African countries. At the last forum in November 2009, it made a new pledge to double its concessional loans to Africa to $10 billion in the next three years, while setting aside $1 billion for loans to SMEs in Africa.

So far, one of the main focuses of China's aid has been on building economic infrastructure, now universally seen as critical to Africa's future, and that contribution is also highly visible. Even with issues encountered in implementation, the country is rapidly expanding its areas of cooperation, going beyond natural resources and infrastructure through the "Angola Mode" to agriculture and sectors such as telecommunications and water, as well as to soft infrastructure projects such as building hospitals and schools. A raft of new financial institutions and facilities has also been created, including the China Development Bank. More than 90 per cent of China's infrastructure projects are still financed by preferential loans from the EX-IM Bank, but some, such as road activities in Botswana and Ethiopia, are now funded by the Ministry of Commerce, which has begun providing investment and trade credit financing.[16]

Large State companies from China may dominate big infrastructure projects and resource extraction sectors, but some private companies have become active in various sectors. With official financial support initially avail-

> *The emergence of China and other economies as new economic partners for Africa has attracted widespread attention and debate.*

able through the China–Africa Fund, an ever-increasing number of small, privately run firms have been setting up in manufacturing and services across the continent, especially in Nigeria and South Africa.[17] These private firms operate mainly outside the close circle of Chinese Government supervision and monitoring. Private firms, initially assisted by concessional loans, have also been told to wean themselves financially off State help.

Private commercial banks, such as the China Merchant Bank and the Industrial and Commercial Bank of China, which acquired a 20 per cent stake in South Africa's Standard Bank in 2007, have started playing a pivotal role in providing commercial loans to a growing number of Chinese private entrepreneurs in Africa. China's State credit insurance agency—Sinosure—has become active in offering cover for country and credit risks.

Chinese–African economic relationships are, in short, complicated, spanning numerous activities and actors, evolving constantly as a critical part of China's overall going-out strategy.

In agriculture, China has targeted its aid at increasing productivity by sending large numbers of experts and setting up extension centres for sharing and transferring technology. African farmers are reported to prefer farming machinery from China to that from the West as it offers technology that is simple and easy to operate. Yet, China's domestic considerations and imperatives sometimes appear to impose themselves also on engagement with Africa in agriculture. For example, there has been a big push for Chinese farmers to focus on opening new lands for plantations in Africa. What lies behind this initiative is reported to be China's own need to relocate the farmers displaced through the dual pressures of WTO trade liberalization and its rapid urbanization, as well as its eyeing Africa as a source of future supply for its own food security. This move has inevitably produced a backlash against large Chinese investments in agriculture.

African smallholders see such initiatives as a threat to traditional farming, dubbing them land grabs.

Overall, aid in a package deal with expanded investment and trade from China (and other new partners), without policy conditionality and cumbersome negotiations, has added impetus to African development against the chequered history of aid relationships with traditional bilateral donor countries and multilateral institutions. The emerging partners' stance offers African countries an opportunity to gain the policy space that is desperately needed for exploring their own path of economic development. It could, potentially, even help to bring to maturity Africa's nascent democracy if it makes African policymakers accountable for policy reforms to their citizens, not just to donors.

Finally, because aid and investment flows from new development partners have targeted not only critical bottlenecks in African economic development—infrastructure and agriculture—but also new activities and sectors—services and manufacturing—there is hope that such engagement could alleviate these bottlenecks, realize the structural transformation of economies and share benefits from economic globalization, in a sustainable manner. For this to become reality, African policymakers have to take proactive, strategic positions in their economic relationships with emerging partners as these partners are engaging in Africa undoubtedly driven by their own business and economic interests.

> *African policymakers have to take proactive strategic positions with emerging partners in their economic relationships.*

Private capital flows

The surge in interest in resource-rich Africa from new partners and creditors has had other tangible "leverage-in effects" from international investors, unseen before in Africa. For the first time, private investors are increasing-ly taking Africa seriously as one of their key destinations. Net flows of FDI and portfolio investment (equity and bonds) to Africa for 1990–2010 are given in figure 5.6.

Figure 5.6

Net private capital flows to Africa, 1990–2010 ($ million)

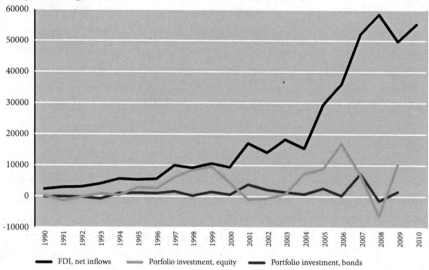

Source: World Bank (2011a).

Foreign Direct investment

FDI to African countries peaked in 2008 at $72 billion—a five-fold increase from 2000 and from just $2 billion in 1990—falling to $59 billion in 2009 and to $50–$52 billion in 2010, owing to the global financial crisis (figure 5.6). FDI now accounts for 20 per cent of gross capital formation in Africa, much higher than in other developing regions (AfDB et al., 2011).

> *Africa still attracts largely natural resource-based FDI or FDI geared toward the lower end of the global value chains of MNEs.*

Africa still attracts largely natural resource–based FDI or FDI geared towards the lower end of the global value chains of MNEs, such as simple assembly-line operations. FDI in the garment industry in Africa is an example of "foot-loose" FDI, attracted by temporary conditions such as preferential market access granted through the African Growth and Opportunity Act (AGOA) or protections accorded under the Multifibre Arrangement before it expired in 2005. These sectors and activities are characterized by fewer dynamic externalities and knowledge spillovers than in other developing regions. Only some of the very recent FDI in new knowledge- and technology-intensive sectors—such as telecommunications, ICT and solar-panel production, or biotechnology-based agricultural products—have raised hopes for a new generation of FDI activities that are local market–based and can therefore be locked firmly with commitments to Africa's future.

In considering the strategic position that the host countries should take to derive maximum developmental benefits from FDI, one should recognize wide asymmetries in market power and access to information, technology and other intangible knowledge assets between MNEs on the one hand, and local entrepreneurs, farmers and traders in developing countries on the other. Indeed, contemporary "corporate-led" globalization has eroded the capacity of governments to raise revenues for redistributional purposes or to enact regulations to protect and enhance labour rights or protect the local environment, for fear of driving away MNEs or capital. This is reflected in the MNE dominance in commodity and value chains of traded goods, as well as in observed conditions such as the sharp decline in real wages in export processing zones.

In such global conditions, the benefits of productivity improvements, instead of going to the fragmented producers and farmers, are largely appropriated by MNEs and global supermarket chains. This has resulted in a hugely skewed distribution of gains from global trade and direct investment, pointing to the need to improve the negotiating positions of governments in developing countries vis-à-vis MNEs—in a strategic, targeted approach to FDI—so that FDI can facilitate skills and technology transfer and generate strong productivity spillovers that also benefit domestic firms.[18]

More specifically, given that most FDI is attracted to Africa by its rich deposits of oil, minerals and other metals, we cannot expect dynamic externalities (through market-based channels) such as the generation of significant forward and backward linkages between upstream and downstream industries, as is the case in manufacturing or services. Hence, the issue of how to manage and distribute resource rents through macroeconomic policy configuration and fiscal mechanisms should take a central place in policy discussions in natural resource-based economies.

There is a need to ensure that a fair share of the resource rents accrues to host countries in the first place—thus, the question of how to conduct negotiations on resource rents with MNEs, becomes critical. In Africa, the position of governments weakened sharply after mineral concerns were privatized in the 1990s, and in an ownership structure dominated by MNEs policy space for autonomous fiscal and monetary management—in bringing about short-run stabilization as well as long-run economic development through fiscal mechanisms—is heavily curtailed. Owing to differences in privatization programmes negotiated with MNE conglomerates, Zambia, for example, found itself in a much less favourable position than Chile in distributing and using mineral rents.[19] Given the public outcry over unfair tax regimes for mineral rents negotiated under earlier secret deals, the Zambian Government was in the end forced in 2008 to renegotiate the initial fiscal concessions accorded to MNEs.

Negotiations between MNEs and host countries on fiscal and tax regimes conducted in secret tend to produce outcomes strongly favouring MNEs, because host countries, too fearful of losing the MNE interested in their location, offer unnecessarily generous fiscal concessions such as tax holidays or lower taxes and royalty payments. Indeed, asymmetric access to information on MNE global strategy and little transparency in negotiations have often prompted competing host governments to "race to the bottom".

Yet, fiscal concessions may not be one of the top criteria for MNE investment-location decisions, compared with other fundamental issues such as the size of the potential national and regional markets or the skills level of workers (with horizontal and vertical integration), the quality or other technical properties of natural resource deposits (with resource-based FDI) or general political and economic stability. For this reason, policymakers need to focus on improving these fundamental conditions in order to influence MNE decisions on where to invest. As chapters 3 and 4 showed, there are numerous other factors as well, including the institutional environment, economic and social infrastructure, and technological capabilities. All these need to be upgraded not only for investment promotion, but also for laying a solid, wider foundation for socio-economic development.

Over the past decade, African governments have taken many investment promotion and liberalization measures to attract foreign investors, with an emphasis on creating "an enabling environment for doing business" in policy

> *The quality of governance over the domestic distribution of resource rents makes a huge difference to the development of resource-based economies.*

discussions led by the IFIs. These measures include reducing transaction costs by cutting unnecessarily cumbersome bureaucratic paper work and strengthening regulatory systems. These measures are naturally important for facilitating private investment generally, by foreign or domestic investors.

However, there is a question mark over the "additionality" in investment flows entailed in various attempts at luring foreign investors by granting too generous fiscal incentives. Aarsnes and Pöyry (2010) argue for more transparency and for host countries to move away from agreements with individual MNEs signed behind closed doors. They stress the merits of establishing open, general, transparent non-negotiable fiscal terms enacted directly in tax law, as in most developed countries. In particular, they recommend that host countries have tax systems and rates that are neutral relative to the MNE home countries or have clear benchmarks for comparable countries in the case of capturing resource rents. Their proposal is specifically intended to avoid unnecessary fiscal competition and to reduce incentives for MNEs to use illicit transfer-pricing mechanisms for repatriating profits.[20]

Finally, there is no doubt that the quality of governance over the domestic distribution of resource rents makes huge a difference to the development of resource-based economies. In fact, the use of resource rents for sustainable economic development is likely to require the formation of a developmental State through a real public–private sector alliance in the name of broad–based, inclusive, socio-economic development.[21]

Portfolio flows

Private portfolio flows to Africa are much smaller than FDI flows (see figure 5.6). South Africa is the dominant destination, taking about 80 per cent of Africa's total, and Egypt comes next. Mauritius is known to be the most active portfolio investor in intra-African portfolio investments (AfDB et al., 2011). With increased private capital flows over recent years, Africa's asset–liability positions with the rest of the world and its debt profile and dynamics may change greatly. In particular, if these flows are properly deployed in productive investment with substantial growth dividends, the absorptive capacity of capital flows and the debt-carrying capacity of African economies could be enhanced.

However, portfolio flows are characterized by very high volatility and are pro-cyclical (see figure 5.6). These charts show net portfolio flows, which already cancel out the extreme volatility exhibited in gross flows. Further, portfolio flows in contemporary financial globalization are more diversification finance (conducted through asset swapping for risk hedging and shedding by financial investors to achieve maximum risk-adjusted returns to asset holders) than development finance, the case under the early phase of globalization in the late nineteenth and start of the twentieth centuries. Mediated through very high-frequency trading activities, portfolio flows are viewed rightly as "hot money".

The pro-cyclicality of portfolio flows is driven by fast changes in investor liquidity preferences and risk appetites or aversion. Hence, the potentially detrimental effects of sudden cross-border movements on the stability of macroeconomic conditions and on domestic asset prices raise serious policy concerns. It is by now well acknowledged that financial globalization proceeded without a proper global governance structure, including an internationally coordinated system of regulation and supervision of the activities of financial institutions. Furthermore, cross-border capital flows are the main culprit for developing unsustainable global macro imbalances and periodical financial crises.

As newcomers to international capital markets, policymakers in Africa can draw many valuable lessons on how to manage cross-border portfolio flows from the experiences of emerging economies in other regions which adopted a regime of full capital-account convertibility earlier. In fact, the best approach for African countries may well be to concentrate efforts on deepening financial markets and strengthening the capacity of financial institutions, rather than on courting international investors excessively out of eagerness to mobilize additional resources.

Remittance flows, and flights of financial and human capital

Given the growing size of workers' remittances to Africa, how can they be used better (UNECA and AUC, 2011) note that remittances represented the most important source of capital flows to Africa after FDI in 2010, equivalent to about 7 per cent of African GDP. Cape Verde, Gambia, Morocco, Nigeria, Senegal and Togo receive some of the larger flows as a share of GDP.

Workers' remittances accrue to private citizens, and are used for various purposes, including: keeping current consumption over subsistence levels among poor households; attending to medical conditions of household members; investing in children's education, nutrition and health; building private housing; and starting and expanding businesses. These uses contribute to socio-economic development, but are not centrally mobilized and are intermediated through informal channels and financial systems to the hands and accounts of the recipients.

Developmental benefits would stem from increased income and enhanced savings from remittances, preferably mobilized through financial institutions or a broadened tax base with an enhanced system of collection of direct and indirect taxes.

Policymakers could also aim to repatriate the huge wealth that has built up in foreign bank accounts or in real assets abroad as a result of capital flight (capital that has left the continent through non-transparent transactions or illicit channels used by high-profile politicians or other government officials with access to public money).

The size of African capital flight is huge, according to Ndikumana and Boyce (2011). On the basis of data re-

> *The size of African capital flight is huge. More than $700 billion fled the region during 1970-2008.*

constructed from balance-of-payments statistics of 33 sub-Saharan countries, they estimate that more than $700 billion fled the region during 1970–2008. If one includes earned interest at market rates on the accumulated wealth, the value of capital flight amounts to $944 billion—close to sub-Saharan Africa's GDP in 2008 of $997 billion.[22] These statistics reveal a major development challenge stemming from unacceptable levels of mismanagement of public resources in Africa.

To this capital flight, we should add the loss of public resources incurred through the brain drain of skilled human resources because of the lack of suitable jobs at home. Many African countries are in effect paying to train medical professionals for developed countries. By one recent estimate, "sub-Saharan African countries that invest in training doctors have ended up losing $2 billion as the expert clinicians leave home to find work in more prosperous developed nations".[23]

Governments could usefully revisit the "the brain drain tax" proposal made in the mid-1970s by Professor Bhagwati. For example, at least some proportion of income tax on skilled and professional emigrants levied in destination economies could be used as a source of development financing for specific projects in education and health or for schemes designed to create job opportunities for skilled and educated youth in home countries.[24]

Such financial haemorrhaging and massive human capital loss from the continent illustrate how much hardship the people of Africa have had to endure unnecessarily because of the "institutional development trap" that has characterized the African continent throughout the post-independence era, despite its immeasurable developmental potential in human and natural resources (box 5.1).[25]

Box 5.2: The institutional development trap

Diagnosing the development trap in Africa as resulting from large-scale pervasive government failure, in the wake of the early 1980s' debt crisis, the IFIs recommended economic liberalization and deregulation, and keeping the size of governments to a minimum, in exchange for aid and debt restructuring. Africa's debt crisis was, however, closely linked to the severe commodity crisis at the time (Maizels, 1992).

The collapse of commodity prices amounted to a loss of real purchasing power of 40–60 per cent for many commodity-dependent economies in sub-Saharan Africa—a deeper crisis than that faced during the Great Depression in the 1930s. For macroeconomic stabilization, the demand management of commodity-dependent economies hit by external shocks should have been countercyclical to commodity price movements. Yet, at that time of an externally induced balance-of-payments crisis, accompanied by a sharp drop in domestic demand, these countries were forced—lacking alternative financial facilities—to adopt the IMF-sponsored pro-cyclical stabilization programme that brought about further contraction in aggregate domestic demand.

In practice therefore, with the debt crisis, as well as severe and deep fiscal retrenchment imposed on them in the reform process, governments were generally left with little capacity and few resources to undertake sustained public investment and little ability to crowd in private investment.[1] In the absence of reliable public goods provisions, transaction costs to engage in productive activities remained prohibitively high. Economic transactions were conducted in highly uncertain and risky environments, which engendered eminently volatile returns to investment.

High uncertainty and instability are powerful deterrents not only to private investment and economic growth, but also to the composition of investment in favour of reversible and safe investments that have a self-insurance character. In such circumstances, African investors systematically chose safe and liquid assets over less liquid but high-yielding assets. While wealthy segments of the population often invested abroad—capital flight—other private investors put their capital in short-term assets in sectors with lower sunk costs and shorter turnover periods, such as trading, rather than in long-term physical investments (Aryeetey, 1994). The resulting low public and private investment together harmed economic growth and development in Africa.

In particular, the political and economic environment in the 1980s and 1990s kept the economic activities of a significant proportion of private agents away from the "official" economy. Since then, the informal economy has become an important source of employment and income for the majority of urban and rural households, and economic activities tend to be restricted to small-scale production and local trade. The majority of the poor, particularly the rural poor, have been left behind. At the same time, a largely informal economy leading to a weak and narrow tax base reinforces fiscal fragility.

The slow but gradual transition from systems of personal or authoritarian rule—characterized by infrequent but often violent turnover of incumbents—to democratic regimes with a multi-party system since the turn of the 1990s was naturally a welcome change. This could potentially lay the basis for creating governments committed to broad-based, equitable and inclusive development.

Yet, in practice continued poor public-goods provision and fragile fiscal conditions developed its own vicious cycle for condemning an economy to low equilibrium, leading to a fragile State with reduced institutional capability to function. Indeed, the scope and quality of public social and infrastructure services progressively deteriorated in many countries in the 1990s.

Thus, without resolving the institutional trap, States could make little progress in mobilizing the energy and resources of their people for commonly shared development objectives. Rather, more often than not, fiscal fragility and retrenchment aggravated distributional tensions and conflicts in ethno-linguistically fractured societies. These factors have acted as serious impediments to structural transformation in Africa's economies.

1. See Nissanke (2011b) for a further analysis of how international and institutional traps are closely interrelated through feedback mechanisms that have created both a low-equilibrium trap of debt-induced growth and an institutional configuration that is detrimental to shared growth and inclusive development through a loop of negative private–public interfaces for economic development.

5.3 Meeting the need—new approaches

SEVERAL INNOVATIVE FINANCIAL instruments have attracted attention as mechanisms for closing Africa's vast infrastructure gap by mobilizing private savings through financial markets. Among them are instruments targeted at global investors who can bear high currency and country risks in their quest for high returns, including debt instruments issued in hard currencies, and private funds or vehicles (Brixiova et al., 2011; Beck et al., 2011).

Ghana's sovereign external 10-year bond issue of $750 million in late 2007, for example, to finance energy and infrastructure projects attracted heavy publicity at the time, as it was the first sovereign bond issued by a sub-Saharan country (apart from South Africa). It was hailed as a success, achieving a B+ rating and four times oversubscribed at the time of issue, with strong demand from asset managers and hedge funds in particular. In the wake of the global financial crisis, however, it was sold heavily at 48 cents to the dollar in the fourth quarter of 2008. It recovered to 80–85 cents to the dollar in summer 2009 but with a yield of about 12 per cent.

This episode, as well as the sovereign debt crisis in the euro area, shows the high volatility in sovereign bond markets and that debt sustainability could be at risk when investor risk appetite shifts rapidly. Indeed, a series of sovereign bonds issues planned in 2009 and 2010 by African countries had to be deferred owing to adverse conditions on global financial markets.[26]

Attention has recently been paid to tapping excess savings in public bodies on the continent or globally for accelerating investment in Africa. Many resource-rich countries in Africa have become net creditors to the rest of the world, as the rapid increase of commodity prices since 2002 and many new discoveries of mineral and oil deposits in Africa have led them to accumulate reserves. Windfalls from these resource rents are often far in excess of a country's absorptive capacity to deploy them effectively for development over a short period. In any case, commodity prices are inherently volatile, so policymakers in these countries require attractive savings instruments to smooth their expenditures and absorption over commodity boom-bust cycles.[27]

In response to these conditions, several governments with large excess reserves have established sovereign wealth funds (SWFs) to manage these savings. SWFs are increasingly seen as one of the potential sources for financing development, in particular infrastructure projects in Africa.

In contrast to private equity funds, which are mostly managed by private investors, or bond issues on international capital markets, SWFs are managed by governments with excess public savings. A number of resource rich countries in Africa, such as Libya and Nigeria, have already used this approach to fund development projects in their own countries or elsewhere in Africa.

African policymakers need to take a strategic position on exploiting all these new opportunities, and negotiate and secure best deals, so that resources in minerals, oil, and precious metals are used in the best interests of the future generations of the African people.

Mitigating risks

A common thorny issue in all these sources potentially available to bring in foreign funds, private or public, is how to mitigate risks associated with long-term investment. Brixiova et al. (2011) propose various risk-mitigating instruments, including:

▸ Debt and equity insurance and guarantee instruments for mitigating commercial and political risks, in addition to partial risk guarantees offered by multilateral institutions.

▸ Viability-gap financing (leveraging in public funds for infrastructure investment by providing public subsidies through partial capital cost financing upfront) for reducing risks to private investors.

▸ First-loss guarantees for portfolios such as the First Loss Investment Portfolio Guarantees developed by AfDB to mitigate country risk premiums.

▸ Currency hedging, government exchange guarantees and devaluation liquidity schemes against currency risks.

These are useful when supporting institutions and when other preconditions are in place. However, residual risks always remain in any inter-temporal financial transactions, and often the excessive application of sophisticated financial instruments and securitization increase systemic macro risks, as seen in many financial crises over the past two decades.[28]

Further, efficient trading of international financial instruments requires deep, highly liquid, markets and developed forward markets for domestic currencies in the first place; such preconditions cannot be developed overnight. Over the past decade, many emerging economies in Asia have focused efforts on deepening bond markets by issuing debt instruments in domestic currencies to attract both domestic and global investors on an experimental basis and by gradually deepening the market with more issues. They have also boosted the capacity of domestic financial institutions and regulatory systems.

In considering the use of risk mitigating instruments, therefore, associated costs and benefits should be carefully weighed. On the one hand, the cost of accessing sophisticated risk-hedging instruments is often prohibitive for low-income countries without subsidies from multilateral public institutions. On the other hand, as the global financial crisis suggests, the effectiveness of the risk-mitigating capacity of some instruments is not guaranteed. These considerations raise the question of whether public resources should encourage use of these instruments, rather than focus on deepening markets and boosting domestic capacity.

Policymakers should be also much more vigilant against accumulating unsustainable private external debt, by carefully monitoring debt through an appropriate debt sustainability analysis framework (under different assumptions and scenarios). In a crisis, it is the government that has to take on private debt obligations and turn them into sovereign debt obligations.

African countries require a long learning period before operating in international capital markets with confidence, on an equal footing. They may consider experimenting with issuing debt instruments in local currencies and aiming primarily at domestic (or diaspora) investors and financial institutions (or those with ties to, or expertise in, countries in Africa).

Since investors in these investment vehicles are more likely to have firm commitments and interests closely aligned with the economic development of African countries, they are probably willing to take currency or other country risks associated with these local currency–de-

> *African countries require a long learning period before operating in international capital markets with confidence on an equal footing.*

nominated instruments issued in domestic capital markets, by positioning themselves with a longer perspective. Hence, these instruments are by nature more geared towards financing long-gestation infrastructure projects.

Recent examples of instruments launched in Africa in this category include four types of bonds (Brixiova et al., 2011):

Local currency infrastructure bonds. The Kenyan Government issued three infrastructure bonds for roads, energy and water, sewerage and irrigation with a total value of $1 billion in 2009/2010. This paved the way for issuance of corporate bonds by private and State companies, including Safaricom (a mobile phone company) and KenGen (an electricity utility). Additional incentive schemes instituted with infrastructure bonds in Kenya: allow bond holders to use infrastructure bonds as collateral for bank loans, and banks can pledge them as collateral for their operations; exempt bondholders from tax on interest payments; and incorporate the practice of Islamic banking, so that banking institutions such as the Gulf African Bank can participate.

Commodity-linked bonds. The Standard Bank Group in South Africa offered rand-denominated, commodity-linked, exchange-traded notes in August 2010, which are listed on the Johannesburg Stock Exchange, with a specific redemption date and returns linked to the performance of precious metals.

Infrastructure and municipal bonds. These seek the participation of domestic pension and other funds, as well as international investors.

Diaspora bonds. Such bonds could raise $5 billion–$10 billion annually by tapping the wealth of 16 million Africans living abroad (Beck et al., 2011). The people of the diaspora are viewed as less risk-averse towards bonds issued in domestic currencies as they know more about their country of origin than other investors. They also have liabilities in their home country and often have a desire to help develop it. Ethiopia, for example, issued Millennium Corporate Bonds targeting Ethiopians at home and abroad.

Realistically, however—for the time being at least—only a handful of "frontier" markets such as Egypt, Kenya, Nigeria and South Africa may issue bonds, because bond markets have to be highly liquid, with appropriate term structures. Many smaller countries would require regional capital markets in subregional hub countries, which are important in accessing finance for cross-border infrastructure projects, as their economies are often too small to justify projects on their own. One way forward, benefiting from economies of scale, can be done through subregional banks, funds and associated instruments, as discussed at recent meetings of the AU and various RECs.

5.4 Meeting the need—taxation

Recent trends in tax revenues

THE AVERAGE TAX to GDP ratio has been increasing since the early 1990s in Africa (figure 5.7). The weighted average of the tax ratio declined from 22 per cent in 1990 to 17 per cent in 1993, but from then it climbed to 27 per cent of GDP in 2007, a 10 percentage point increase in 15 years. Africa's average tax ratio is quite high relative to developing countries in East Asia and the Pacific and Latin America and the Caribbean, whose ratios were 10–17 per cent in 2007–2009.

The tax ratio differs hugely among African countries depending on the country's natural resource endowments and income. The recent increase in Africa's average tax ratio is largely driven by windfalls to governments in oil-producing countries. Classified by income (figure 5.9), the tax ratio in upper middle-income countries in Africa in 2007 was 30 per cent, nearly achieving the average of 35 per cent in OECD countries. Lower middle-income countries had a ratio of 20 per cent and low-income countries only around 15 per cent (AfDB, OECD and UNECA, 2010).

Figure 5.7

Tax share of GDP in Africa, 1990–2007 (weighted and unweighted averages, %)

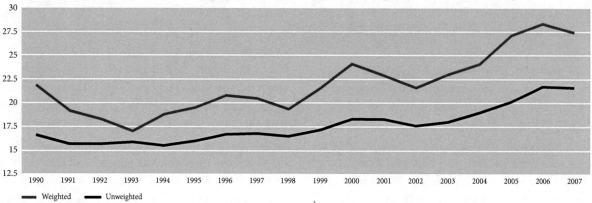

Source: AfDB, OECD and UNECA (2010).

Figure 5.8

Tax share of GDP in Africa, 1990–2007 (by income group, %)

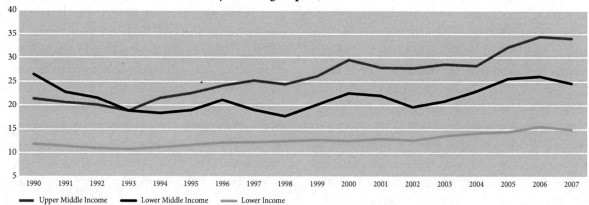

Source: AfDB, OECD and UNECA (2010).

As expected, there are clear overlaps in groupings between resource-rich countries and upper middle-income countries.

What makes tax systems in Africa different from those in other developing regions are a heavy reliance on resource-based taxes in resource-rich countries, particularly among oil-producing countries; a small share of direct taxes (personal income and corporate income taxes combined) in most African countries; and a high share of trade taxes in poorer countries.[29]

Trends in 1996–2007 were as follows: the increase in the weighted average tax ratio for Africa (see figure 5.7) was driven almost entirely by the rise in resource-based taxes in resource-rich countries, in particular in oil-producing

countries.[30] The share of resource-based tax revenues as a share of GDP tripled from 3 per cent in 1998 to 15 per cent in the late 2000s. In Libya and Angola, this share was 66 per cent and 39 per cent, respectively, in 2007.

The share of corporate income tax remained stable but low relative to potential revenues because of too many tax concessions and exemptions granted to corporations. In indirect taxation, lower-income countries showed a marked increase despite its regressive nature. The share of trade taxes declined in the period, but the rate of the decline decelerated. In the earlier years, the effects of trade liberalization strongly affected government revenues.[31]

Structural tax issues

The critical structural issues in domestic public resource mobilization may be summarized under three headings (AfDB, OECD and UNECA, 2010):

> Unresolved cross-cutting structural bottlenecks: high levels of informality, a lack of fiscal legitimacy and huge administrative capacity constraints.

> Further erosion of the already shallow tax base by excessive granting of tax preferences, inefficient taxation of extractive activities and inability to fight abuses of transfer pricing by MNEs.

> Unbalanced tax mix: excessive reliance on a narrow set of taxes to generate revenues, disproportionate representation of some stakeholders in the tax base, and emergence of a critical gap in public resources due to declining trade taxes.

The two key features of most African countries—the shallow tax base and unbalanced tax mix—are largely outcomes of the unresolved cross-cutting structural bottlenecks.

The informal economy, which remains stubbornly high in Africa, is less productive than the formal sector, and people in it have no labour or social protection schemes. Many informal economic activities are very fragile, and by the nature of their activities, they function outside the tax net, although they may pay indirect taxes, such as value-added tax.

Many informal operators may not feel much benefit from paying taxes—direct or indirect—gaining little tangible payback in high-quality public services or provision of public goods. Thus, as AfDB, OECD and UNECA (2010) note, informality often arises where the costs of legal employment outweigh the benefits for producers, employers or employees. Further, if entry costs in a regulated economy are unaffordable, people and businesses are forced to remain outside the system (Jütting and de Laiglesia, 2009).

The institutional changes required to move out of this type of behavioural impasse are usually slow to come.

Concerted efforts on all fronts would, however, make a difference and would lead to lifting institutional constraints and freeing the traps discussed above (box 5.1). In particular, enhanced and sustainable provision of public goods is essential for domestic stakeholders to feel tangible returns from their tax contributions.

Another outcome of the structural bottlenecks is that public resource mobilization cannot be improved by just increasing tax rates from the existing narrow base. Yet, policymakers in Africa tend to take an easy short cut by adjusting the tax rate at margin to increase revenues. For example, UNECA and AUC (2011) point to tax-related problems, citing several assessments such as "African countries tend to enforce easy taxes, particularly trade taxes, and impose high taxes on the formal sector or both" (Aryeetey, 2009). The finding by Gauthier and Reinikka (2006) suggested that "a high tax burden is imposed on a limited number of taxpayers, and on medium-size firms, which already bear a disproportionately high share of taxes". Indeed, UNECA and AUC (2011) argue that "A fundamental tax difficulty in Africa is the trilemma between the demand for higher tax revenue to finance development; the unwillingness of those with political power and economic ability to pay additional tax; and the rest who have no assets to be taxed and who resist paying taxes."

AfDB, OECD and UNECA (2010), among other studies on tax in Africa, discuss detailed policy measures for overcoming the weaknesses in the tax system such as establishing an independent revenue collection body

Many informal operators may not feel much benefit from paying taxes—direct or indirect—gaining little tangible payback in high quality public service or provision of public goods.

and enhancing the administrative and technical capacity of tax-collecting institutions. Beyond such proposals, tax issues should be considered as deeper structural concerns that require fundamental changes in public resource management. The unbalanced and shallow tax base in African countries today, in particular, their strikingly heavy reliance on resource-based tax revenues is not only a testimony to the continuous susceptibility of fiscal revenues to commodity boom-bust price cycles but is also a result of the historically evolved weak incentives for governments to engage in forging a meaningful partnership with domestic stakeholders for advancing the socio-economic agenda.[32]

Mobilizing and managing domestic resources better

A distributional fiscal mechanism should therefore be used so that a genuinely functional partnership between the State and domestic stakeholders can be forged. Policy discussions should go well beyond the technical issues looked at above. Mobilizing domestic public resources should be discussed in the context of a broader debate on how to mainstream the informal economy into the country's development agenda as part of the strategy of improving public resource management at large. Broadening the tax base through improved fiscal distribution mechanisms is the best way forward in the long run.

Further, to avoid past experiences with forced fiscal retrenchment in crisis, resource-rich countries should strengthen their macroeconomic management over commodity cycles—now, while their economies enjoy the commodity boom. Countercyclical macroeconomic management through commodity stabilization funds, as practised in Chile and Norway, is undoubtedly a critical tool for managing resource rents for economic development.[33]

But the practicality and efficacy of implementing such policies depend heavily on how mineral rents are distributed between domestic stakeholders and MNEs, and how they are used and managed. Many low-income countries find it hard to conduct successful countercyclical macroeconomic policy, not just because it requires high technical knowledge, but because they regard the opportunity cost of holding savings abroad as too high in the light of immediate pressing needs to accelerate economic development and to reduce poverty.

5.5 Conclusions and policy recommendations

SEVERAL POLICY IMPLICATIONS can be drawn from the analysis and discussions in this chapter, summarized as follows:

› Windfalls from commodity booms and newly available resources should be deployed purposely to help diversify and transform economic structures, while resource rents should be distributed to ensure that an inclusive growth pattern emerges.

› African policymakers should take a strategic position with all the categories of external actors and investors. They should seize on their newly acquired, stronger position by presenting their home-grown development visions and strategies as a basis of negotiations.

› To mobilize private domestic and foreign savings through financial systems, it is important to concentrate efforts on deepening financial markets and strengthening the capacity of financial institutions so that mobilized funds are effectively intermediated and used for productive investments and socio-economic development.

› It is critical to forge a truly productive partnership between the State and domestic stakeholders. This requires making substantial changes in the political economy of public resource management, to address at core the structural weaknesses in domestic public resource mobilization.

> Policymakers should broaden the tax base by improving fiscal distribution, such as better provision of public goods, and by mainstreaming the informal economy into development processes.

> Mechanisms of regional cooperation for countercyclical macroeconomic management should be explored and deepened.

With changes in external economic conditions and the geopolitical landscape for Africa, the aspirations of domestic stakeholders have been rising. Young generations of Africans in particular are eager for a better future and are rightfully demanding inclusive development, politically and economically. Policymakers should take up this challenge and turn emerging opportunities into reality by accelerating the process of structural transformation, as well as by facilitating wider engagement of domestic stakeholders in economic policymaking, so as to build an inclusive society.

References

Aarsnes, F., and E. Pöyry. 2010. "Taxation of multinationals: fiscal competition and profit repatriation (including transfer pricing)." Paper presented at the conference "Public Resource Mobilization & Aid" for the African Economic Outlook 2011, African Development Bank, Tunis.

Adam, C., and O'Connell, 1997. "Aid, taxation and development: Analytical perspectives on aid effectiveness in sub-Saharan Africa." Mimeo. Centre for the Study of African Economies, University of Oxford.

AfDB (African Development Bank), 2006. "Infrastructure Development and Regional Integration: Getting the Policy Framework Right." Concept Note Paper for the 2006 Annual Meetings, Ouagadougou, Burkina Faso, May 16.

AfDB, OECD (Organisation for Economic Co-operation and Development), and UNECA (United Nations Economic Commission for Africa). 2010. *African Economic Outlook 2010.* Paris: OECD Publishing.

_____. OECD, UNDP (United Nations Development Programme), and UNECA. 2011. *African Economic Outlook 2011.* Paris: OECD Publishing.

Al-Alamo, R. 2011. "The Arab Spring: corruption and revelations." *Energy& Geopolitical Risk* 2(12), December.

Alden, C. and Hughes, C., 2009. "Harmony and Discord in China's Africa Strategy:

Some Implications for Foreign Policy", The China Quarterly, September 2009, 563-584.

Aryeetey, E.,1994. "Private investment under uncertainty in Ghana." *World Development* 22 (8): 1211–21.

_____. 2009. "The global financial crisis and domestic resource mobilization in Africa." Working Paper 101. African Development Bank, Tunis.

Beck, T., S.M. Maimbo, I. Faye, and T. Triki, 2011. "Financing Africa: through the crisis and beyond." Making Finance Work for Africa, African Development Bank, Tunis.

Bhagwati, J. 1976. "Taxing the brain drain." *Challenge* 19 (3).

Borensztein, E., O. Jeane, and D. Sadri. 2009. "Macrohedging for commodity exporters." Working Paper WP/2009/229. International Monetary Fund, Washington, DC.

Brauner, Y.2010. "Braindrain tax as development policy." Research Paper 2010–17. University of Florida Levin College of Law, Gainesville, FL

Brixiova, Z., E. Mutambatsere, C. Ambert, and D. Etienne. 2011. "Closing Africa's infrastructure gap: innovative financing and risks." Africa Economic Brief2 (1). African Development Bank, Tunis.

Brunnermeier, M. 2009. "Deciphering the liquidity and credit crunch 2007–2008." *Journal of Economic Perspectives* 23 (1): 77–100.

Cohen, D., H. Djoufelkit-Cottenet, P. Jacquet, and C. Valadier. 2008. "Lending to the poorest countries: a new counter-cyclical debt instrument." Working Paper 269. OECD Development Centre, Paris.

Commission for Africa Report. 2005. UK Government, 11 March 2005

Gauthier, B., and R. Reinikka. 2006. "Shifting tax burdens through exemption and evasion: an empirical investigation of Uganda." *Journal of African Economies* 15(3):373–98.

Gunther, B., 2009. "Towards an MDG-consistent debt sustainability concept." One Pager 87. International Policy Centre for Inclusive Growth, Brasília, Brazil.

Jütting, J., and J.R. de LaIglesia. 2009. "Is informal normal? Towards more and better jobs in developing countries." OECD Development Centre, Paris.

Keen, M., and M. Mansour. 2009. "Revenue mobilization in Sub-Saharan Africa: challenges from globalization." Working Paper 09/157. International Monetary Fund, Washington, DC.

Kelland, K. 2011. "Doctor Brain Drain Costs Africa $2 billion."*Reuters News,* November 25.

Krugman, P. 1988. "Financing vs. forgiving a debt overhang." *Journal of Development Economics* 29 (3): 253–68.

Maizels, A. 1992. *Commodities in crisis.* Oxford: Clarendon Press.

Ndikumana, L., and J.K. Boyce. 2011. *Africa's odious debts.* London and New York: ZED Books.

Ndulu, B. 2006. "Infrastructure, regional integration and growth in Sub-Saharan Africa: dealing with the disadvantages of geography and sovereign fragmentation." *Journal of African Economies* 15 (2): 212–44.

Nissanke, M. 2007. "Aid effectiveness to infrastructure: a comparative study of East Asia and Sub-Saharan Africa." Framework Paper. Japan Bank for International Co-operation, Tokyo.

_____. 2009. "The global financial crisis and the developing world: transmission channels and fall-outs on industrial development." Working Paper 06/2009. United Nations Industrial Development Organization, Vienna.http://www.unido.org/fileadmin/user_media/Publications/RSF_DPR/WP062009_Ebook.pdf.

_____. 2010a. "Commodity market structures, evolving governance and policy issues." In *Commodities, governance and economic development under globalization,* eds. M. Nissanke and G. Movrotas, 65–97.Hampshire, UK: Palgrave/Macmillan.

_____. 2010b. "Engaging in the economic development process in low-income countries through participatory sovereign debt management: a critical review of the joint Bank-fund debt sustainability framework." Commonwealth Secretariat, London.

_____. 2011a. "Commodity markets and excess volatility: sources and strategies to reduce adverse development impact." Paper commissioned for the International Conference on Commodity Price Volatility, Common Fund for Commodities, May 2011. Available at http://www.common-fund.org/data/documenten/CFC-Nissanke-Commodity-MarketVolatility_Feb_2011.pdf.

_____. 2011b. "International and institutional traps in Sub-Saharan Africa under globalisation: a comparative perspective." Paper presented at the International Workshop on Advancing Knowledge in Developing Economies and Development Economics, Hitotsubashi University, Tokyo, September 23–24.

_____. 2012. "Commodity Market linkages in the global financial crisis: excess volatility and development impacts." *Journal of Development Studies* 48 (6).

Nissanke, M., and M. Soderberg. 2011. "The changing landscape in aid relationships in Africa: Can China's engagement make a difference to African development?" Working Paper. Swedish Institute for International Affairs, Stockholm.

Nissanke, M., and E. Thorbecke. 2010. *The poor under globalization in Asia, Africa and Latin America.* Oxford: Oxford University Press.

UNECA. 1999. Economic Report on Africa: Poverty Reduction and Sustainable growth in Africa, Addis Ababa.

UNECA and AUC. 2010. *Economic Report on Africa 2010: promoting high-level sustainable growth to reduce unemployment in Africa.* Addis Ababa.

_____. 2011. *Economic Report on Africa 2011: governing development in Africa—the role of the state in economic transformation.* Addis Ababa.

Wang, J.-Y.2007. "What drives China's growing role in Africa?" Working Paper WP/07/211. International Monetary Fund, Washington, DC.

World Bank. 1994. *Infrastructure for Development. World Development Report 1994.* Washington, DC.

Notes

1   See Nissanke (2012) for detailed discussion on factors behind recent commodity price dynamics.

2   These groupings have a few overlapping countries such as Mauritania and Sudan, owing to the differences in the way the World Development Indicators and UNECA classify countries.

3   The portfolio element in capital inflows is very volatile, and exaggerates commodity price cycles. It can disappear quickly as market sentiment shifts, making it unreliable as development finance.

4   There are some discrepancies in the volume of each of the flows reported in AfDB et al., (2011) and the discussions in this section depend on the source of data used for analysis. However, all the data, irrespective of source, reveal common trends.

5   Our analysis on ODA is based on OECD-DAC data, which report total aid flows to Africa and for countries "South of Sahara" and "North of Sahara" separately as well as to individual countries. Under its classification, Sudan and Mauritania are grouped into North Africa, as in the UN classification. In this chapter, we use countries in sub-Saharan Africa (Africa excluding North Africa) for countries "South of Sahara".

6   See Nissanke (2010b) for detailed arguments and the cases for incentive-compatible loan contracts and an efficiently structured contingent financing facility along the lines originally proposed by Krugman (1988), but specifically adapted for use as a mechanism to avoid recurrence of debt-overhang conditions in low-income countries prone to exogenous shocks (such as commodity prices shocks). The objective of such a facility is to provide low-income countries with an automatic debt-relief mechanism incorporated in the original contracts. See also Cohen et al. (2008) for an alternative contingency scheme—the countercyclical loan facility.

7   See Ndulu (2006) for a discussion on this effect.

8   The diagnoses offered by the donor community for development failures in Africa have in fact evolved from "capital shortage" in the 1960s and 1970s to "policy failures" in the 1980s to the "institutional failures" in the 1990s (Adam and O'Connell, 1997). Only in the 2000s has the "infrastructure" failure in Africa received due attention.

9   See Beck et al. (2011).

10   Africa's top emerging partners are China, India, Brazil, Republic of Korea and Turkey (AfDB et al., 2011).

11   Traditional partners' share in Africa's overall trade totalling $673 billion in 2009 was 64 per cent (AfDB et al., 2011).

12   India at the first India-Africa Forum Summit promised to provide $5.4 billion in loans and $500 million in grants over the following five or six years.

13   Brixiova et al. (2011).

14   See Nissanke and Soderberg (2010) for more detailed discussions of China's drive in Africa. It looks at such areas as China's domestic imperatives for its drive in Africa, its adoption of the economic cooperation model practised by the Japanese Government in Asia as its chosen aid modality (with some notable variations), and its impacts on African development, which have raised both hopes and fears in the region.

15   Detailed statistics and information on Chinese aid and cooperation are hard to obtain. Indeed, the paucity of information and the unfamiliarity or non-transparency of the Chinese engagement have led to some misunderstanding, confusion, and occasionally unfounded accusations against Chinese aid in Africa. Offered as a package together with trade and investment, aid cannot be disentangled from other economic deals and relations, and hence it is difficult to analyse on a par with bilateral aid from other DAC countries. This must be one of the

reasons why aid flows from non-traditional partners are not properly captured in the OECD-DAC data, on which figure 5.4 draws.

16 See Wang (2007) for further discussion of financial facilities.

17 The China–Africa Fund, China's State-owned private equity fund, was set up in 2006 with an initial $5 billion. The fund was given a promise of further expansion at the FOCAC meeting in 2009. Alden and Hughes (2009) suggest that much more than three quarters of a million Chinese have migrated to Africa in recent years, following the lure of African riches.

18 See Nissanke and Thorbecke (2010) for detailed discussions of recent trends in MNEs' activities and changes in their relative positions versus host countries.

19 See Nissanke (2010a and 2011a) for more detailed discussion on recent developments in governance of commodity markets and production, and their effects on economic development in low-income commodity-dependent countries.

20 See Aarsnes and Pöyry (2010) for discussions of various components of tax systems for resource rents.

21 See UNECA and AUC (2011) for detailed analysis of the developmental State.

22 Similarly, it has emerged that former Presidents Ben Ali of Tunisia and Mubarak of Egypt (and their families and associates) have embezzled billions of dollars over many decades, much in capital flight. Former President Ben Ali and his entourage are reported to have expropriated over $5 billion, while wealth totalling $10 billion–$11 billion has been amassed by former President Mubarak (and his associates). Al-Alami (2011) compares these figures with an education budget of $2.5 billion and capital spending of $1 billion for 2007 in Tunisia and an education budget of $5.8 billion for 2007 in Egypt.

23 Kelland (2011). South Africa and Zimbabwe suffer the worst brain drain of medical staff.

24 See Bhagwati (1976) for a rationale for the brain drain tax, and Brauner (2010) for designing the tax to make it administratively and legally feasible in the current international tax regime.

25 See Nissanke (2011b) for conditions characterized by the two traps that have impeded African development over five decades.

26 Similarly, private equity funds, in their quest for high, private returns, may not be the appropriate vehicle for development financing. If African policymakers do use them, they should put in place necessary measures to safeguard the interests of projects and people in Africa against instability originating from these destabilizing cross-border movements of funds.

27 Some emerging countries in Asia and Latin America now hold large international reserves resulting from their desire to have liquid assets for self-insurance purposes against currency attacks or financial crises. A large part of these excess savings are held in safe assets with low returns such as US Treasury bills, entailing substantial opportunity costs.

28 In the global financial crisis, for example, sophisticated derivatives and instruments such as collaterized debt obligations or special-purpose vehicles to securitize original credit transactions gave an illusion that risks had been removed from their portfolio. If anything these instruments amplified aggregate systemic risks. See Brunnermeier (2009).

29 AfDB, OECD and UNECA (2010).

30 AfDB, OECD and UNECA (2010).

31 See Keen and Monsour (2009) for detailed discussion of the sharply declining share of trade taxes in tax structures in sub-Saharan Africa for 1980–1982 to 2003–2005.

32 See UNECA and AUC (2011) for discussion on institutional deficits in the early post-independent years which made it difficult to advance developmental agenda collectively.

33 See Nissanke (2011a) for a critical assessment of the proposal for using macro-hedging with derivative instruments as an effective substitute for countercyclical macroeconomic management through commodity stabilization funds. For such a proposal see Borensztein et al. (2009).